WRITTEN AND ILLUSTRATED BY

TOM SCHMIDT

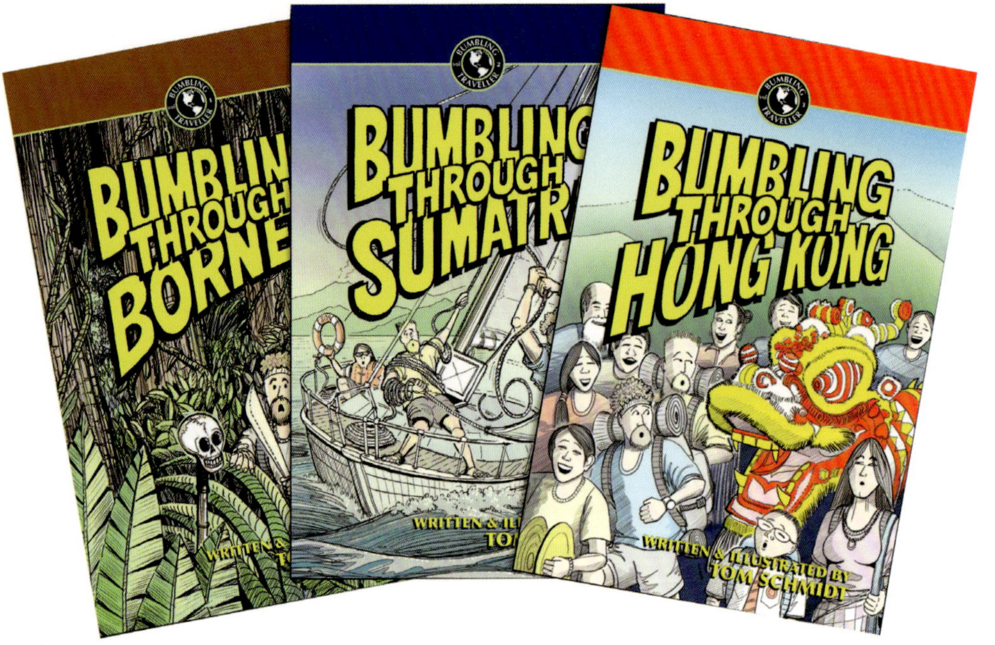
BUMBLING
THROUGH
BORNEO
BUMBLING
THROUGH
SUMATRA
BUMBLING
THROUGH
HONG KONG
WRITTEN & ILLUSTRATED BY
TOM SCHMIDT

WRITTEN AND ILLUSTRATED BY

TOM SCHMIDT

KAKIBUBU
MEDIA
LIMITED

Hong Kong

THE BUMBLING TRAVELLER

Published by Kakibubu Media Limited
Hong Kong

www.kakibubu.com

ISBN 978-988-18066-4-2

Bumbling Traveller logo by Pamela J. Trail

Dedicated to Catherine ...

The world is your oyster!

-- William Shakespeare

Acknowledgments:

I would like to thank the following individuals who assisted and inspired me in the production of this publication:

My parents and family for their unending support; Kate for her love, patience and understanding; my young daughter Catherine who demands I explain the world around us; Johan and all of the varied travel companions in my past backpacking adventures; my former university professor, mentor and friend David Barrett who encouraged me to sketch and keep a sketchbook; Erica Arakawa for urging me to keep a travel journal on the first day of my European adventure all those years ago; Jimmy Tablante who has kept the art of sketching and watercolor alive and well in Hawaii; Ray Hirohama who continues to defy modern conventions with his stellar hand-drawn architectural drawings; Peter Basmajian for his eagle-eye editing; all those who donated their valuable time throughout the whole process, and of course, the kind and hospitable residents of the various places I've visited in my travels throughout the years ...

TRAVEL SKETCHING

WHY TRAVEL?

See the world before you leave it.

The travel bug bites everyone at some point or another -- whether it's a short weekend holiday or an extended trek through faraway lands.

Throughout our lives, there are often transitional times or personal circumstances that allow us to travel for an extended period of time. Perhaps it's after graduating from a course of study at a university, or after quitting a job. Maybe it's after breaking up with a significant other, or an exploratory journey during a mid-life crisis.

In my own experience, I have typically tried to "backpack" independently for longer uninterrupted periods of time, and as cheaply as possible. I also prefer to travel alone much of the time to maximize my interaction with locals and become acclimated to a given culture. Like with any travel, the more of the world you see, the more you realize you haven't seen.

In this book, I've dusted off my sketchbooks and shared some of my travel sketches from their yellowing pages.

ENJOY!

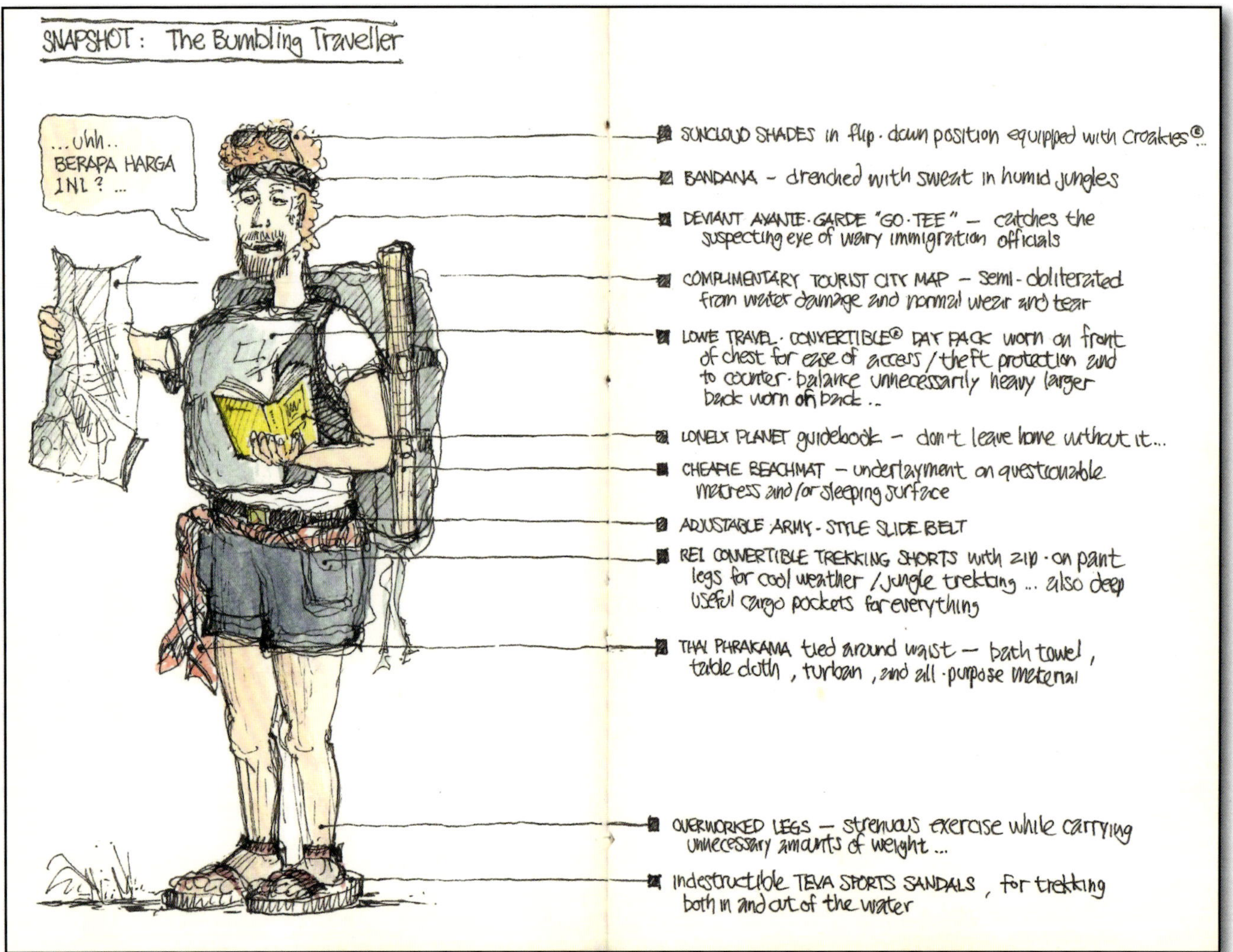

Sketchbook Self Portrait: This is how I travelled in the "old days" before the advent of digital devices.

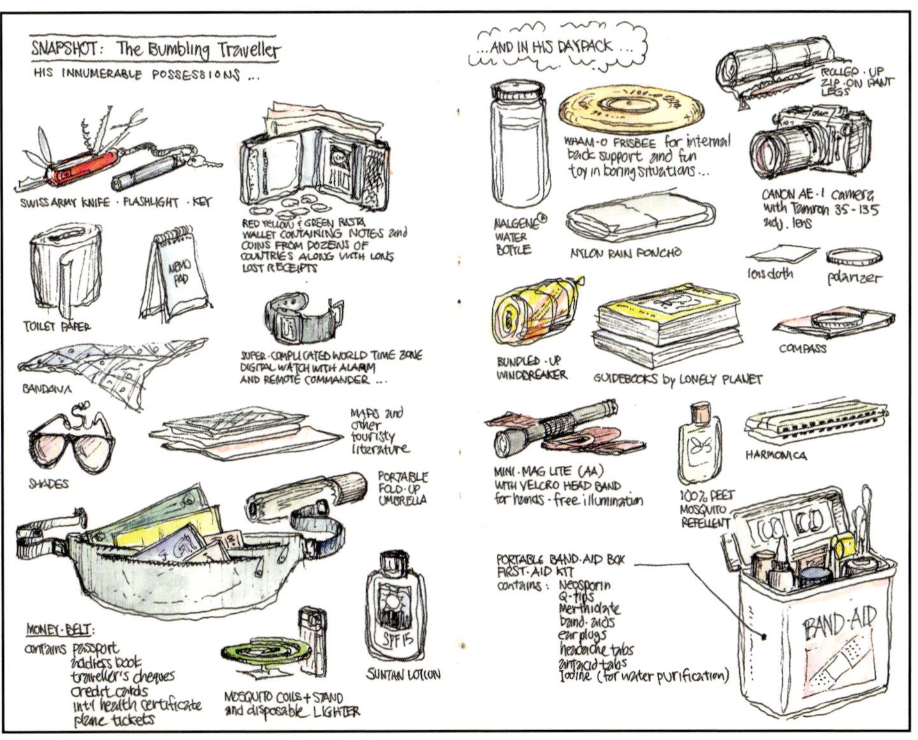

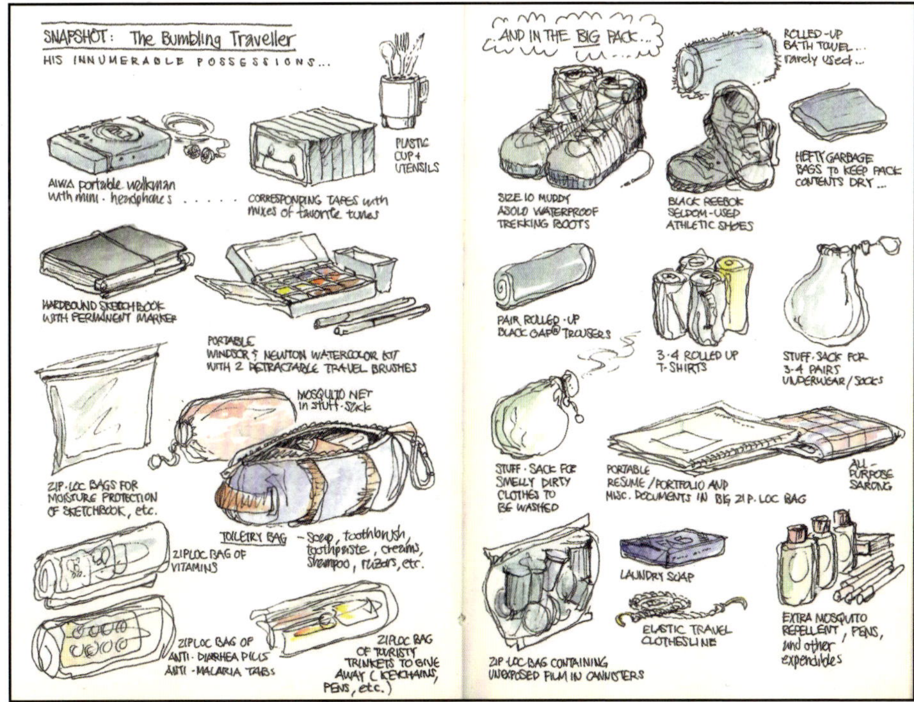

WHAT SHOULD I PACK?

As little as possible!

The choice of what to bring on an extended trip is subject to many variables including your personal level of comfort, where you'll be travelling, the climate there, and the availability of travel supplies at your destination.

Personally, I choose to "backpack" and keep my load as light as possible. For maximum flexibility, I still prefer to use an actual wearable backpack, rather than wheeled luggage. You'll always need to climb a mountain or wade through a river with all of your gear when you least expect it.

In the "old days," the use of a hefty guidebook and all kinds of accessories were almost mandatory. In today's digital and interconnected world, a smartphone can eliminate the need for a guidebook, dedicated musical device, flashlight, compass, a clunky camera and film, a means of payment, and many other sundry travel items.

But the trade-off for bringing a smartphone is the need for chargers, batteries, adapters, and other peripherals. And needless to say, if you lose or damage a smartphone that has not been backed up, then you'll find yourself up a river filled with excrement. This is all the more reason to build in redundancy for your trip by taking along a travel sketchbook and a separate camera to document your journey.

WHY SKETCH?

A picture tells a thousand words.

I once studied Environmental Design at the University of Colorado in the USA. As students, we were always encouraged to get into the habit of sketching the built environment and keeping a sketchbook containing our creative ideas. This practice carried over into my travels, but only after a friend urged me to keep a travel journal as I embarked on one of my first trips abroad. And now years later, I am glad I did!

A solo sketcher becomes an attraction in his or her own right. Sketches transcend language barriers, and the act of sketching can open the door to new friendships and invitations into the homes of locals who value someone expressing interest in their corner of the world.

In today's digital age, many people have traded in their sketchbooks for electronic tablets, or have simply relegated themselves to documenting their journey through photographs and videos with frequent uploads for the world to see. While many people may feel they are not artistically inclined, basic sketching can be learned and honed through practice. On-the-spot sketching, sometimes called "urban sketching" or "plein air painting," is alive and well throughout the world. I would encourage everyone to try their hand at sketching while they travel -- you might just surprise yourself!

WHAT DO I NEED?

Just the basics.

If you're ready to try your hand at sketching while travelling, you don't need much. A pencil and paper is a good start. A borrowed pen and a beer mat from a local pub also works.

For more serious sketchers, an assortment of pens, pencils, paints and sketchbooks allows for a wide range of options to depict the world as you see it.

When I backpack, I like to keep things as light as possible: A small A4 or A5 size bound sketchbook, a few permanent felt-tip markers, pencil and eraser, and a portable folding travel watercolor set to add a splash of color when I'm so inclined.

Watercolor postcard blocks are useful in that you can do a quick sketch, add some color, scribble an address on the back, and mail it from the local post office to provide a "hard copy" surprise for someone back home. If you're staying in one place for an extended period, you might consider experimenting with bulkier items, larger watercolor blocks or larger format media -- but these tend to weigh more.

It's also very important to stay hydrated while you sketch, especially if sitting in the sun. A bottle of water is essential, and a cold beer might help get the creative juices flowing.

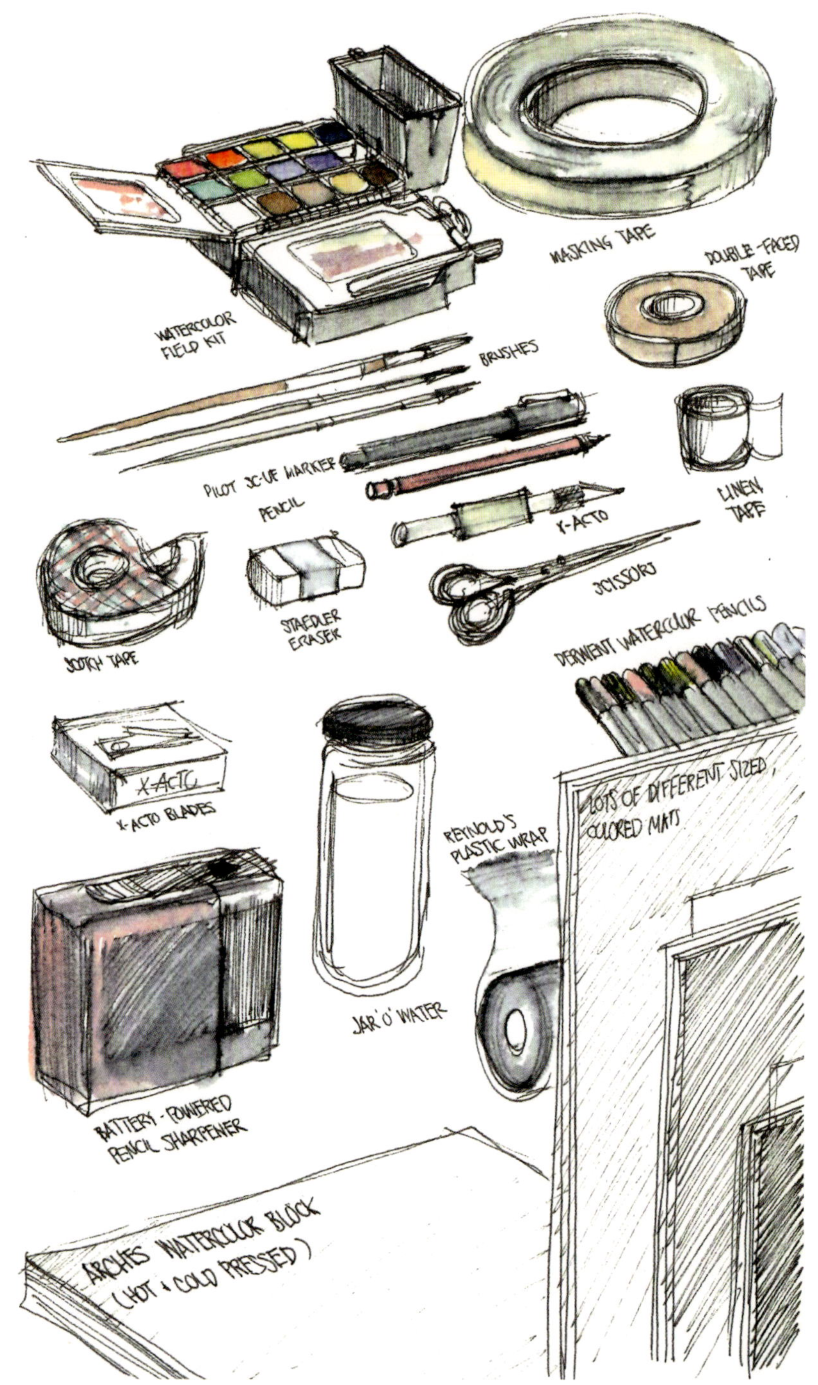

Sketching in Sumatra: Small Indonesian children clinging to me as I sketch, convinced my "magic" pen was the thing responsible for making the sketch!

Forever Waiting: As a traveller, you are always waiting for *something*. Sketching the environment around you while you wait is a great way to pass the time.

IS SKETCHING DANGEROUS?

It can be.

Over the years, I've had to endure a variety of antics while huddled over my sketchbook:

- Being talked about as if I was not even there ...
- Jostled by harried passersby, ruining my work ...
- Hassled by shop owners for blocking their display windows ...
- Questioned and detained by suspicious security guards ...
- Stalked by attractive members of the opposite sex ...
- Photographed as an odd attraction for the local newspaper ...
- Surreptitiously filmed for inclusion in a Chinese KTV music video ...
- Innocently groped by gangs of small curious kids ...
- Inadvertently spat upon from a balcony far above ...
- Having cigarette smoke repeatedly blown in my face ...
- Pelted with cigarette butts ...
- Stung by seen and unseen insects ...
- Become drenched in sudden, frigid downpours ...
- Having beer sloshed onto me and my sketchbook ...
- Chased away by angry buskers defending their turf ...
- Urinated upon by small animals ...
- Other events not suitable for publication.

Sketching can be fun, but proceed with caution!

HOW DO YOU SKETCH?

It depends how I feel.

Almost all of the sketches in this book are what I call "in situ" sketches -- or sketches drawn on the spot. While more polished renderings can be achieved by simply tracing over a photo, these in-situ sketches take anywhere from 15 minutes to 4 hours, depending upon how much time I have, remaining hours of sunlight, weather conditions, and what level of detail I am trying to achieve. It's important to stake out a spot with an interesting vantage point. There also needs to be a relatively comfortable place to sit for an extended period of time without blocking pedestrian traffic.

For most sketches, I generally commit pen to paper upon commencing the sketch. However, for other subjects with more complicated proportions, I will sometimes block out the basic proportions in light pencil before inking in the details, and erase the pencil after completion of the linework. If I have time (or the subject lends itself to color), I then add very quick watercolor wash to the sketch. Some sketches are "vignettes" without hard borders, and others use masking tape to frame the composition and contain the watercolor wash. There's no right way or wrong way to sketch. It all comes down to personal preference.

See my step-by-step example on the following pages.

HOW DO YOU CREATE A QUICK IN-SITU SKETCH?

STEP 1: BLOCK OUTS

For a rectilinear subject like a building, I generally start by sitting in a position that is slightly oblique to the subject in order to create a two-point perspective. In this example, I begin sketching with a graphite pencil before applying ink at a later stage. I first establish a horizon line and estimate the nearest vanishing point. I then block out the basic proportions of the facade and determine how it is subdivided. While this method of "eyeballing" is not as accurate as tracing over a photo of a building, the intent is to provide the rough proportions -- it's well worth estimating the overall proportions as carefully as possible at this early stage since any major errors will become apparent later in the sketch.

STEP 2: SUBDIVISIONS

After the major shapes and elements are penciled in, I begin to further subdivide each subsection and identify architectural elements. This forces your eye to do a constant comparison between what you see and what you just drew, which often results in eye strain. You then need to make minor adjustments as you visually check to see how some elements are aligned with adjacent elements.

I sometimes hold the sketchbook out at arm's length to do a side-by-side comparison of my drawing and what my eye sees. I then flip the sketch upside down as this will often expose any major errors in perspective that your eye had ignored when working right-side up.

STEP 3: DETAILS

More detail is added at the pencil stage, especially if the subject has a fair amount of intricate architectural details. If you're right handed, it is generally advantageous to start at the left side of the drawing and work your way to the right to prevent the smudging of pencil work that has already been laid down. If you're left-handed, the opposite holds true.

After the major elements of the composition are laid in, I pencil in significant "entourage" elements (for example, trees, people, plants, and other things that might help define scale and context) before starting the ink linework.

STEP 4: INK LINEWORK

After I'm satisfied with the overall proportions depicted in the pencil block outs, I then begin the ink linework. This is the point of no return -- once the inking begins, there is no turning back.

There are hundreds of types of pens available, but I generally try to use pens with permanent, waterproof, fadeproof ink that will not bleed excessively onto the sketchbook paper. The Japanese and Germans are arguably the world leaders in producing such pens, and I'd encourage you to experiment with as many types of pens and papers as you can to see what suits your personal tastes. Note, however, that if you choose a water soluble ink, this may result in unexpected results should you get caught in a sudden rain shower!

STEP 5: INK & ERASE

I often use broken lines when inking to provide a slight "fudge" factor which I can adjust later. When you're crouched down on a step beneath the pounding sun, and being jostled by passersby, it's exceedingly difficult to maintain a high level of accuracy.

When all of the major elements are inked in, I generally erase the pencil guidelines with a soft eraser resulting in a crisper drawing. At this point, I often make a decision whether to stop any further linework and use this as a base for adding watercolor -- in which case the paint will provide details and values -- or simply continue adding linework and working in a black and white format as I've done in this example.

STEP 6: DETAILS & ENTOURAGE

After the basic ink outlines are complete, I then do a second pass and add more details and textures, depict building materials, add cross-hatching to indicate different values, and provide indications of shade and shadow.

One of the last things I do is add entourage around the edges of the sketch where appropriate. This helps define the scale of the subject, "ground" the sketch, and provides an idea of the distance of the subject from the viewer.

But beware, as one of my former professors once warned: The last thing you do to your sketch is sometimes the thing that ruins it!

At this stage, I either stop and call it a day, or perhaps I might provide a very quick watercolor wash to provide an indication of color -- if the subject lends itself to color.

This sketch of the *Hong Kong Museum of Medical Sciences* in the Mid-Levels of Hong Kong took roughly two hours to complete.

Many sketches where I omit the underlying pencil work were executed in less time. It all depends upon how much time you are willing to spend on your sketch, and your choice of media.

Every sketch is a grand experiment, and you never know what you'll end up with.

REMEMBER: Every sketch is a learning experience.

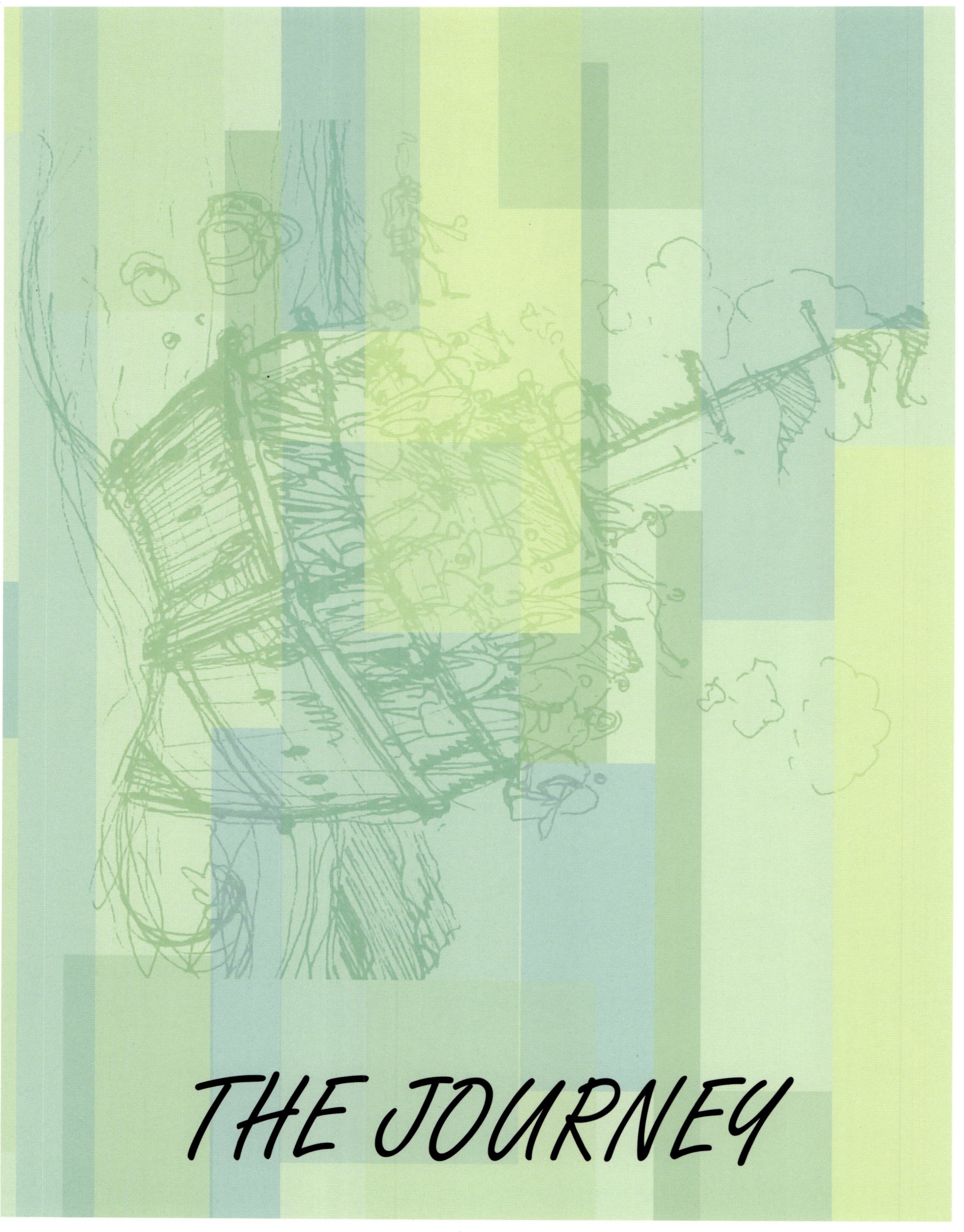
THE JOURNEY

HOW DO WE GET THERE?

Now that your bags are packed, remember that Ralph Waldo Emerson got it right when he proclaimed, *"It's not the destination, it's the journey."*

Often, it really is the methods of transportation that end up being the more memorable parts of a travel adventure. Human and animal-powered modes of transportation can be remarkable ways to reach a particular destination, as are suicidal bus rides at high speeds down darkened icy roads and overloaded ferries across turbulent seas.

Throughout the world, there are countless ways to move humans through their environment, from the basics of unassisted walking to being propelled through the air at diabolical speeds.

While some choose to write and blog about their transportation-related adventures, I prefer to illustrate my experiences to capture the apprehension, emotions and, often, the sheer absurdity of what it takes to get from Point A to Point B.

Human Transport: This is what happens when you travel alone -- you begin thinking about your various transportation options when you have no idea how you'll get to where you want to go.

I hadn't driven a motorcycle since I was 15...
yet this mode of transport seemed to be an
appealing way to get out of Ubud and explore
the surrounding countryside...

Tom & Johan rent bicycles for the day...

it sounded like a good idea at the time... after a delicious
Roti Canai for breakfast, we set off in search of some
bicycles to pedal around this relatively uncrowded town.

Local Transport: Indulging in local systems of transport provides an exciting way of experiencing a destination -- instead of being trapped in the protective bubble of a tour bus.

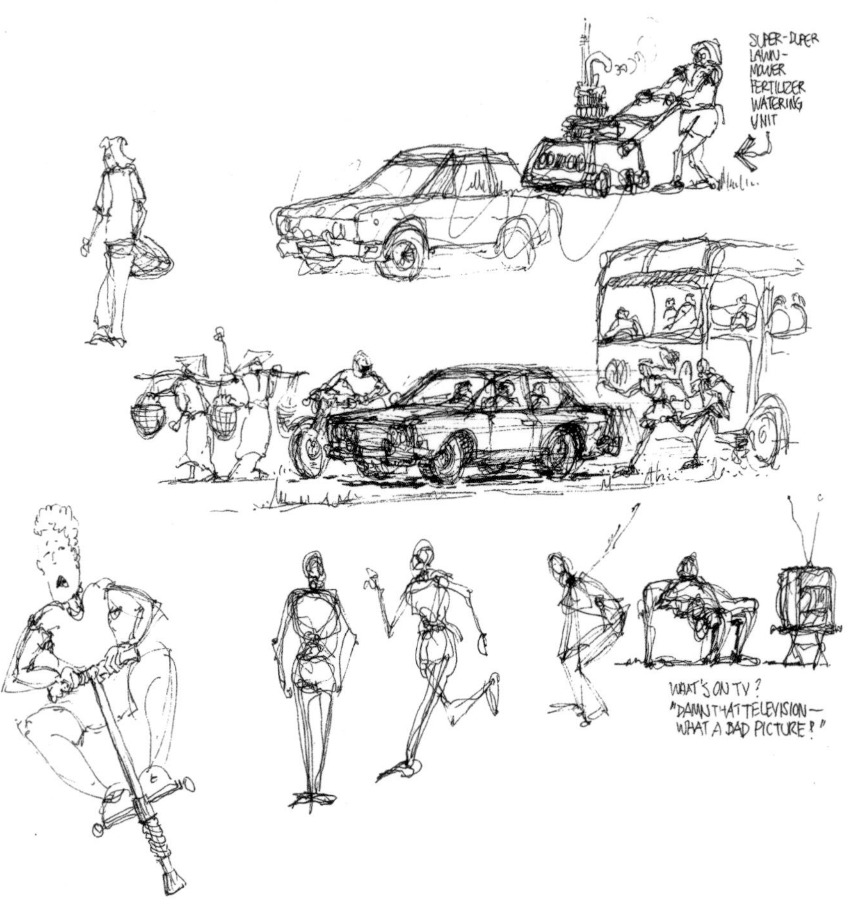

We thought about renting snorkelling equipment....

FERRY to
KOH PHA NGAN

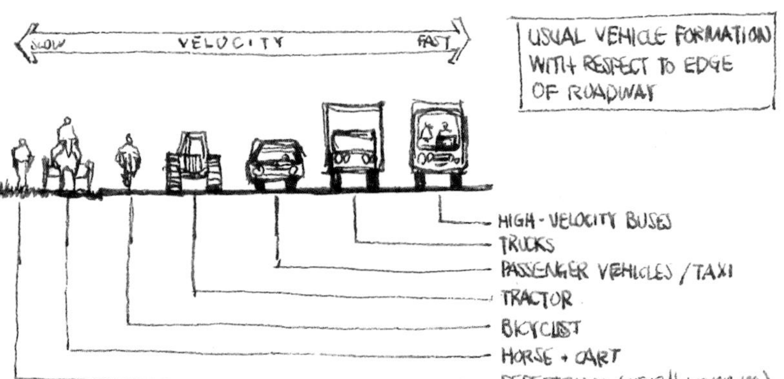

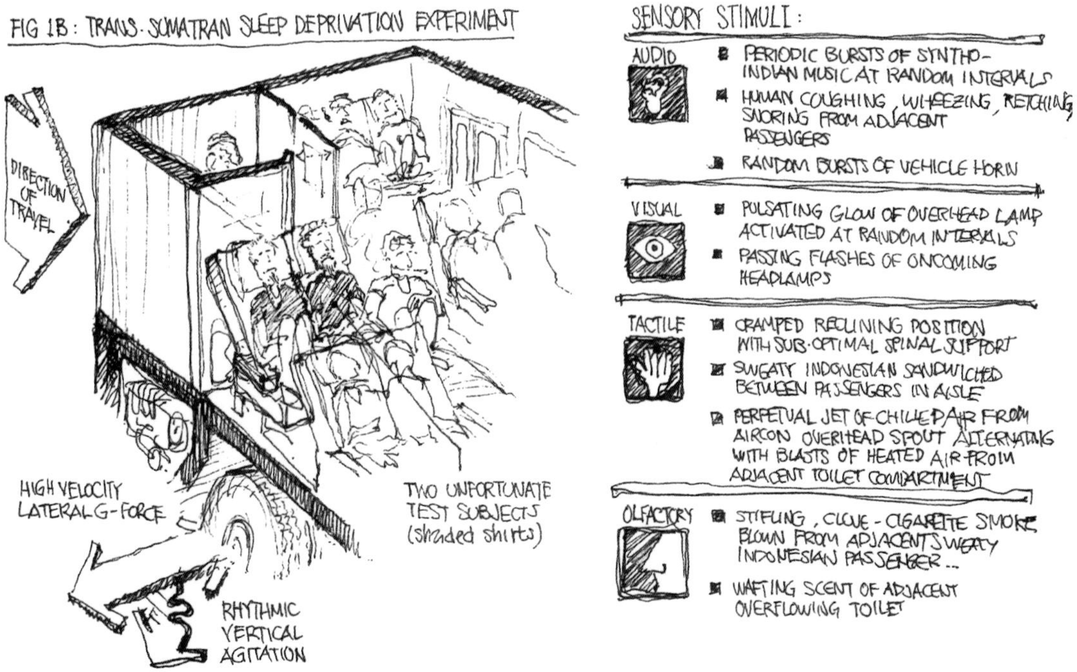

FIG 1B: TRANS-SUMATRAN SLEEP DEPRIVATION EXPERIMENT

SENSORY STIMULI:

AUDIO 
- PERIODIC BURSTS OF SYNTHO-INDIAN MUSIC AT RANDOM INTERVALS
- HUMAN COUGHING, WHEEZING, RETCHING, SNORING FROM ADJACENT PASSENGERS
- RANDOM BURSTS OF VEHICLE HORN

VISUAL 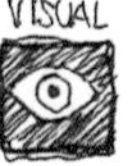
- PULSATING GLOW OF OVERHEAD LAMP ACTIVATED AT RANDOM INTERVALS
- PASSING FLASHES OF ONCOMING HEADLAMPS

TACTILE 
- CRAMPED RECLINING POSITION WITH SUB-OPTIMAL SPINAL SUPPORT
- SWEATY INDONESIAN SANDWICHED BETWEEN PASSENGERS IN AISLE
- PERPETUAL JET OF CHILLED AIR FROM AIRCON OVERHEAD SPOUT ALTERNATING WITH BLASTS OF HEATED AIR FROM ADJACENT TOILET COMPARTMENT

OLFACTORY 
- STIFLING, CLOVE-CIGARETTE SMOKE BLOWN FROM ADJACENT SWEATY INDONESIAN PASSENGER...
- WAFTING SCENT OF ADJACENT OVERFLOWING TOILET

THE BIG PICTURE:

As you travel, it's often interesting to look beyond your particular vehicle or mode of transportation to see how you fit into the overall scheme of things.

I sometimes depict my relative position in space by drawing small sections, or 3D sketches, and note the various influences around me. After all, travel is a multi-sensory experience, and we are all affected by stimuli coming at us from many directions.

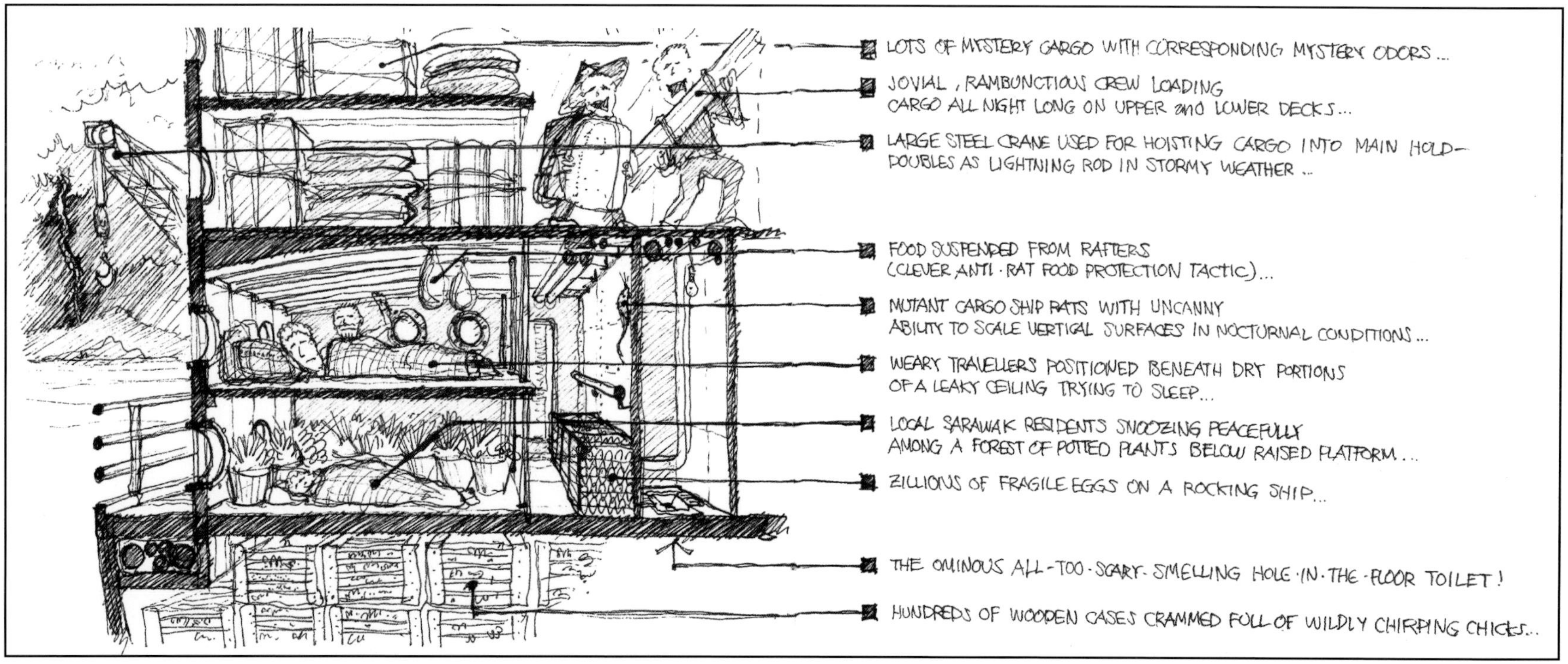

AS IT HAPPENED ...

Who says a 36-hour bus journey needs to be boring?

Travel sketches can make even the most arduous and uncomfortable journeys a bit more tolerable and ultimately memorable.

When I embarked on a 28-hour long-distance bus ride from Sumatra to Java in Indonesia years ago, I had a sneaking suspicion it might just take a tad longer than advertised. I had therefore planned to document the journey "as it happened" as a way to pass the time -- and this proved to be the only thing that kept me sane during the trip.

Sketching can visually describe the passage of time and commemorate key milestones of a journey that may have long since been forgotten.

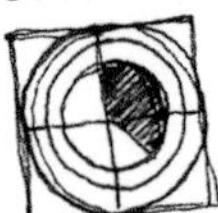

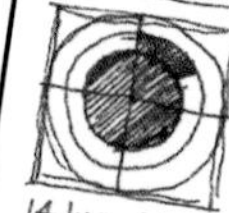

Mystery stop... driver hops out, makes illegal transaction with uniformed men in middle of the night... suddenly, loud Indo-synth pop as torture device from stereo?

14 hrs. 11 min.

Blurred food stop... wandered beneath fluorescent lights in dream-like state sipping teh susu to soothe my increasingly sore throat...

17 hrs. 14 min.

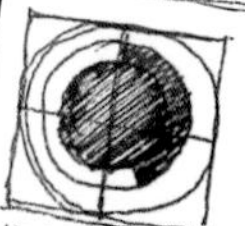

On the road again... trying to fall asleep as first officer of bus sleeps where my legs are supposed to go...

17 hrs. 46 min.

Sunrise... happily chatting and crunching peanuts purchased day before... semi-rested... a few good hours of sleep... still in Sumatra...

20 hrs. 13 min.

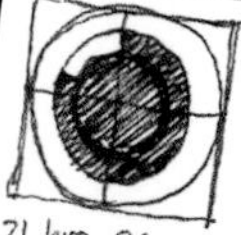

Breakfast stop... arrive at a RUMAH MAKAN for Makan Pagi... sipped down only a teh susu for my scratchy throat

21 hrs. 26 min.

On the road again... persuade friendly driver to play my alien western music on bus cassette deck... soon curious passengers are bobbing their heads to the rhythms of Talking Heads and UB-40...

22 hrs. 03 min.

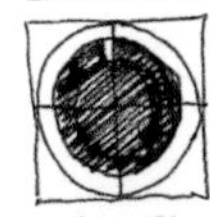

Side 2 of my tape... themes from Batman and Mission Impossible enhance maximum G-force hairpin corner turns on twisty roads in dry South Sumatra... the BAT-BUS blasts off?

23 hrs. 26 min.

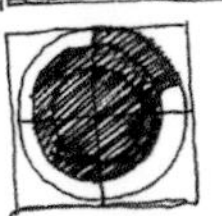

BUS OVERHEATS... short roadside break...

26 hrs. 25 min.

MAINTENANCE STOP... bus rolls into remote bus yard as pit stop crew changes front bald tire to new one with visible tread... also light Padang meal to burn my tongue...

27 hrs. 15 min.

On the road again... sweltering heat of a Tuesday afternoon... still playing my music... driver seems to have an affinity to reggae selections; but orange to heavy-metal/punk...

27 hrs. 43 min.

End of the road at the tip of east Sumatra... disembark as our bus rolls onto large vehicle/passenger ferry to Sumatra... another glowing orange sunset...

29 hrs. 24 min.

Drifting past the smoking Krakatoa volcano as we huddle on the top deck playing a heated game of 7500... we attract a cheering section of dozens...

30 hrs. 39 min.

Set foot on the island of JAVA... On the road again... it's dark now... thinking about Jakarta

32 hrs. 45 min.

20 km out of Jakarta... FLAT TIRE... left rear tire is quickly changed by weary driver and first-officer/co-pilot guy...

35 hrs. 09 min.

FINISH... arrive JAKARTA

Projected trip duration : 28 hrs.
ACTUAL trip duration : 36 hrs. 26 min.
< +8.5 hrs. >

26 min.

SNAPSHOT: Trans-Sumatran Bus

The scene was a typical one: a behemoth air-conditioned bus barrelling down the wrong side of the road — an attempt to achieve the coveted pole position — as it's first officer/co-pilot daringly hangs out of an open door frantically waving hand signals to the vehicle being overtaken... with a quick swig of a colorless alcoholic beverage from an unlabeled bottle and a carefully-timed jerk of the steering wheel in a deadly game of "chicken" the driver narrowly escapes an imminent head-on collision with oncoming traffic skidding to the side of the road...

ARCHITECTURE

WHY WAS IT BUILT LIKE THAT?

As an architect, I've always been fascinated with the built environment. Unsurprisingly, a large number of my travel sketches over the years have revolved around architectural settings.

Travel sketching provides an excellent way to study a given architectural subject, dissect its components, analyze its proportions, and appreciate the details. As opposed to taking a few seconds for a photograph and then moving on, sitting on a doorstep across from a building forces you to observe and understand a structure in its entirety and to soak up the surrounding context.

Small details will become apparent as they are sketched, which then prompts the inevitable question in one's mind: *Why was it built like that?*

Was it a function of climate?
Was it religious or symbolic in nature?
Was it purely decorative?
Was it actually designed in advance, before it was built?

Understanding architecture is analogous to peeling an onion whereby the layers removed, or sketched, slowly reveal what's to be discovered below. In most cases, the buildings we pass by on a daily basis were painstakingly conceptualized, designed, constructed and crafted by a large team of people -- most of whom, sadly, have been forgotten in the mists of time.

HONOLULU HALE / 21 AUG 93
4.0
SCHMIDT 1993

Honolulu, Hawaii, USA: Perfect weather is very conducive to sitting beneath a shady tree to study the details of some of the island's more picturesque buildings.

Honolulu, Hawaii, USA: Experimenting with various media and drawing techniques may inadvertently lead to interesting and unexpected results.

Double Take: On rare occasions, I have had the opportunity to return to the same place years later, and do a sketch from the same vantage point, sometimes using different media. This intimate outdoor cafe in Ubud on the island of Bali, Indonesia, keeps drawing me back.

Bali, Indonesia: A land rich in color and detail is a sketcher's paradise.

TEMPLE BALE (DRUM HOUSE)
UBUD, BALI
20 NOV 91 / 1.0

"PASIK"
SMALL OFFERING TEMPLE BY THE SEA
PADANGBAI , BALI   22 NOV 91 / 1.0

Indonesia: This diverse island nation provides some of the most picturesque and culturally intriguing environments in the world to sketch.

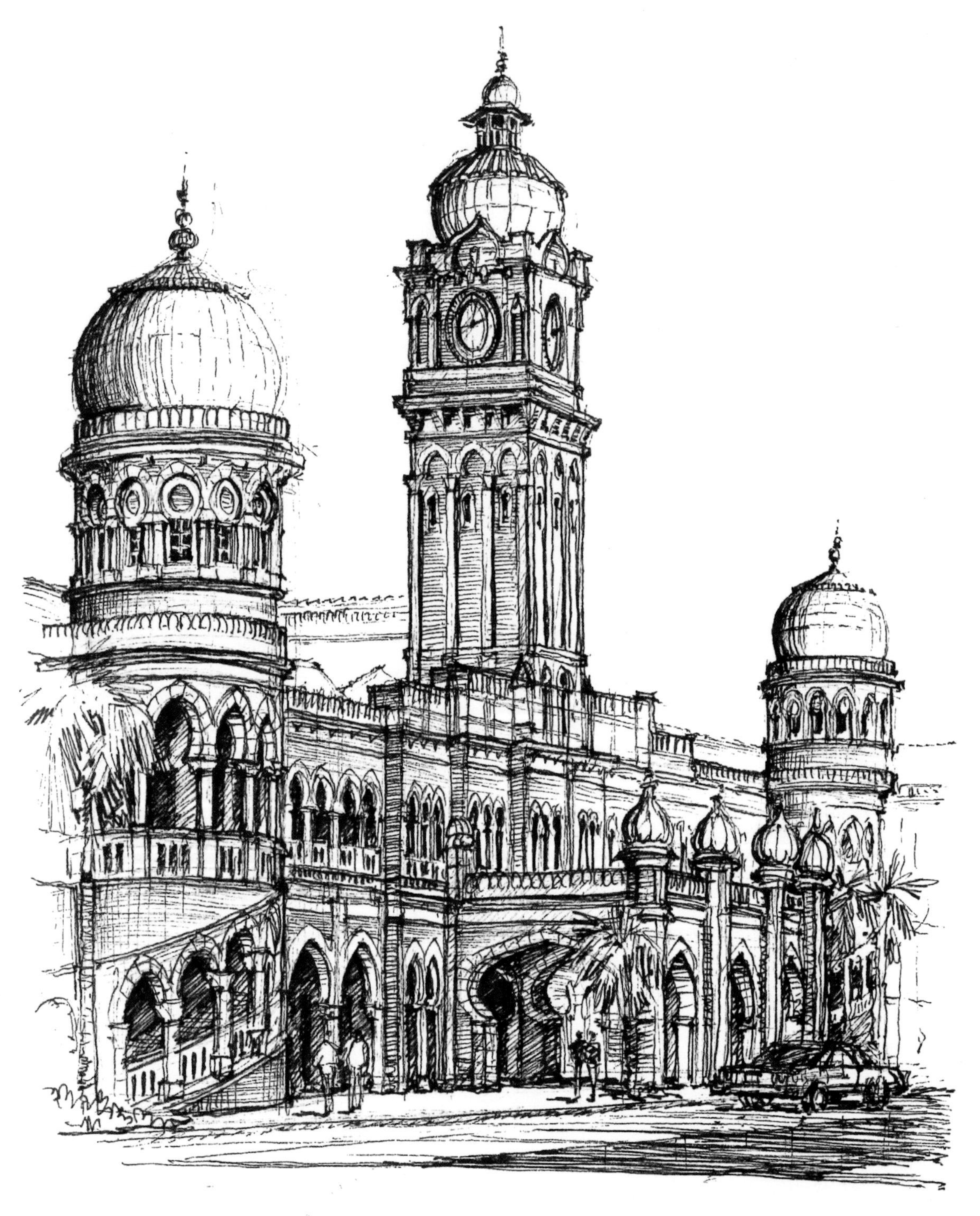

Malaysia: This multi-ethnic and multi-cultural country provides stunning architectural treasures around every corner.

Thailand: The cultural legacy of a country, religious beliefs and adaptations to it's climate extremes are often expressed through architecture.

Singapore and Hong Kong: In some places, as
in these two former British colonies, the local
vernacular is a blend of local and imported design
elements -- adding to the unique "sense of place"
and cultural richness of both destinations.

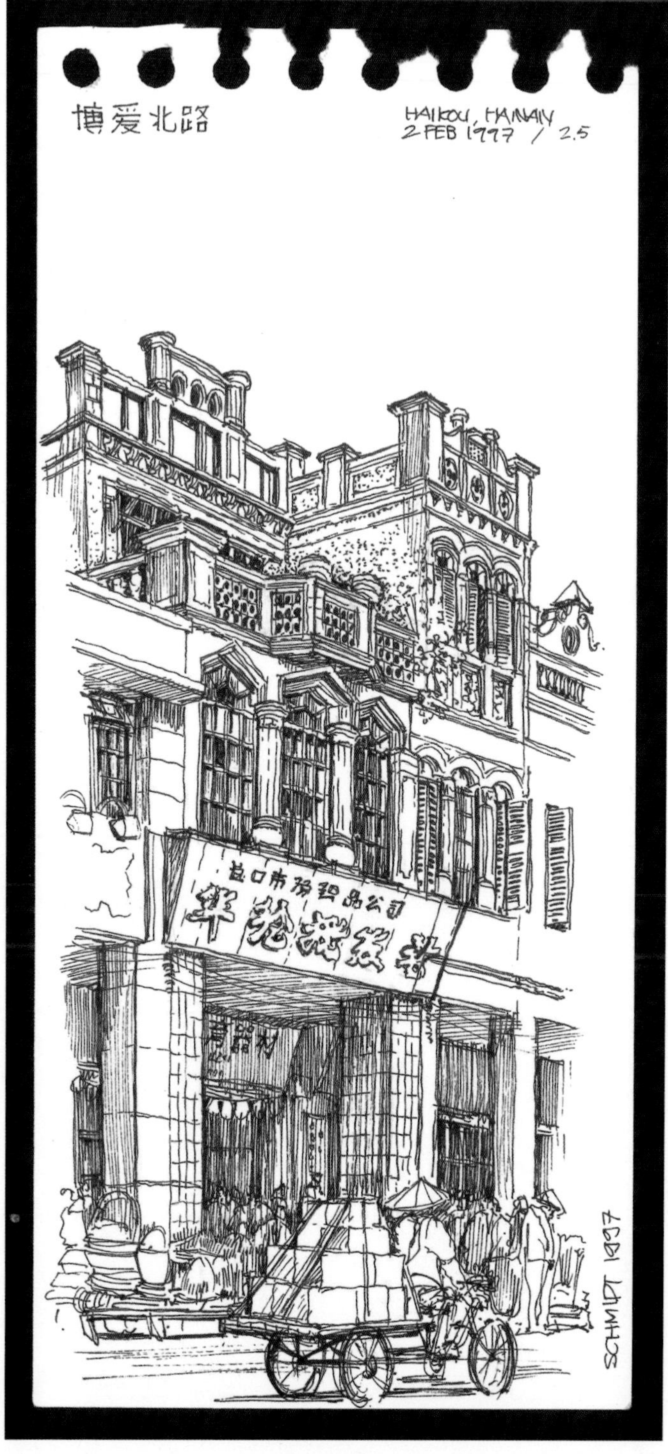

Haikou, China: Rapid urban redevelopment often results in disappearing cities. These street scenes from Hainan Island's capital city were captured at a brief moment in time, only to vanish, unexpectedly, just a few years later.

Summer of Sketches:
In the USA, I once spent a summer holed up in the picturesque mountain resort town of Vail, Colorado, doing quick watercolor sketches and selling them to tourists on the street.

As the "resident street artist," I also obtained a few commissions from local shopkeepers and homeowners, and eventually raised enough money from selling my sketches to fund the next stage of my journey.

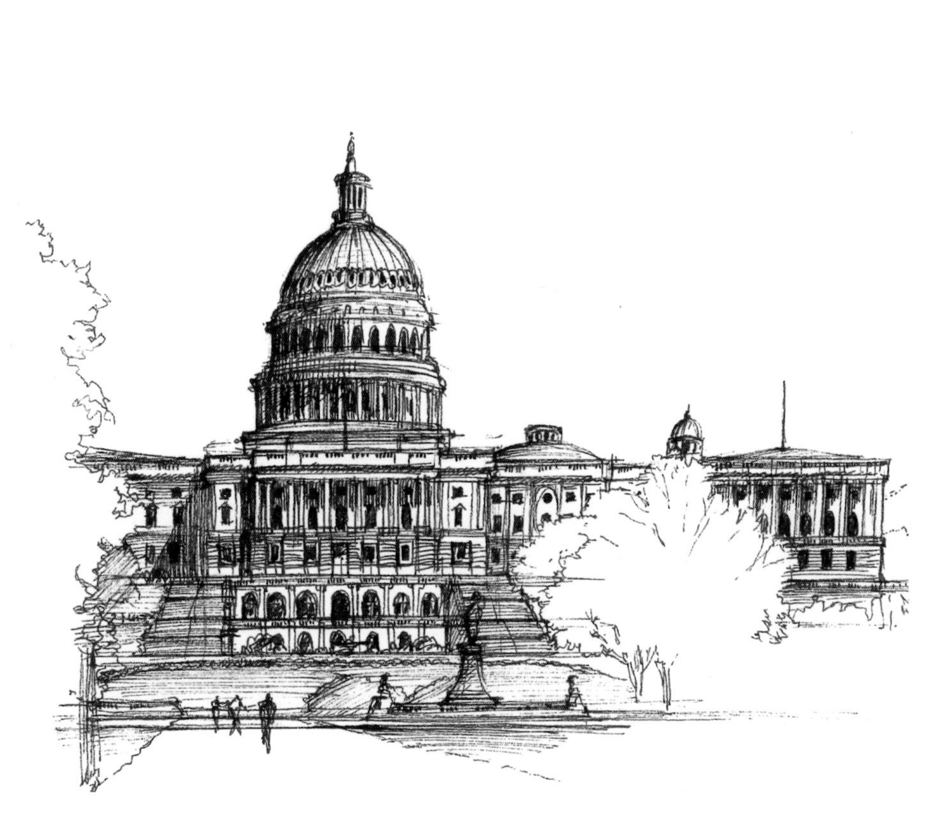

SMITHSONIAN CASTLE / WASHINGTON D.C.

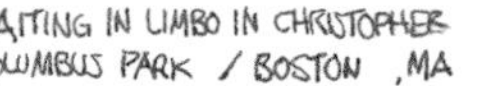

WAITING IN LIMBO IN CHRISTOPHER
COLUMBUS PARK / BOSTON , MA

* SKETCH WITH RAINDROP INK -WASH ENHANCEMENTS

Cold Feet: Sketching in Istanbul, Turkey
on a very chilly November day --
when it's cold, you need to work fast ...
before your extremities freeze up!

ISTANBUL UNIVERSITY ON A CHILLY NOVEMBER DAY ..

Thailand: Postcard-sized watercolors without supporting linework; these paintings were contained within masking tape borders that frame each image.

Vignettes: Sketching without defined borders can help you focus on a particular subject without being distracted by the surrounding context.

Europe: Many regard this part of the world as the Holy Grail of architecture. A lifetime could be spent sketching the countless historic treasures of Europe.

BATH ABBEY (ENGLAND)
23 · JUNE · 1988

7 AUG 1988 - took a walking tour through old Drager just now - really cool little village... but now I'm in...
KØBENHAVN
7 AUG
sitting along the harbor looking at a tower after consuming a litre of beer that cost me 25 dkr which works out to about $4!

CHRISTIANSPOR TOWER
(houses Parliament of Denmark)

ENVIRONMENTS

THE SPACES IN BETWEEN:

While the architecture of a particular place is often iconic and defines a destination, for a traveller, the spaces *between* the buildings and the surrounding natural environment often have the biggest impact on the travel experience.

Movement through the built environment can vary from the wide axial boulevards of Paris to the narrow pathways that meander through rural settlements.

Some parts of the built environment have been designed with a very choreographed progression between spaces, while others have evolved in a more chaotic, organic manner.

Mapping out pedestrian and vehicular circulation systems helps in understanding how people get around and how towns and cities might have evolved. Parks, gardens, infrastructure, and other landscape elements all add to the "sense of place" that makes a destination unique.

Architecture and nature sometimes become blurred.

Wide Angle View: A panoramic sketch created by periodically rotating while drawing.

Nature: Natural environments and the interplay of light during a particular time of day provide inspiration to sketch

Street Cafe: Transitional areas between indoors and outdoors are always teeming with life.

GOLDEN GATE
BRIDGE
SCHMIDT
OCTOBER 13

HAIKOU / HARBOR BOATS / 26 MAR 96 / 1.0

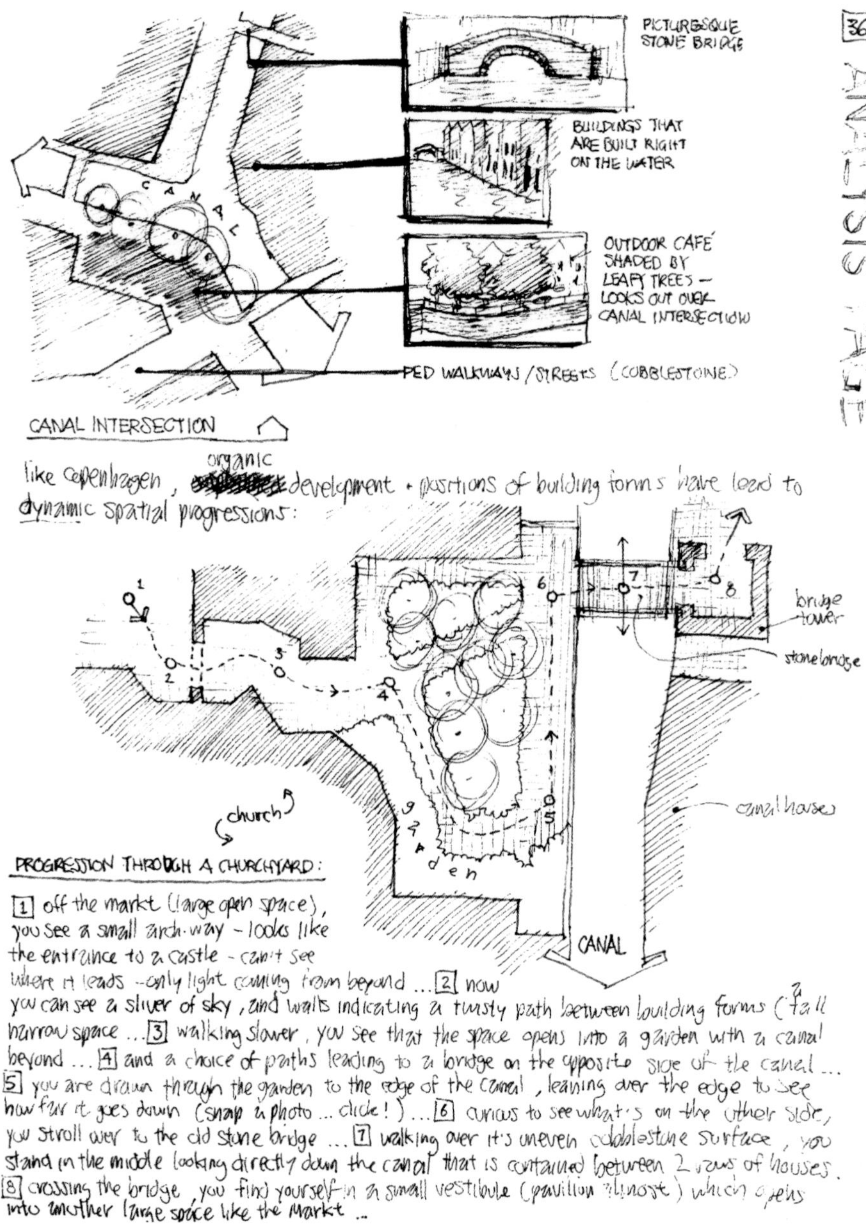

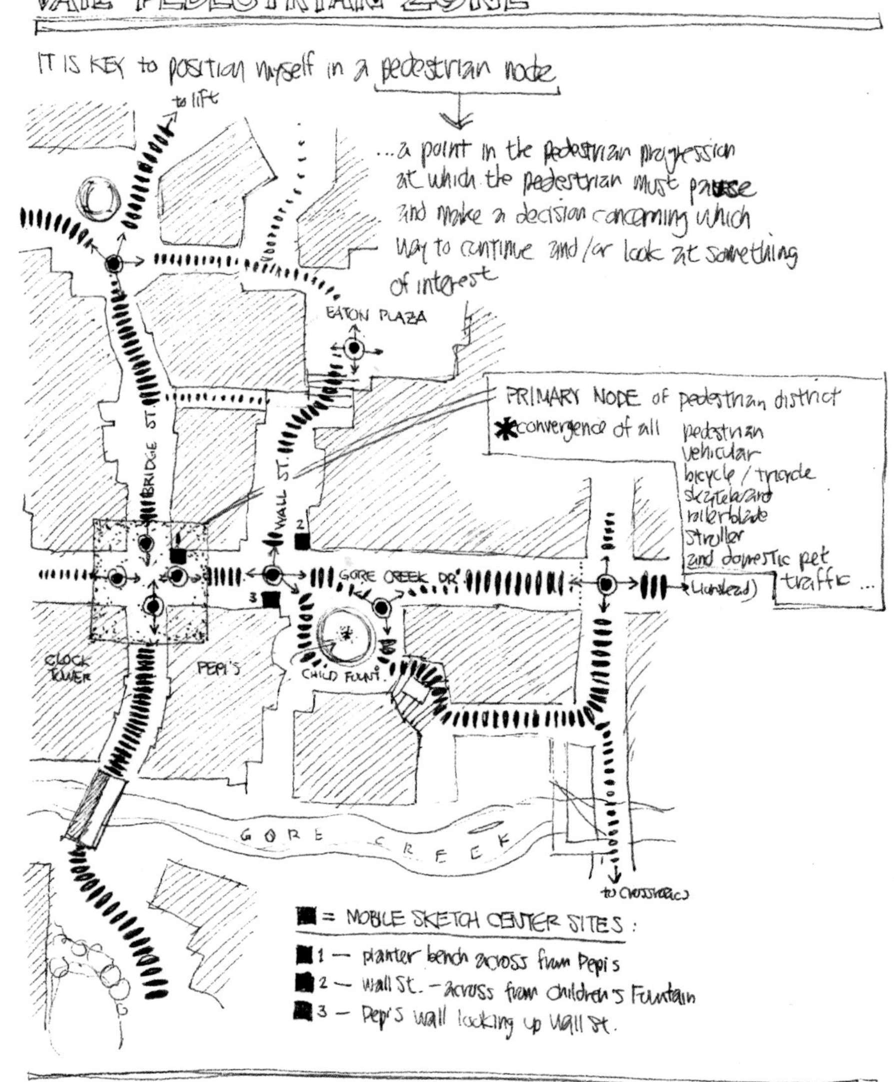

Spatial Progression: Sketching can be used to document progressions through the built environment and to understand how people move between buildings.

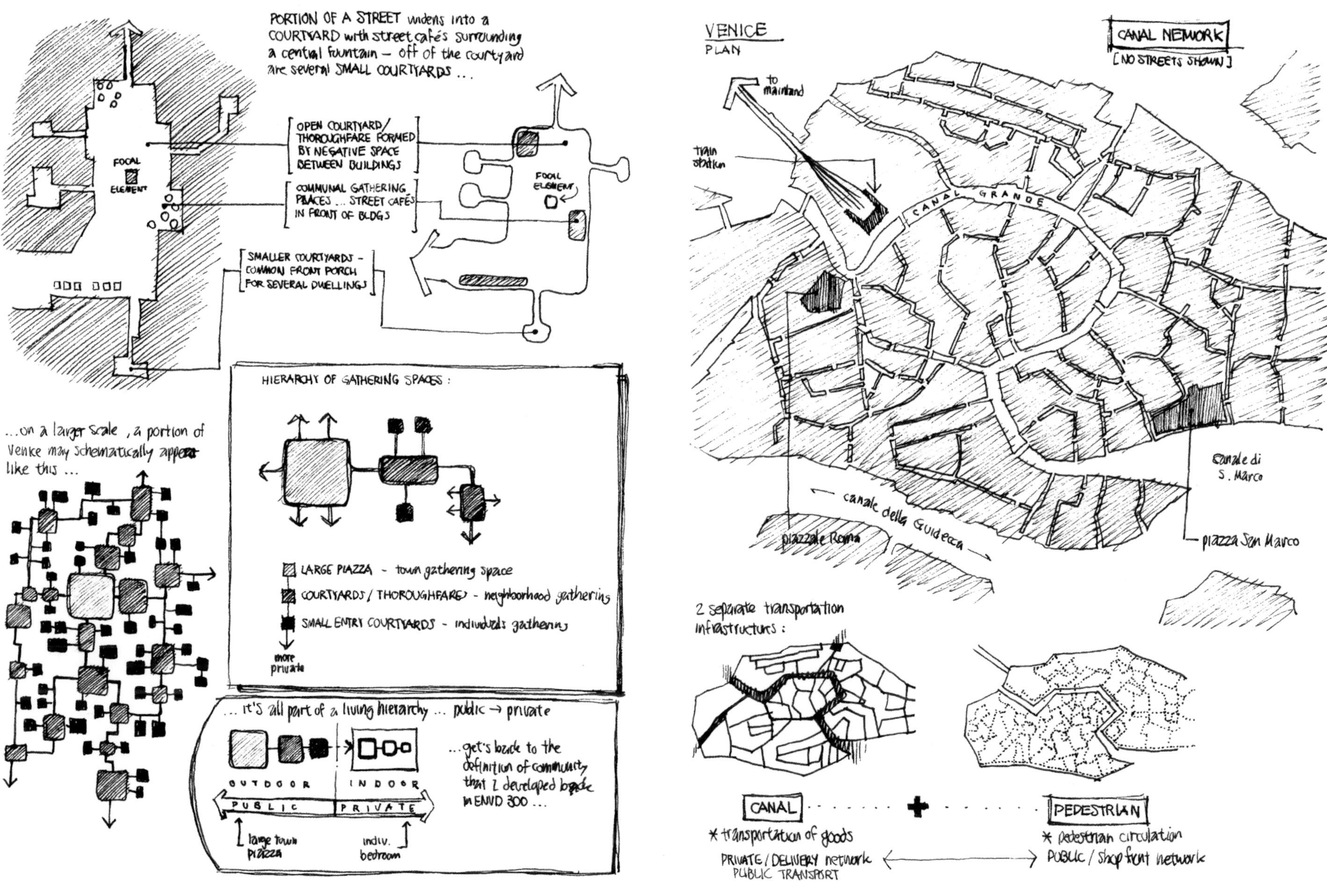

Circulation: Like the human body, urban environments can be analyzed relative to circulation systems and hierarchies of elements.

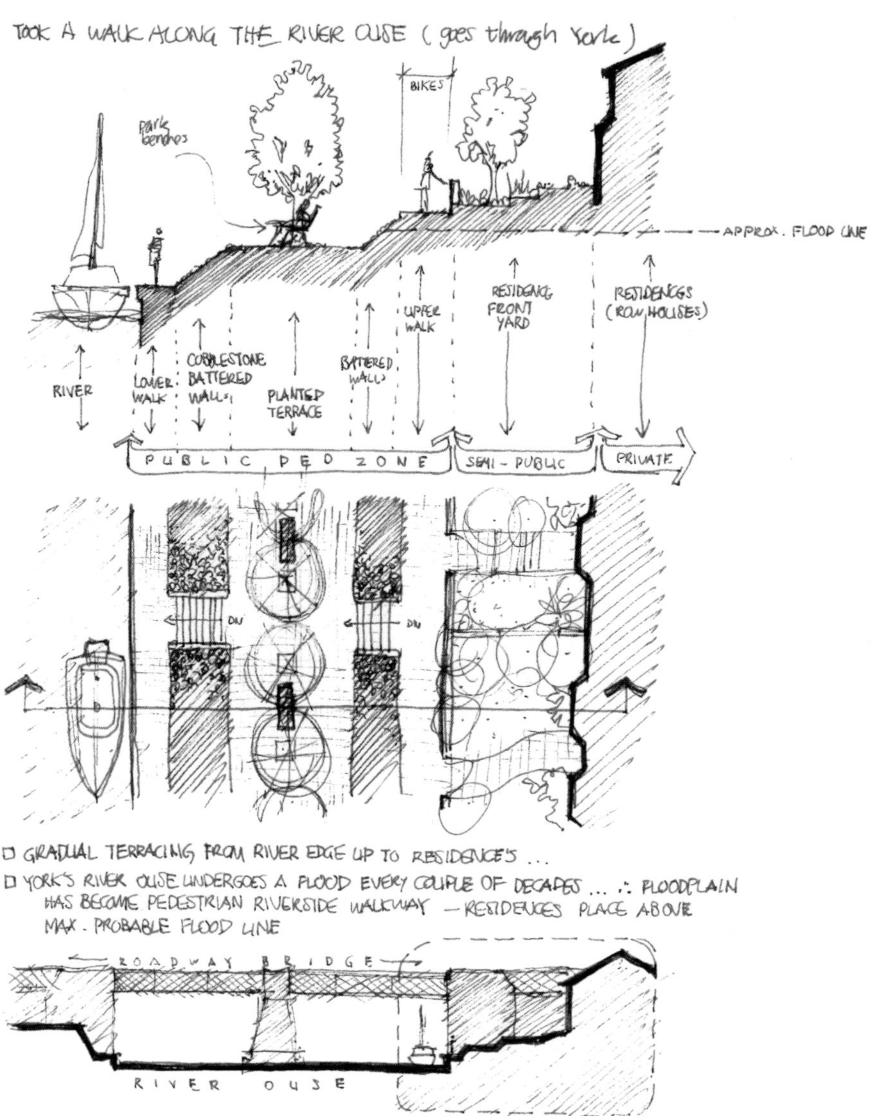

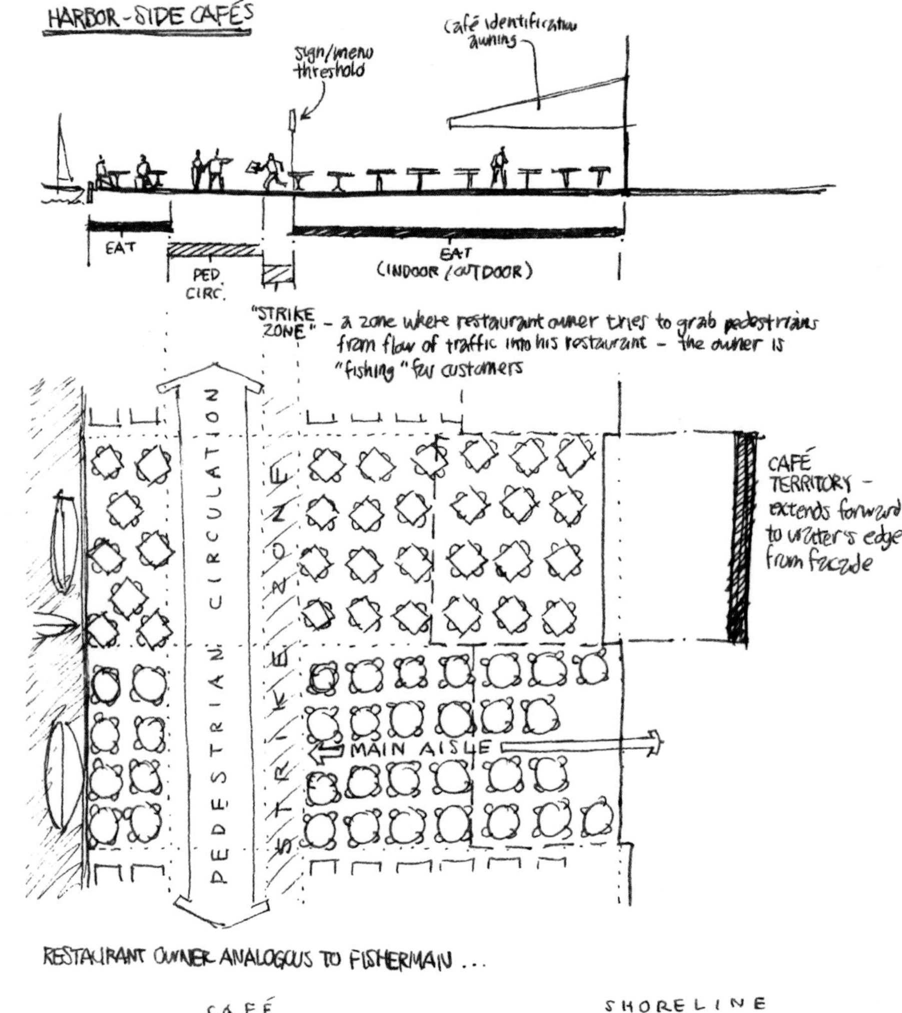

Pathways: The edges of water bodies, pedestrian paths, bicycle paths, roads and other linear elements often regulate our movement and help differentiate public and private space in the built environment.

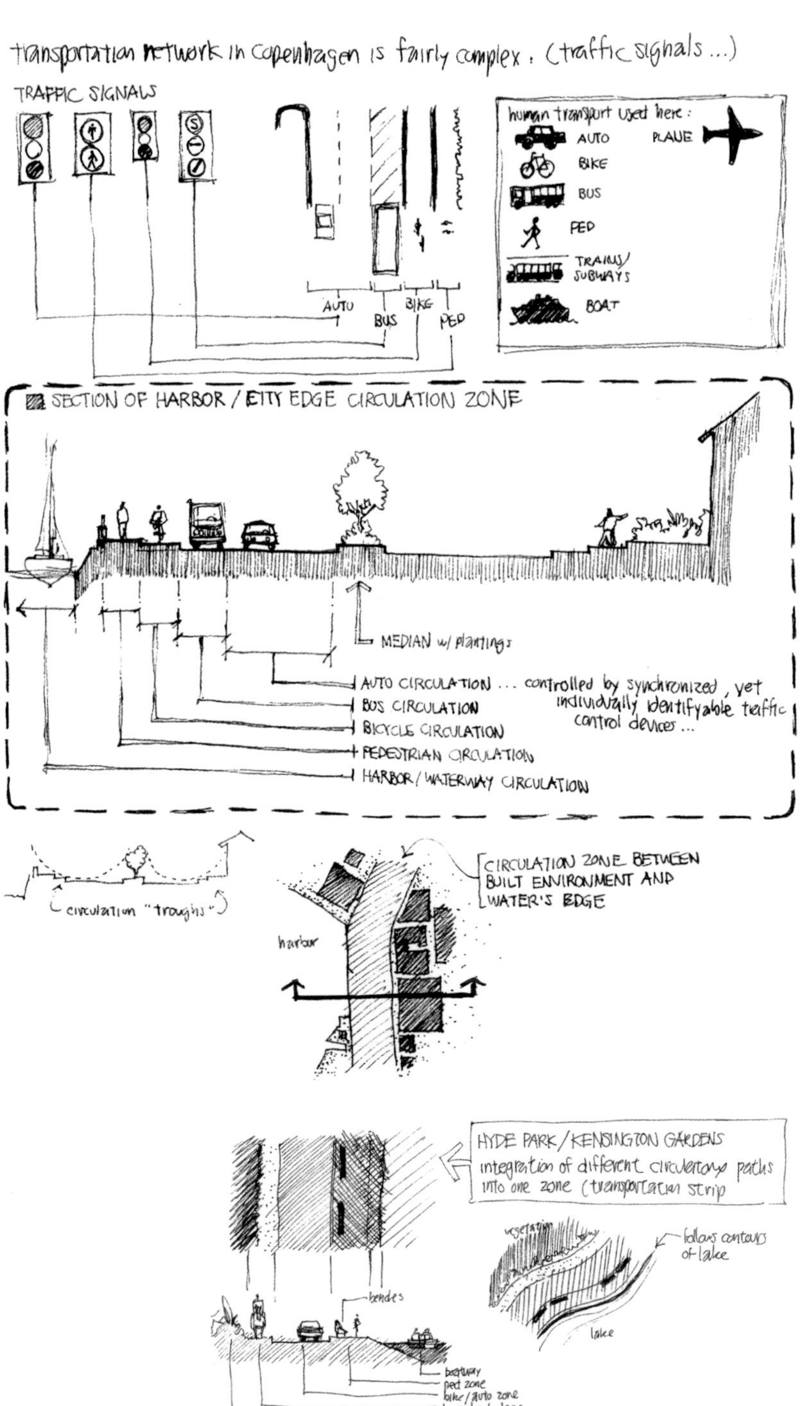

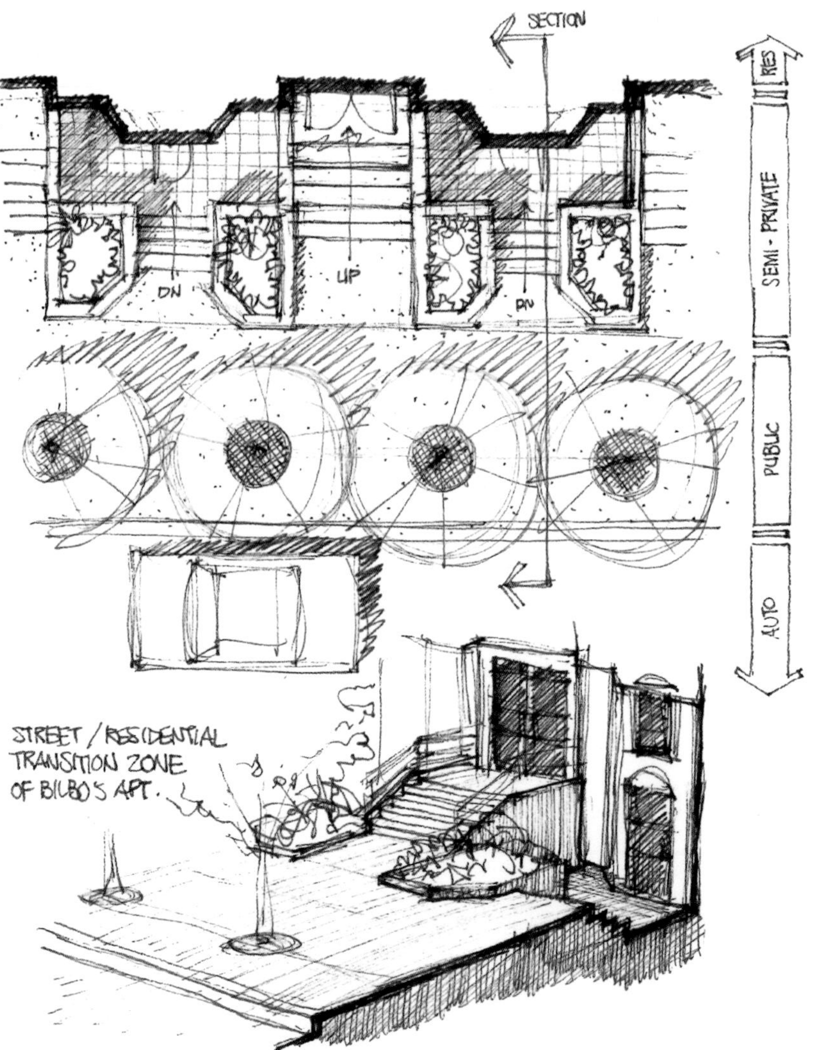

Getting Around: What started out as a simple pathway long ago may have evolved into a modern thoroughfare with separate lanes for different modes of transportation travelling at differing speeds.

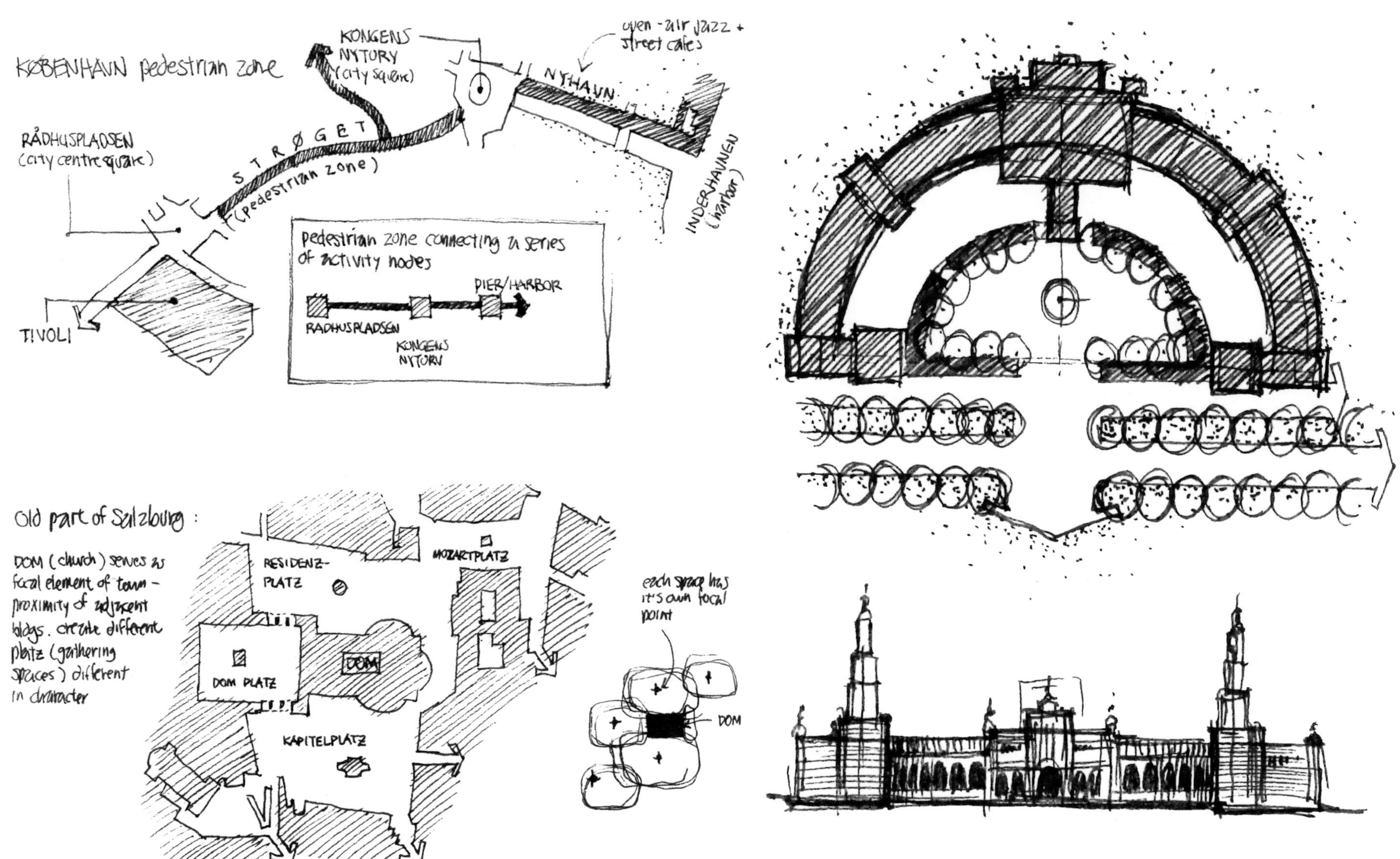

Nodes: Many circulation systems through urban areas are punctuated by a series of "nodes." Sometimes these take the form of plazas, fountains, squares or parks, all of which can assist way-finding through the built environment.

- there is a town code that most buildings (historic ones from 1600's) keep original/orange/yellow pastel color with burnt orange -colored roof tiles — produces an architectural unity throughout town ...

- layout of town was due to eccretively-grown dwellings from an original fishing port [irregular / non-uniform spaces are formed — this makes for a dynamic sensation of movement between bldgs. — in negative space formed by dwellings] — DYNAMIC CIRCULATION —

also provides a perpetually changing scene

despite the random appearance of the maze here, there seems to be some logic to it — an unplanned logic — spaces formed by the needs of the people at a particular moment in time ...

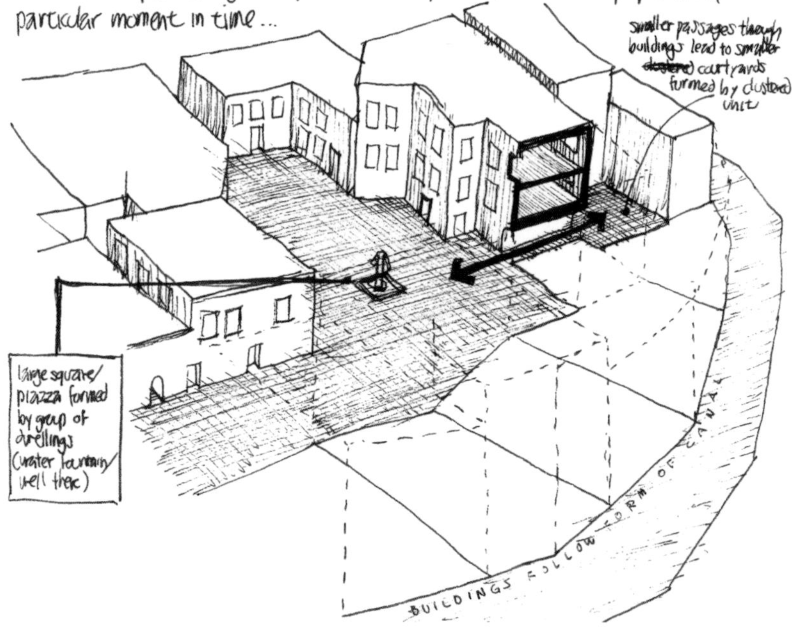

Dynamic Circulation: Places that evolved organically often have circulation paths of varying widths that result in a constantly changing scene as one moves through the environment.

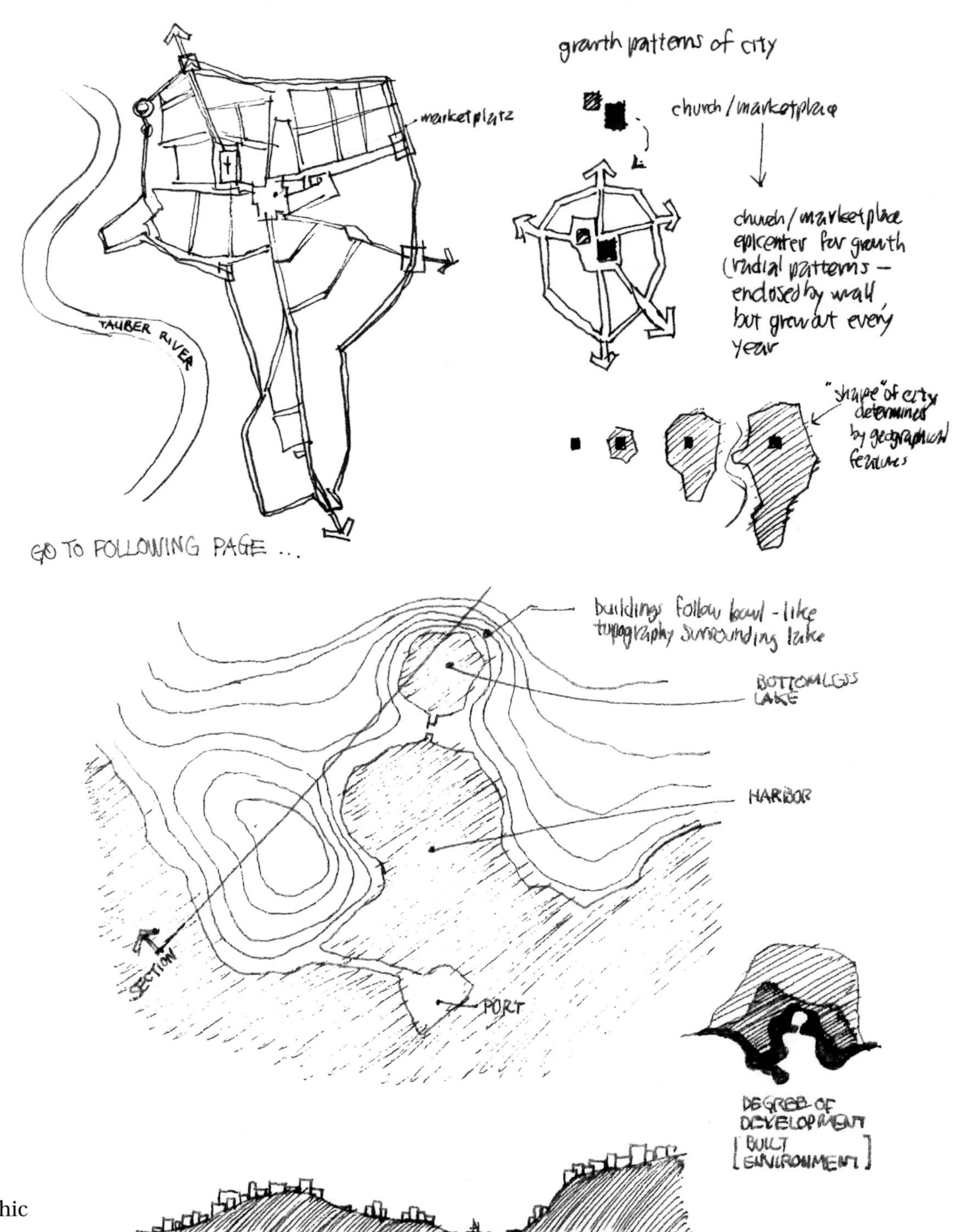

Historical Development: Many of the world's cities have evolved organically from a central core, which, over time, radiated outward and around topographic obstacles.

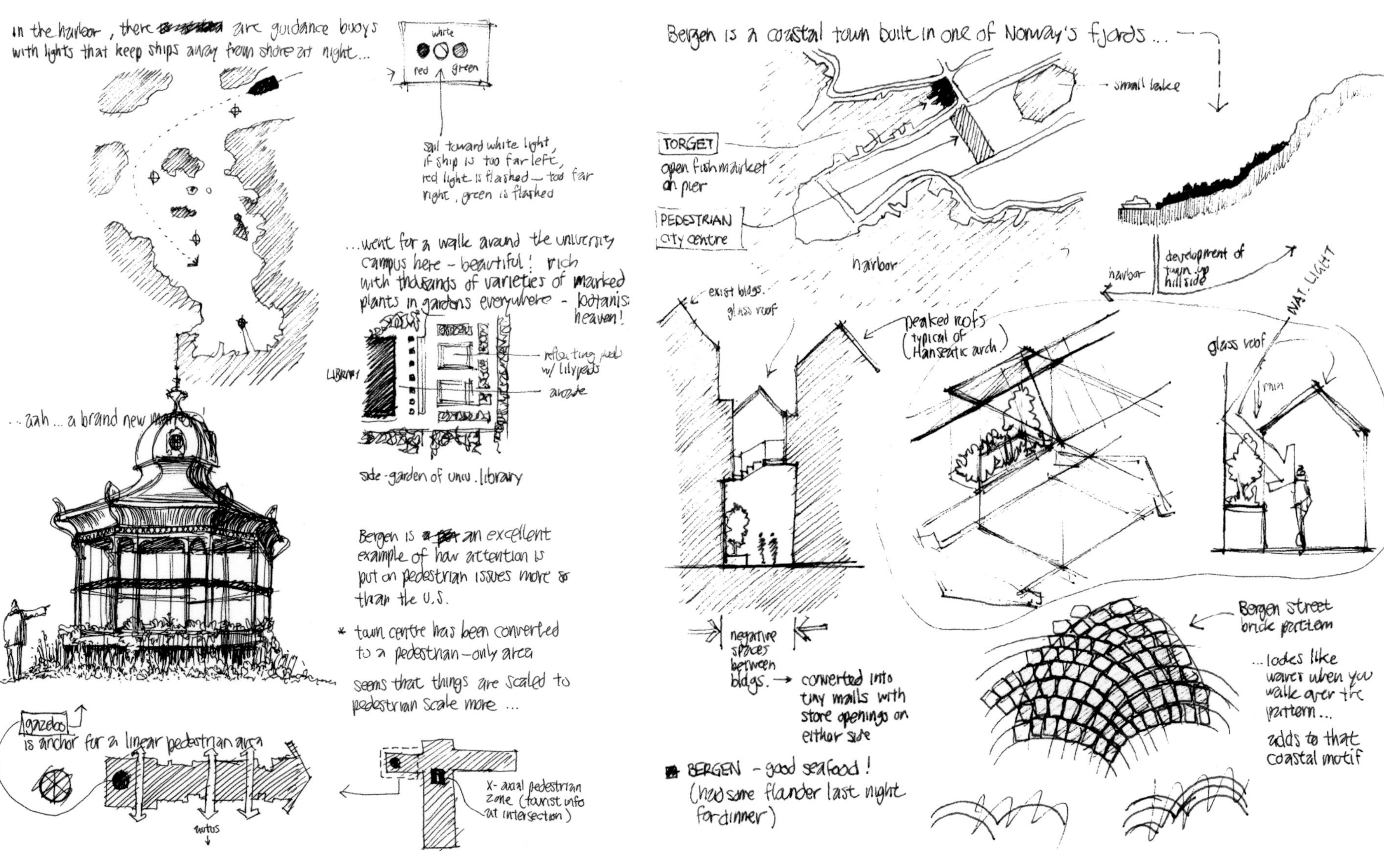

Pedestrianization: Some cities like Bergen, Norway have converted portions of their city centers into pedestrian-only zones.

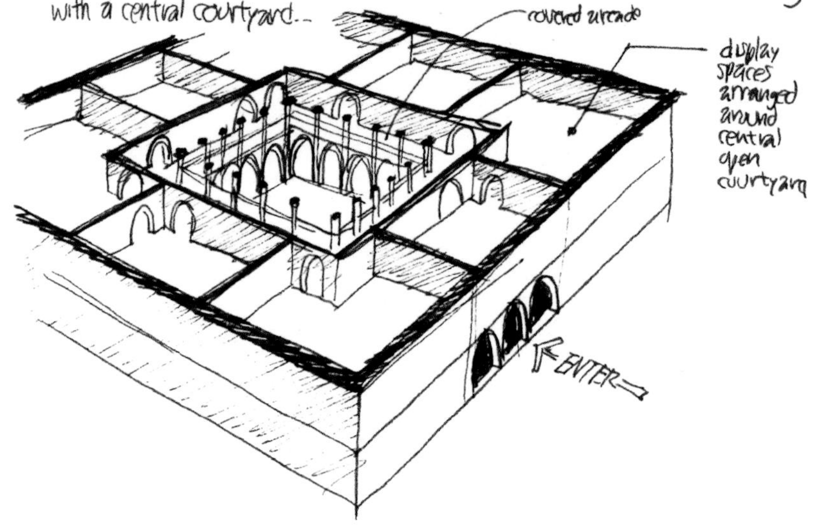

Adaptive Reuse: Ancient fortifications and defensive walls are sometimes converted into pedestrian-friendly areas, while retaining their historic value.

It seems that Sunday mornings are a special time for Italian men ... they go to a nearby café and meet with other men over glasses of wine – the women must either be at home or at church or something ...

Urban Canals: Other cities have incorporated waterways into their urban fabrics, which also serve as important transportation networks.

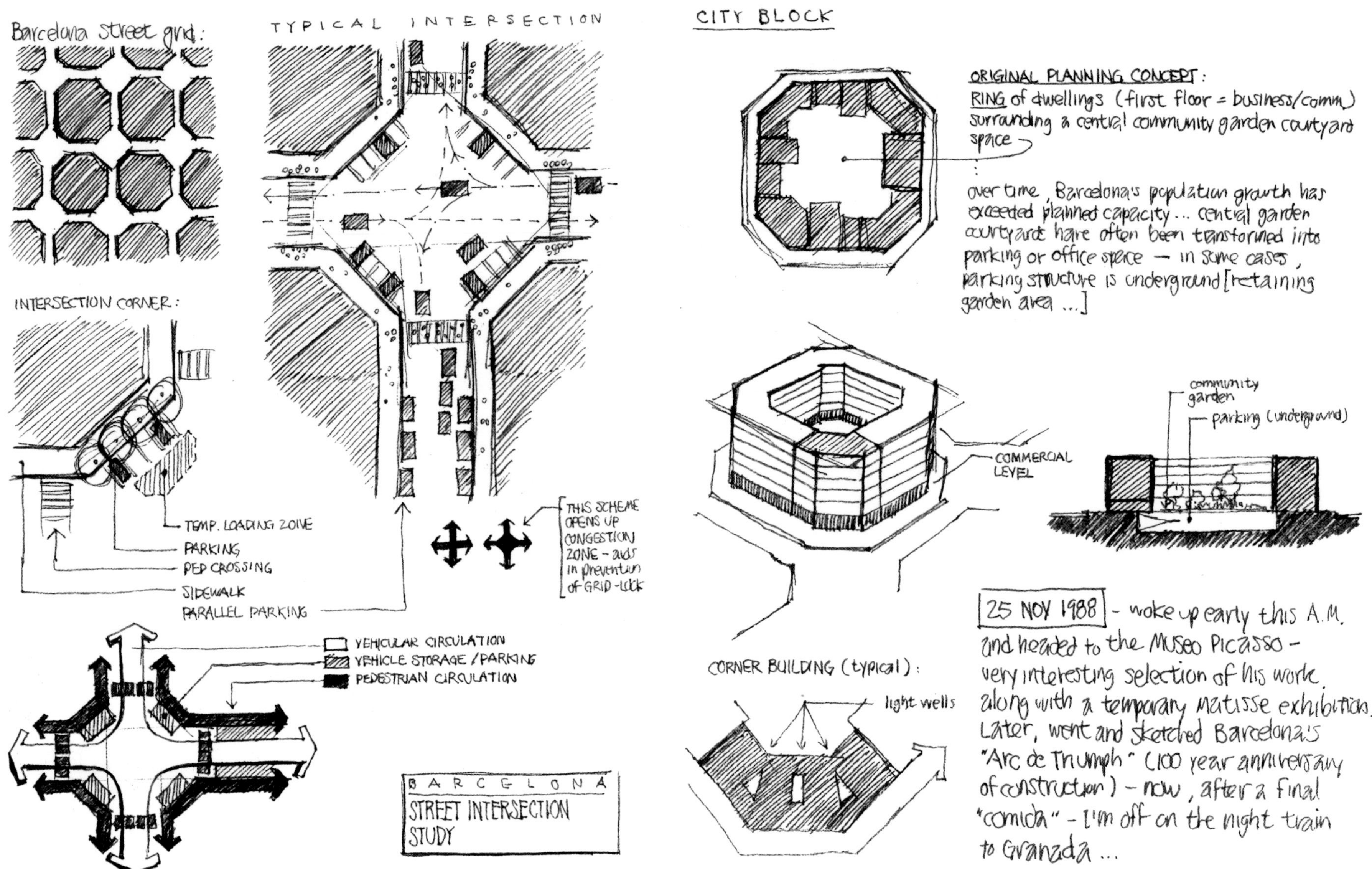

Urban Planning: Places like Barcelona, Spain, have experimented with interesting planning concepts both for urban housing and for easing traffic congestion.

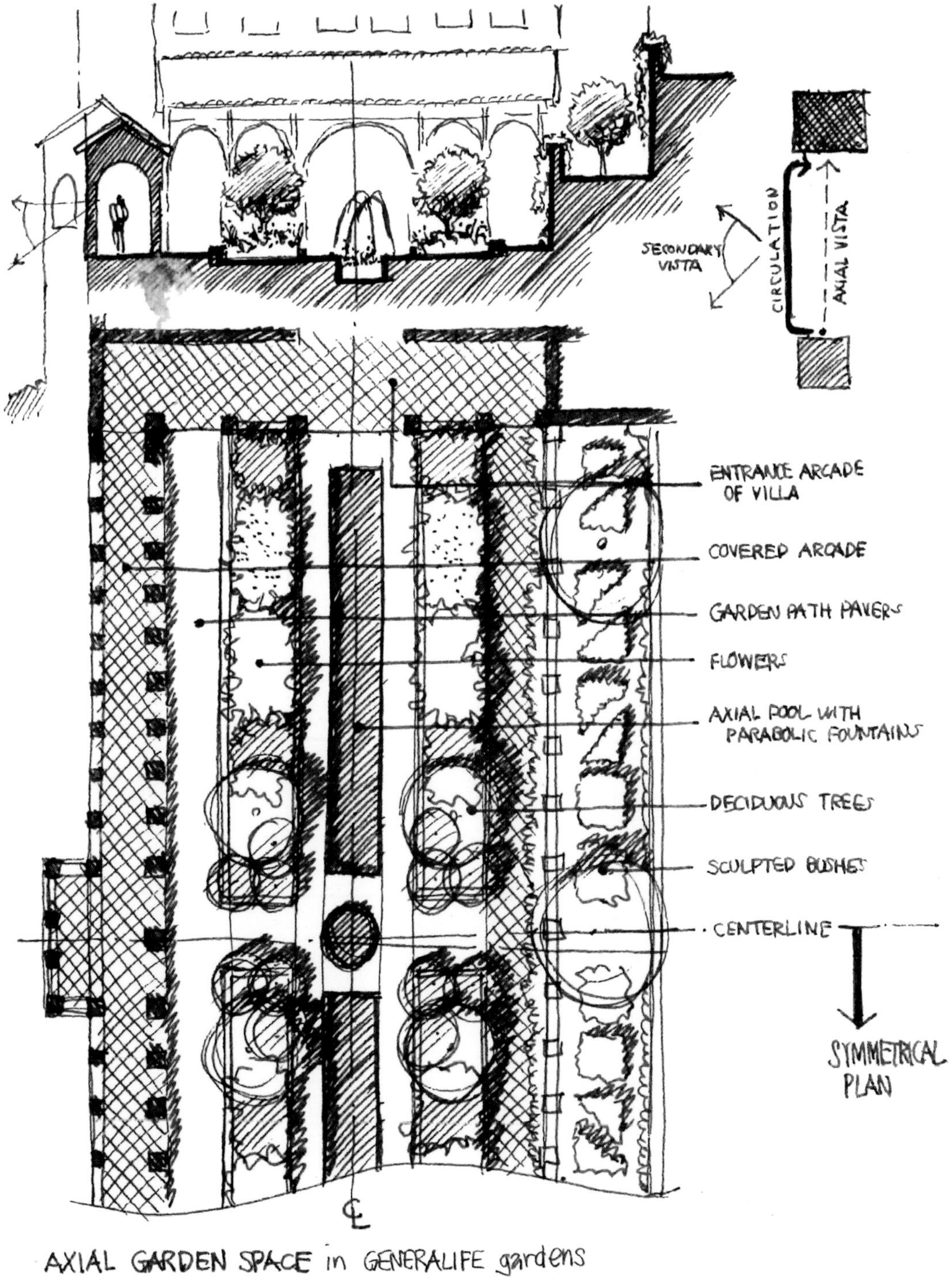

Formal Gardens: The Generalife Gardens in Granada, Spain, provide a contemplative, natural setting within a formal framework.

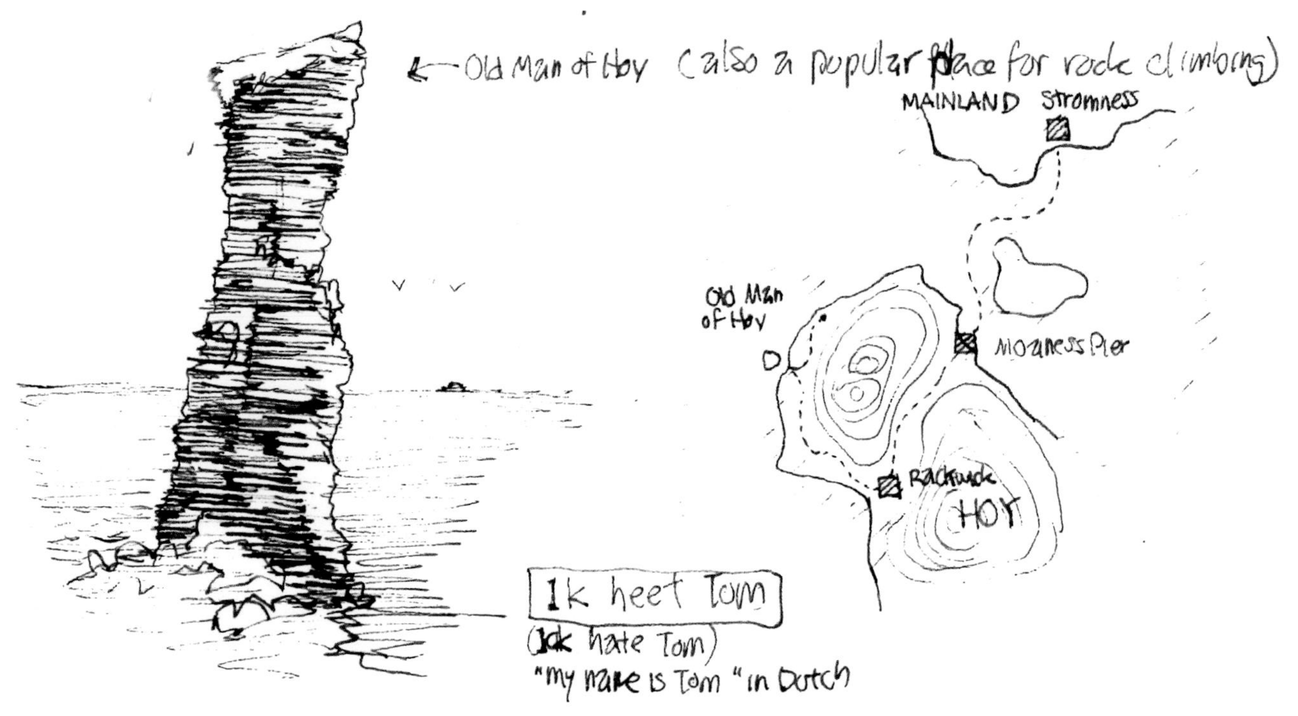

 – this morning, took the early train to Koblenz where I'm now sitting on a boat waiting to float down the Mosel valley. The weather is slightly overcast & gloomy, but I think it may get better as the day goes by...

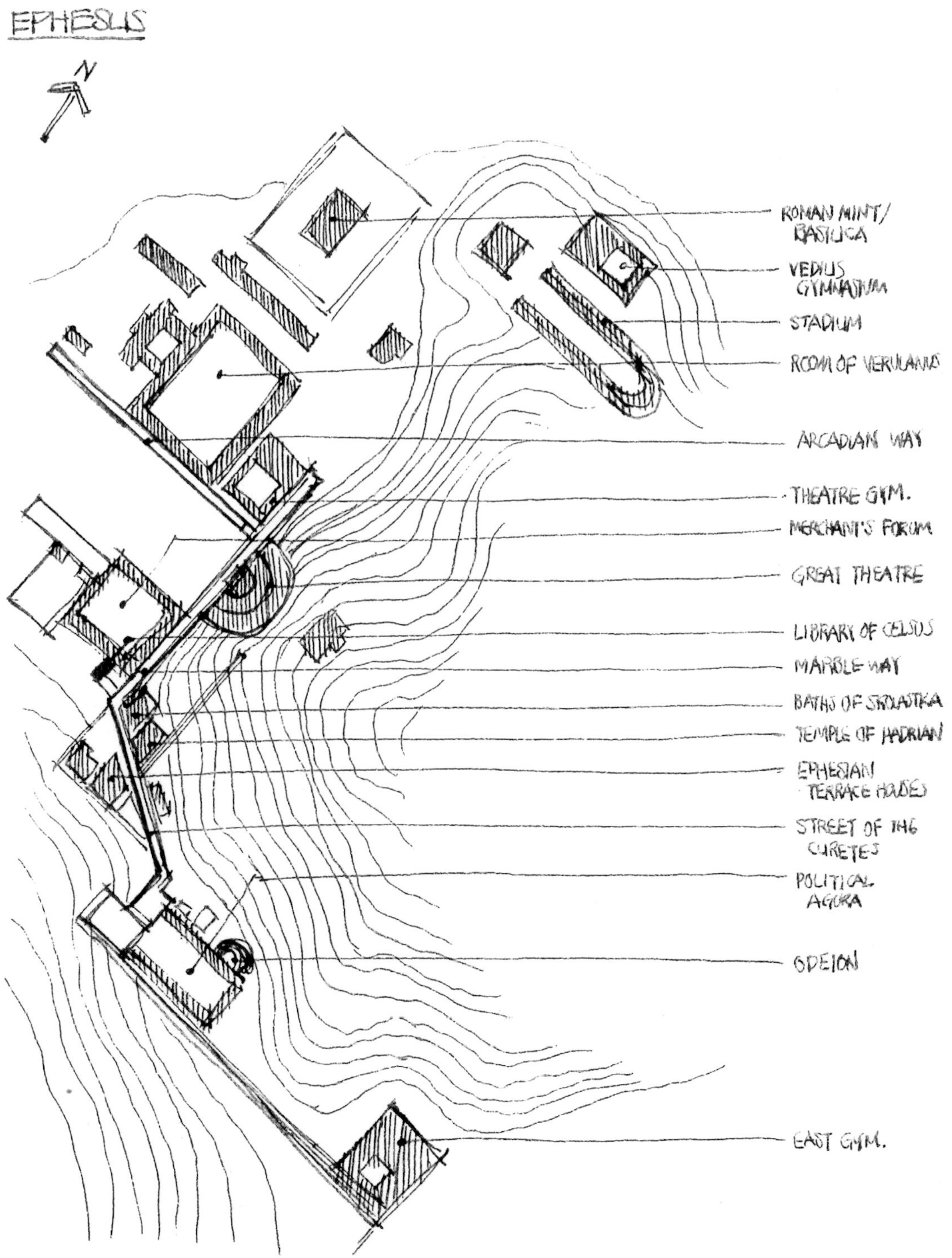

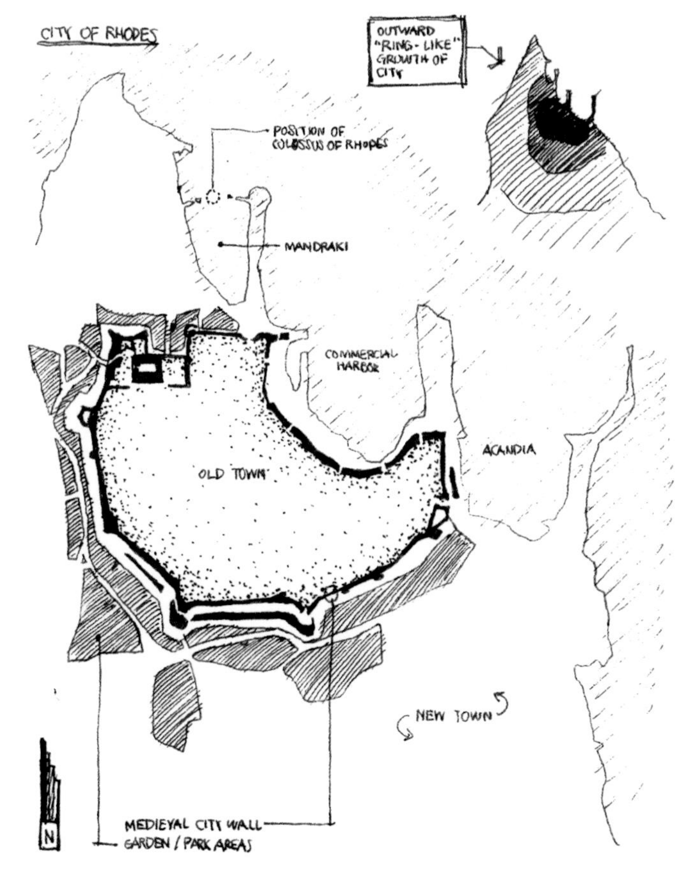

Taming Nature: Humans have modified the natural environment to suit their needs throughout the ages. Defensible hilltops became fortified citadels, caves became shelter, islands became steppingstones between land masses, and anything that could be climbed, was climbed.

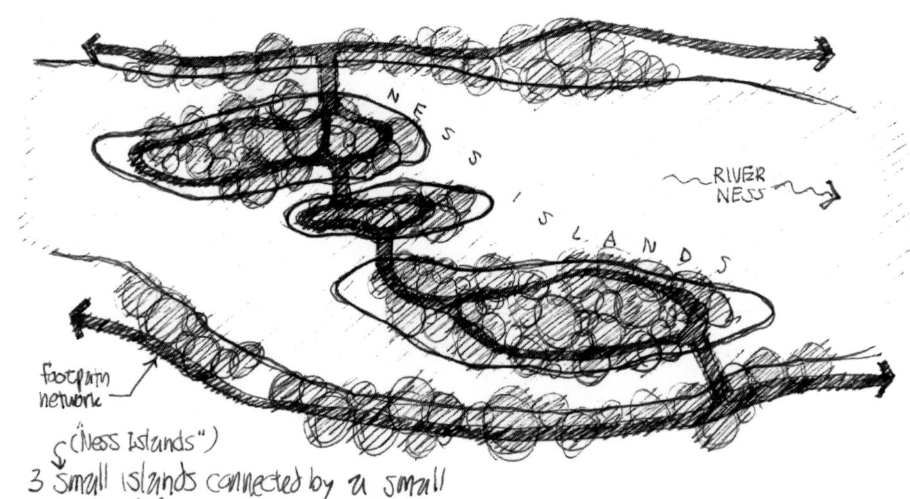

("Ness Islands")
3 small islands connected by a small
network of footpaths — island ↔ island link is by white bridges
(bright contrast against lush green vegetation — similar to Richard Meier's
work (white bldg. reflects surrounding landscape ...)
(riverside benches + picnic tables scattered throughout isles)

NIAH CAVES

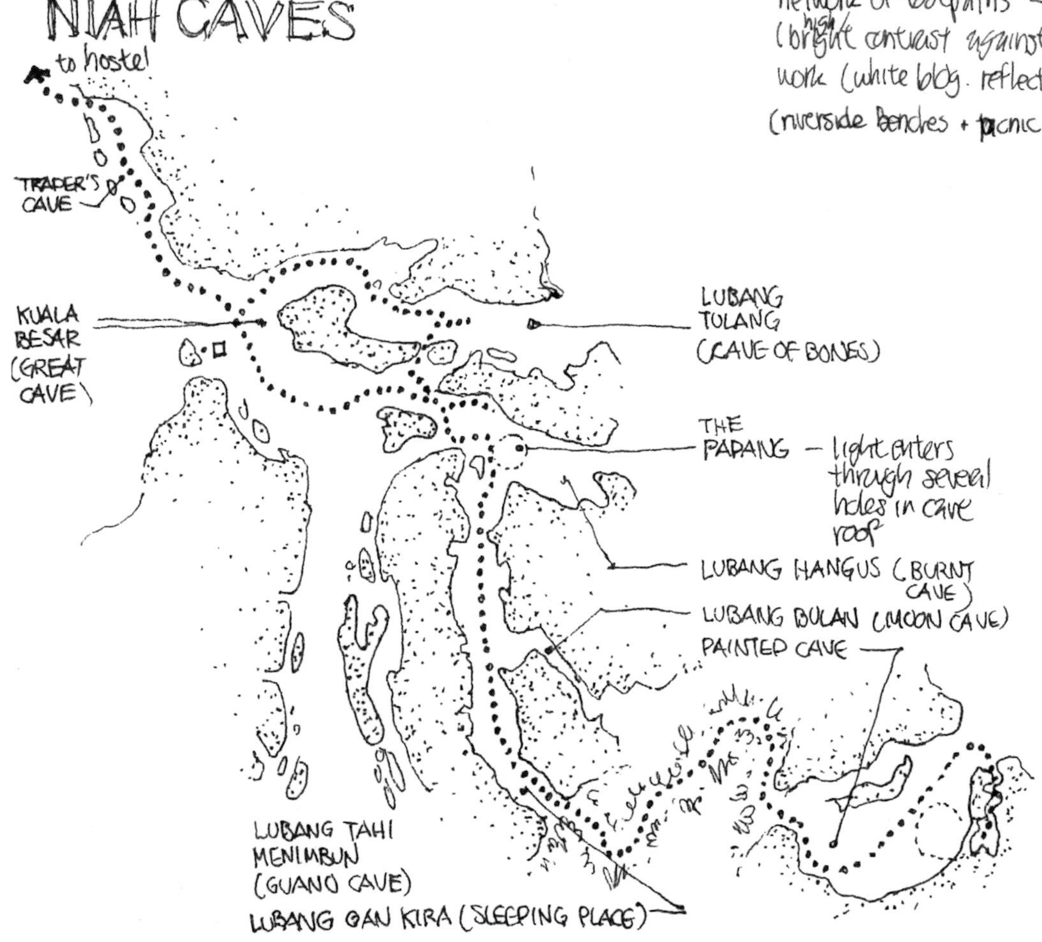

...just went for a sunset walk on the beach here in Radcwide, after a tasty meal prepared by Anne + George (couple at the hostel) – some kind of stew... "but good when you have no food, except for a can of pears...

the sea here is quite chilly – saw one interesting rock formations in cliffs:

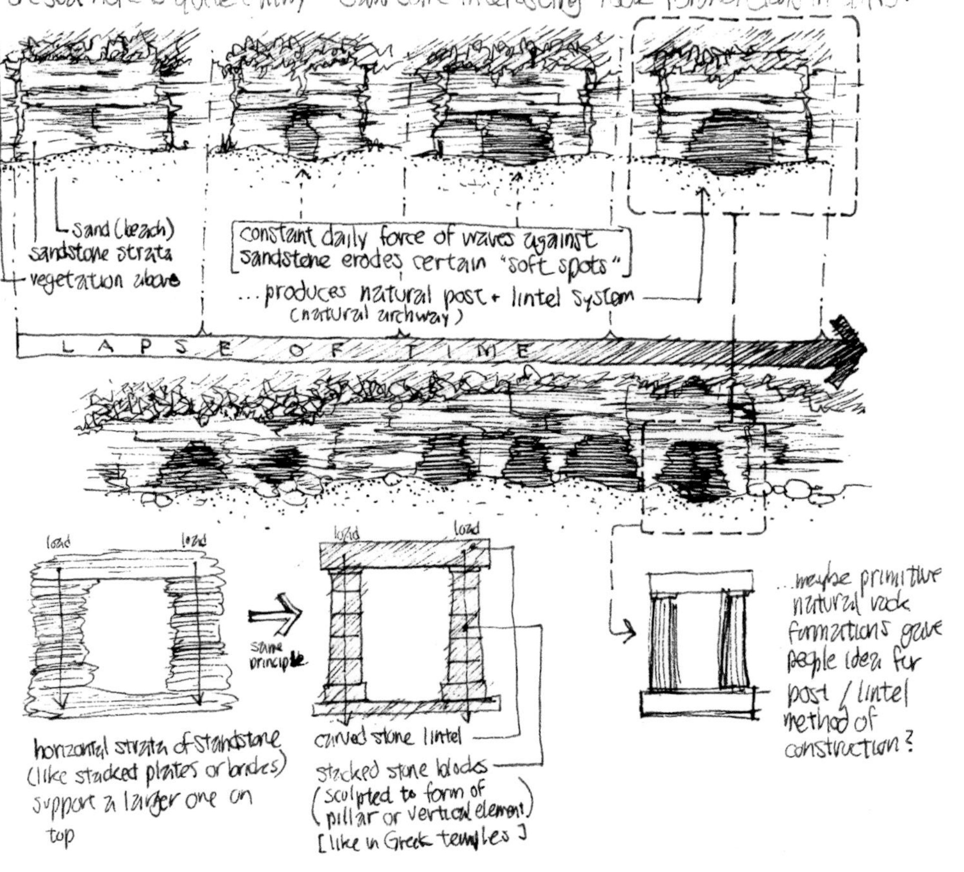

Le Château is a large rock outcropping affording spectacular views of the coastline – the top is covered with parks and a magnificent cemetery.

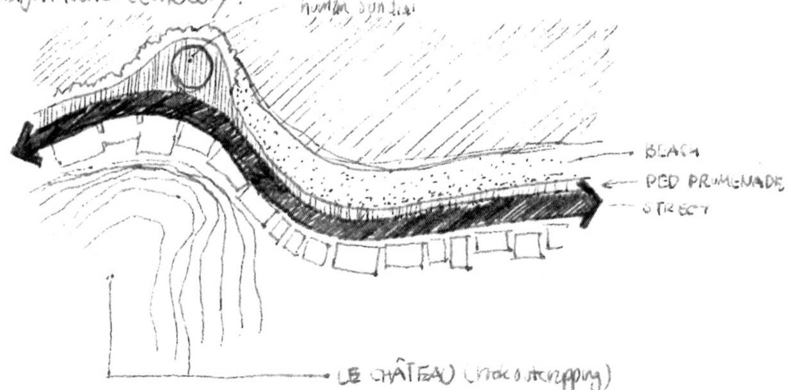

HUMAN SUNDIAL (acts as a gathering node in beach promenade)

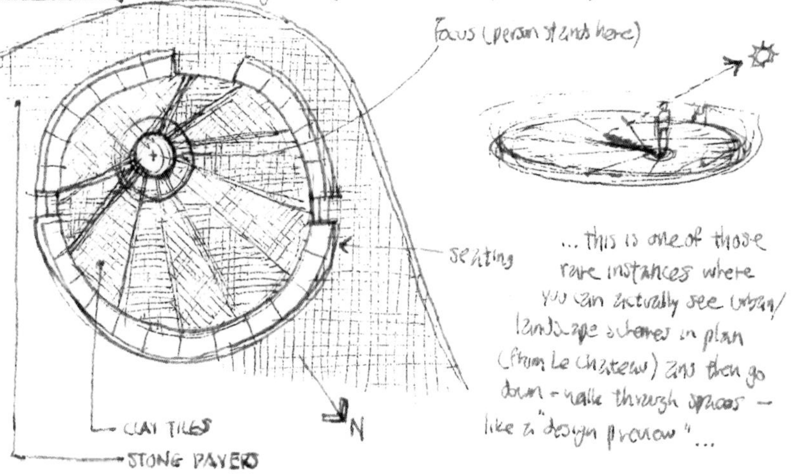

...this is one of those rare instances where you can actually see urban/ landscape schemes in plan (from Le Chateau) and then go down + walk through spaces – like a "design preview"...

MYSTERIOUS PLACES

MYSTERIOUS PLACES

Ever since I was a child, I have been fascinated with enigmatic places that could not be fully explained, or were steeped in history. How many of us have marveled over how and why the pyramids of Egypt were built? Or the mysteries surrounding ancient religious buildings? And what about those huge stone heads on Easter Island?

Destinations shrouded in history and mystery have topped my travel bucket list from an early age. Over the years, I've been very fortunate to have had the opportunity to independently visit many such destinations, find a comfortable vantage point, and leisurely sketch them without being herded onto a bus with other time-starved tourists. As a traveller with your own schedule, you are able to slowly soak up obscure local legends while reading up on why a place "is" the way it is.

Whether you are a historian, or a curious, bumbling traveller like me, mysterious places across the planet attract people from all walks of life.

As Oscar Wilde once wrote, *"The true mystery of the world is the visible, not the invisible."*

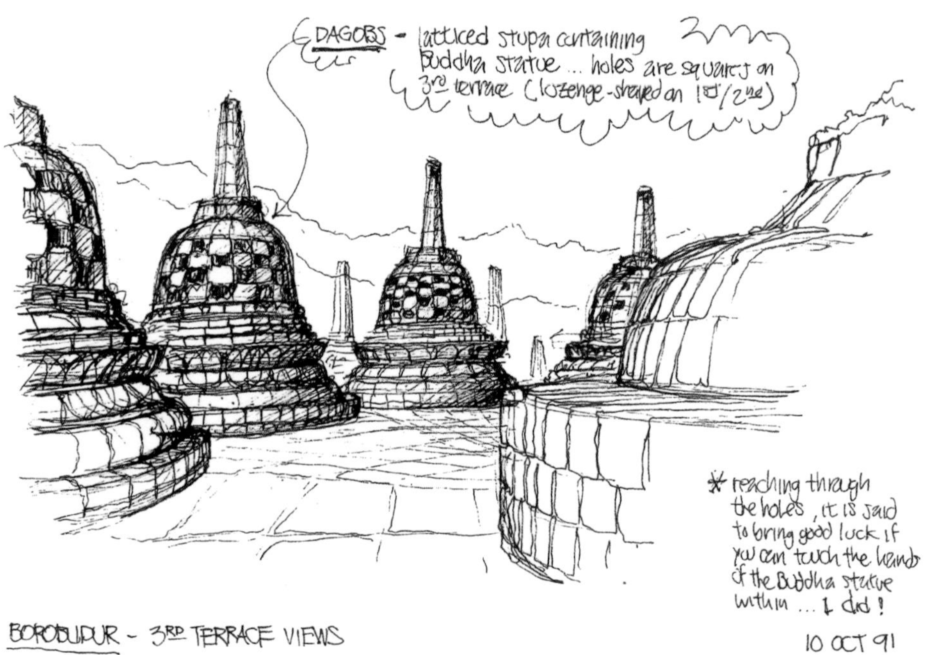

BOROBUDUR - 3RD TERRACE VIEWS

10 OCT 91

BOROBUDUR - view from bukit dagi

9 OCT 91

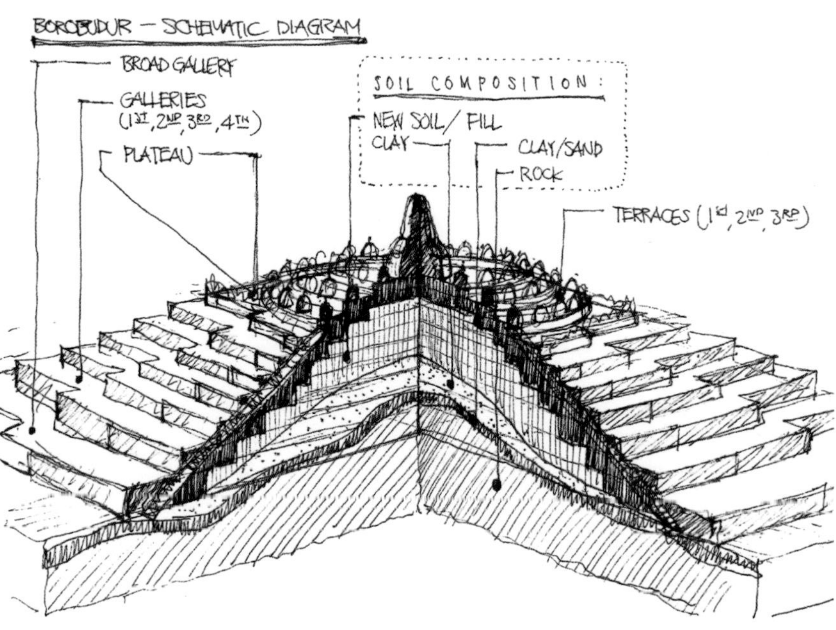

Borobudur, Indonesia: Wandering amongst ancient ruins at sunrise before anyone else arrives offers a chance to meditate and ponder the meaning of life.

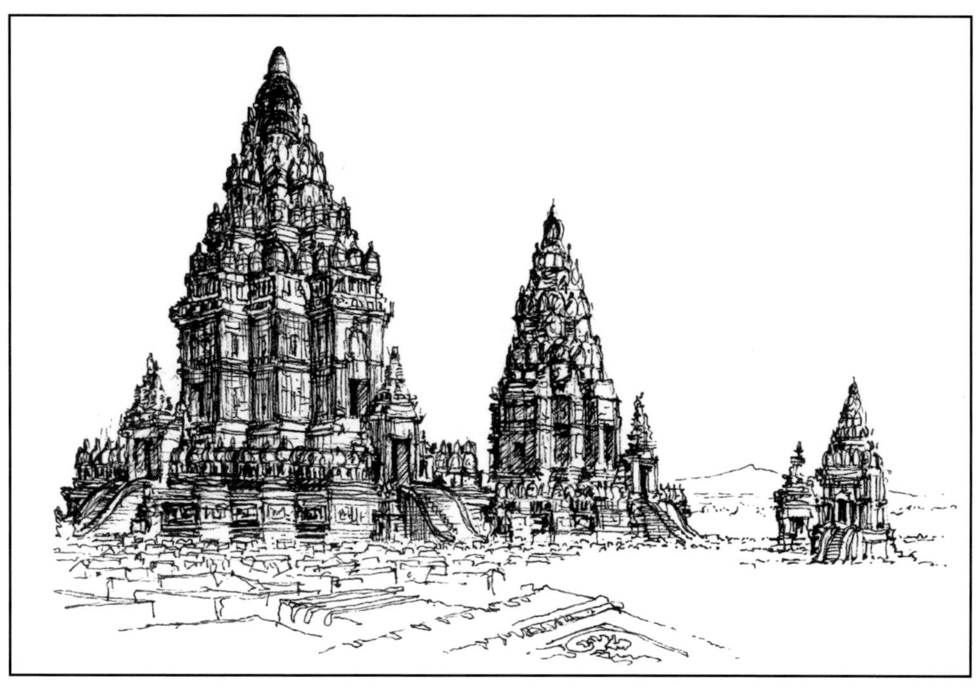

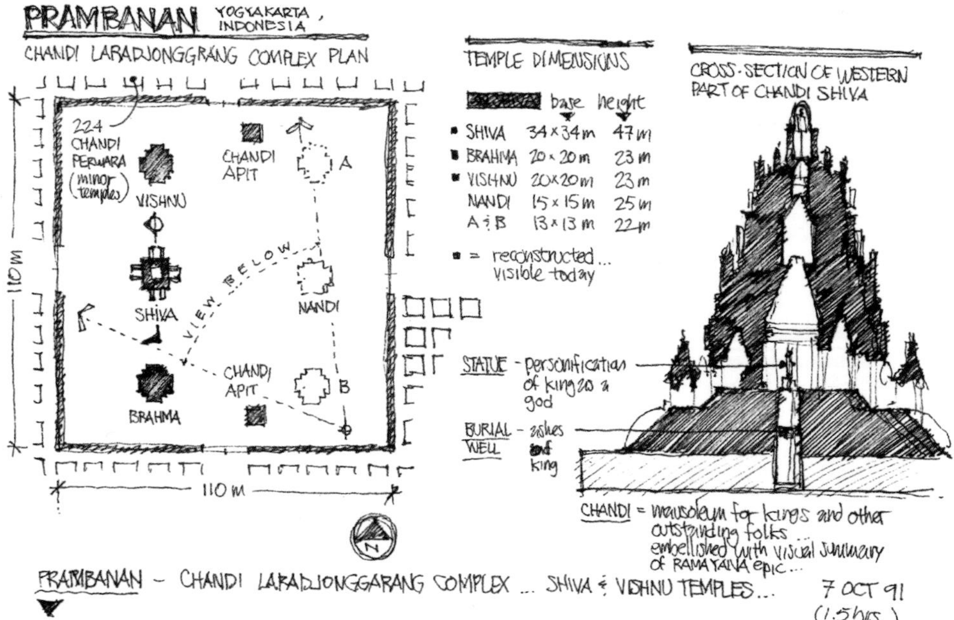

Prambanan, Indonesia: Intricately detailed stone temples reveal a complex ancient religion.

MUANG KAO SUKHOTHAI　　• 25 JAN 1992
(Old Town of Sukhothai)

Sukhothai = "Dawn of Happiness"
independent kingdom of Sukhothai – mid 13th – mid 15th centuries
in present-day Thailand ...

WAT SRI SAWAI ▲
※ features three prangs built in Lopburi style
(style of Hindu art that resembles that of
Khmer art in Cambodia)

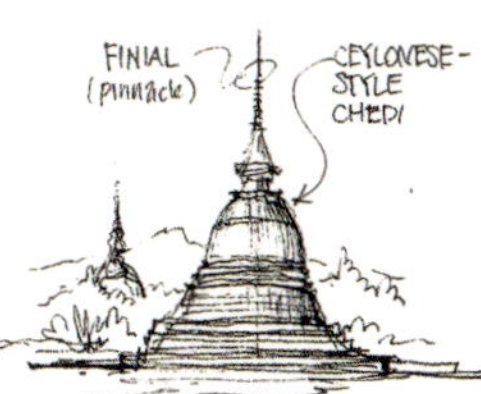

ARCHITECTURAL BACKGROUND:

▣ MID 13TH CENTURY:
 – architectural styles adapted
 from earlier presence of Khmer
 Buddhist & Hindu influences

▣ LATE 13TH CENTURY:
 – distinctive "Sukhothai" expression
 of art & architecture ...
 also Khmer-style prang and
 Ceylonese bell-shaped chedi

▣ END OF CLASSIC PERIOD:
 – new kingdom of Ayudhya founded,
 viharas (edifice enshrining
 images of Buddha where merit-
 making ceremonies were
 performed) were built higher...
 sometimes 2 stories...

(source: "Guide to Sukhothai Historical
 Park," published by Promotion
 and Public Relations Office of
 Fine Arts Department)

ARCHITECTURAL TERMS:

▣ CHEDI – (also called "stupa" or
 "pagoda"). The Monument which
 enshrines relics of the Buddha and/
 or his disciples, also to contain
 ashes of the dead.

▣ FINIAL – pinnacle on top of a Chedi

▣ LATERITE – red-colored porous soil
 which hardens when
 exposed to air – building material
 for Sukhothai structures..

▣ MONDOP – square structure with
 stepped pyramidal roof used to house
 religious relics (Buddha image, etc.)

(continued on following page)

WAT MAHATHAT • SUKHOTHAI, THAILAND • 25 JANUARY 1992 (2.0)

SUKUH TEMPLE ...near Solo, Indonesia... (40 min.)　　　16 OCT 91

Sukhothai, Thailand:
Sometimes a place is so awe-inspiring that, more than one sketchbook page is required to capture its grandeur, as with Wat Mahathat.

WAT MAHATHAT
SUKHOTHAI RUINS
SUKHOTHAI , THAILAND
23 JAN 92 / 3.25

CATACOMBS OF KOM ASH-SHUQQAFA

23 OCT 2002   ALEXANDRIA, EGYPT

DEPTH: 35m BELOW GRADE

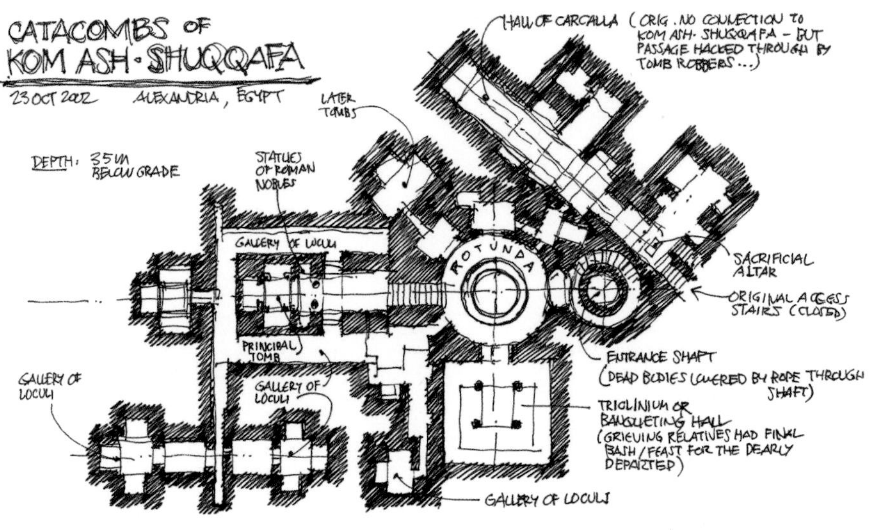

- LARGEST KNOWN ROMAN BURIAL SITE IN EGYPT
- DISCOVERED ACCIDENTALLY IN 1900, WHEN A DONKEY DISAPPEARED THROUGH A HOLE IN THE GROUND!
- 3 TIERS OF SUBTERRANEAN TOMBS (LOWEST TIER FLOODED)
- ORIG. CONSTRUCTED 2ND CENTURY AD AS FAMILY CRYPT
- ULTIMATELY EXPANDED TO CONTAIN 300 CORPSES
- "LOCULI" = PIGEON HOLE CORPSE CONTAINERS
- SPOOKY OLD CRYPT HAS BEEN LIKENED TO A SET FOR A HORROR FILM... I WOULD AGREE ... BORIS KARLOFF...WHERE ARE YOU??

ABU SIMBEL

9 OCT 2002   ASWAN, EGYPT

THE GREAT TEMPLE OF RAMSES II:

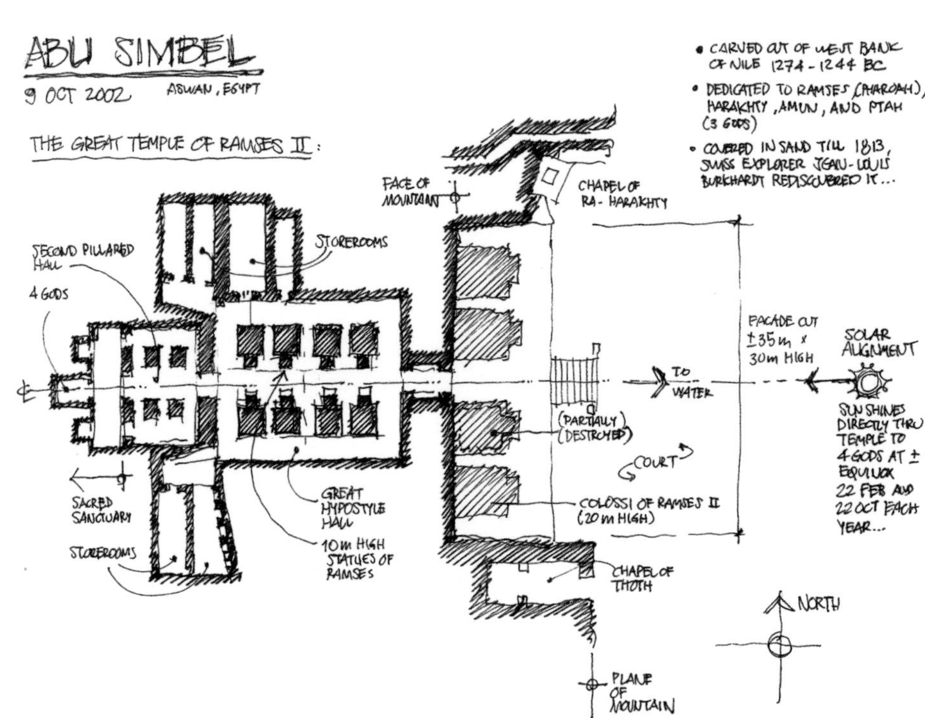

- CARVED OUT OF WEST BANK OF NILE 1274 - 1244 BC
- DEDICATED TO RAMSES (PHAROAH), HARAKHTY, AMUN, AND PTAH (3 GODS)
- COVERED IN SAND TILL 1813, SWISS EXPLORER JEAN-LOUIS BURKHARDT REDISCOVERED IT...

- ENTIRE COMPLEX DISSECTED, MOVED, AND RECONSTRUCTED C. 1960 TO HIGHER GROUND IN RESPONSE TO INUNDATION BY CONSTRUCTION OF ASWAN DAM AND SUBSEQUENT FLOODING OF ORIGINAL SITE. (INTERNATIONAL EFFORT HEADED BY UNESCO)

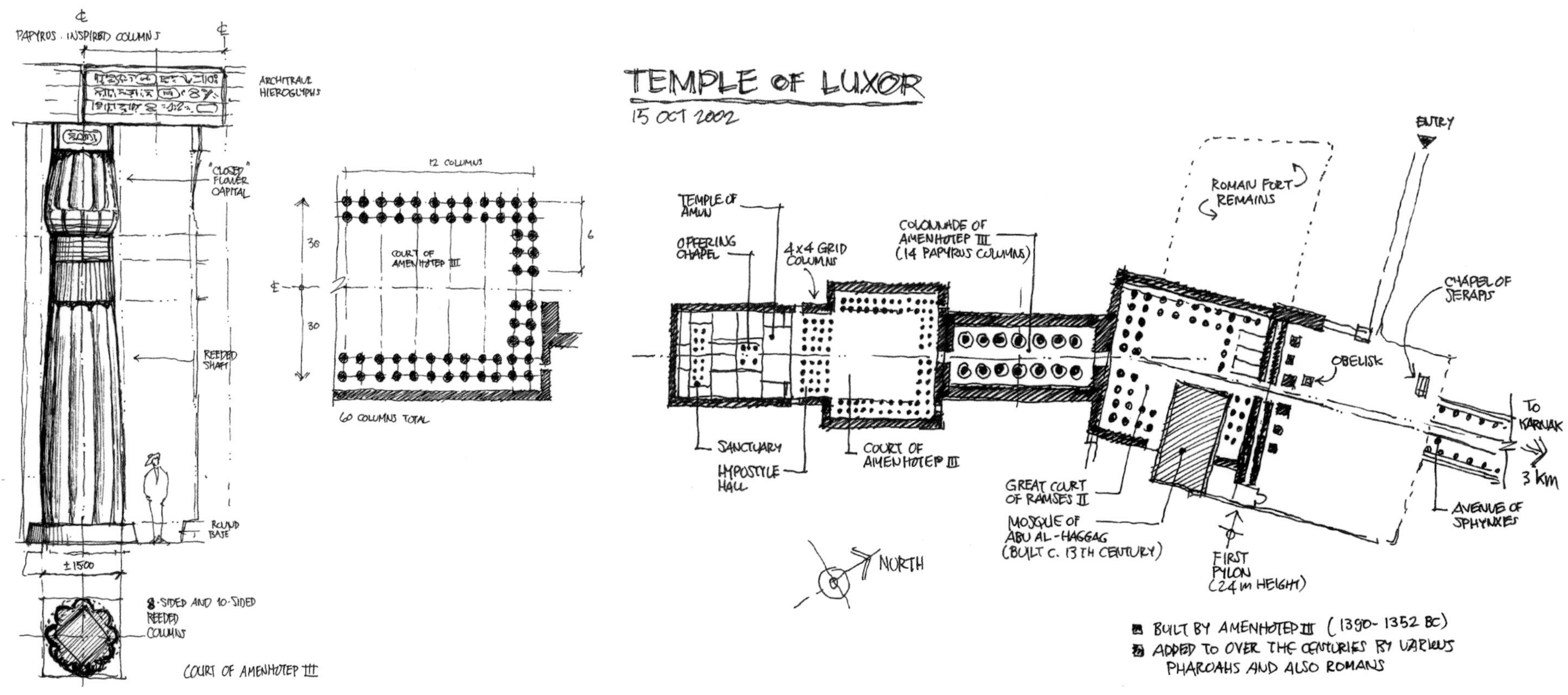

Egypt: Braving the hot desert sun to understand the layout and organizational structure of some of the world's oldest temples is not easy or pleasant, but such sketches will help the viewer better understand a culture and assist in memory recall later on.

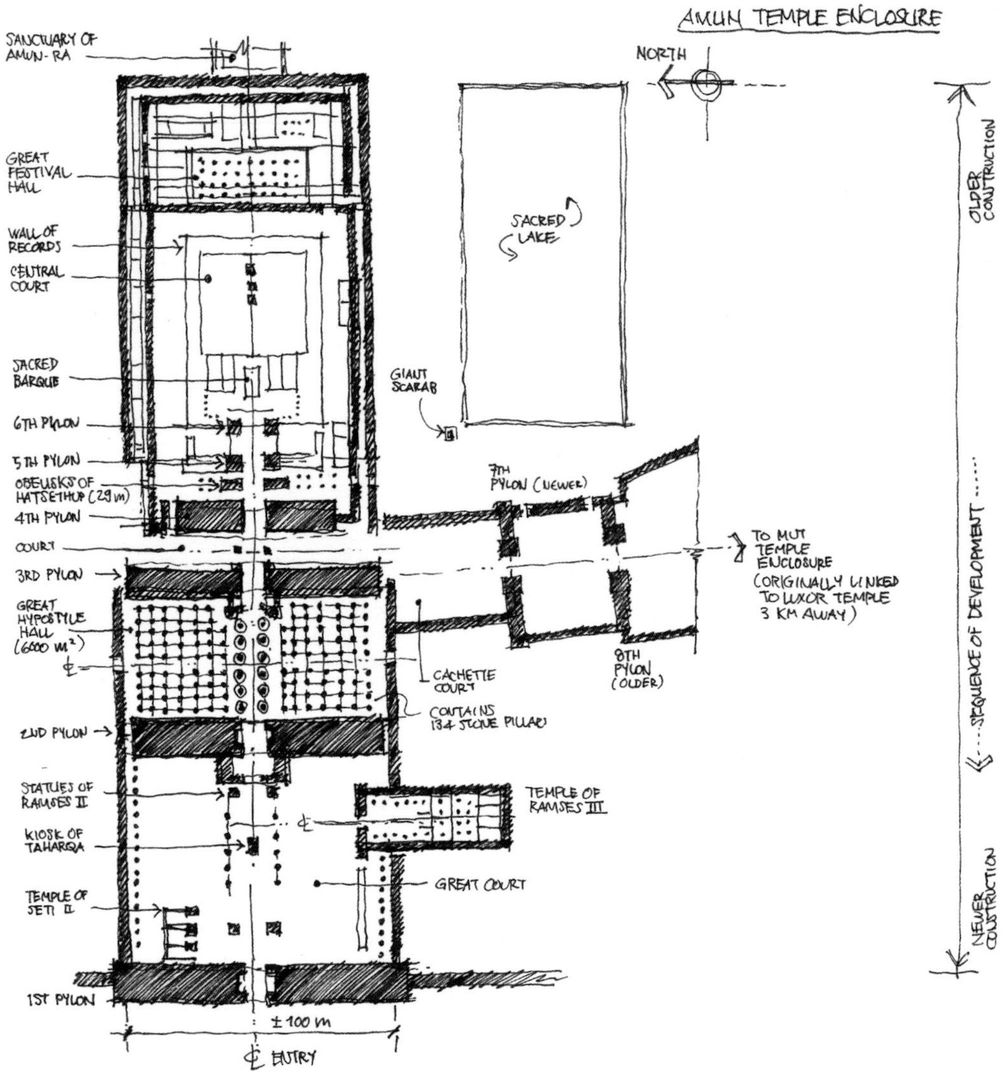

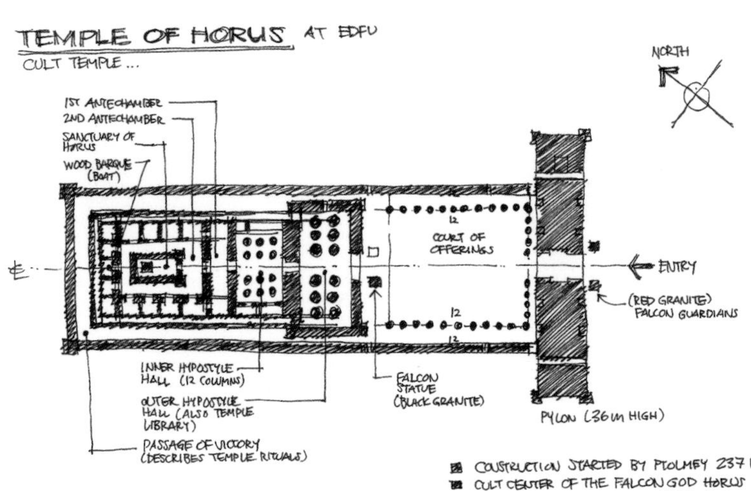

AMUN TEMPLE ENCLOSURE
NORTH
SANCTUARY OF AMUN-RA
GREAT FESTIVAL HALL
WALL OF RECORDS
CENTRAL COURT
SACRED BARQUE
6TH PYLON
5TH PYLON
OBELISKS OF HATSHEPSUT (29 m)
4TH PYLON
COURT
3RD PYLON
GREAT HYPOSTYLE HALL (6000 m²)
2ND PYLON
STATUES OF RAMSES II
KIOSK OF TAHARQA
TEMPLE OF SETI II
1ST PYLON
± 100 m
ENTRY
SACRED LAKE
GIANT SCARAB
7TH PYLON (NEWER)
8TH PYLON (OLDER)
CACHETTE COURT
CONTAINS 134 STONE PILLARS
TEMPLE OF RAMSES III
GREAT COURT
TO MUT TEMPLE ENCLOSURE (ORIGINALLY LINKED TO LUXOR TEMPLE 3 KM AWAY)
OLDER CONSTRUCTION
SEQUENCE OF DEVELOPMENT
NEWER CONSTRUCTION
TEMPLE OF HORUS AT EDFU
CULT TEMPLE ...
NORTH
1ST ANTECHAMBER
2ND ANTECHAMBER
SANCTUARY OF HORUS
WOOD BARQUE (BOAT)
COURT OF OFFERINGS
ENTRY
(RED GRANITE) FALCON GUARDIANS
PYLON (36 m HIGH)
INNER HYPOSTYLE HALL (12 COLUMNS)
OUTER HYPOSTYLE HALL (ALSO TEMPLE LIBRARY)
FALCON STATUE (BLACK GRANITE)
PASSAGE OF VICTORY (DESCRIBES TEMPLE RITUALS)
CONSTRUCTION STARTED BY PTOLEMY 237 BC
CULT CENTER OF THE FALCON GOD HORUS
COMPLETED 200 YRS LATER (57 BC) BY PTOLEMY XII (FATHER OF CLEOPATRA)
13 OCT 2002

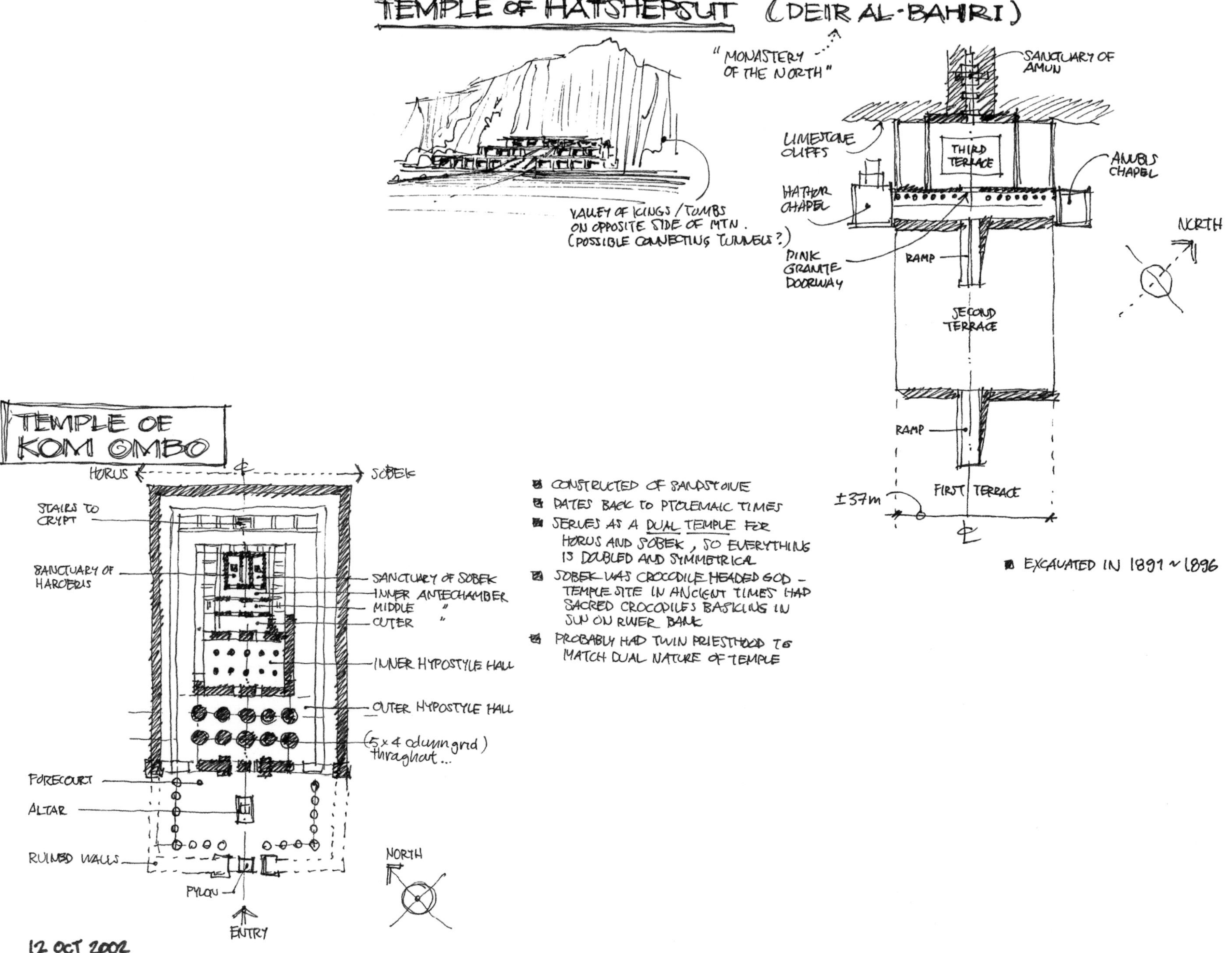

TEMPLE OF HATSHEPSUT (DEIR AL-BAHRI)
"MONASTERY OF THE NORTH"
SANCTUARY OF AMUN
LIMESTONE CLIFFS
THIRD TERRACE
ANUBIS CHAPEL
HATHOR CHAPEL
VALLEY OF KINGS / TOMBS ON OPPOSITE SIDE OF MTN. (POSSIBLE CONNECTING TUNNELS?)
PINK GRANITE DOORWAY
RAMP
NORTH
SECOND TERRACE
RAMP
FIRST TERRACE
±37m
EXCAVATED IN 1891 ~ 1896

TEMPLE OF KOM OMBO
HORUS
SOBEK
STAIRS TO CRYPT
SANCTUARY OF HAROERIS
SANCTUARY OF SOBEK
INNER ANTECHAMBER
MIDDLE "
OUTER   "
INNER HYPOSTYLE HALL
OUTER HYPOSTYLE HALL
(5 x 4 column grid) throughout...
FORECOURT
ALTAR
RUINED WALLS
PYLON
NORTH
ENTRY

CONSTRUCTED OF SANDSTONE
DATES BACK TO PTOLEMAIC TIMES
SERVES AS A DUAL TEMPLE FOR HORUS AND SOBEK, SO EVERYTHING IS DOUBLED AND SYMMETRICAL
SOBEK WAS CROCODILE-HEADED GOD — TEMPLE SITE IN ANCIENT TIMES HAD SACRED CROCODILES BASKING IN SUN ON RIVER BANK
PROBABLY HAD TWIN PRIESTHOOD TO MATCH DUAL NATURE OF TEMPLE

12 OCT 2002

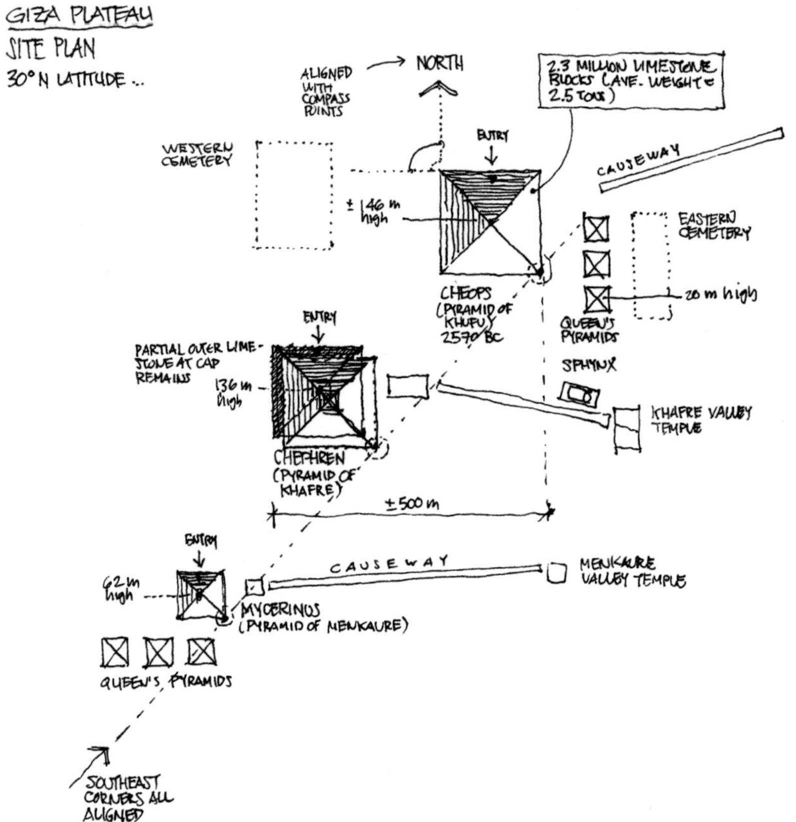

GIZA PLATEAU
SITE PLAN
30° N LATITUDE ..
ALIGNED WITH COMPASS POINTS
NORTH
ENTRY
2.3 MILLION LIMESTONE BLOCKS (AVE. WEIGHT = 2.5 TONS)
CAUSEWAY
WESTERN CEMETERY
± 146 m high
EASTERN CEMETERY
CHEOPS (PYRAMID OF KHUFU) 2570 BC
QUEEN'S PYRAMIDS
20 m high
SPHYNX
ENTRY
PARTIAL OUTER LIMESTONE AT CAP REMAINS
136 m high
CHEPHREN (PYRAMID OF KHAFRE)
KHAFRE VALLEY TEMPLE
± 500 m
ENTRY
62 m high
CAUSEWAY
MYCERINUS (PYRAMID OF MENKAURE)
MENKAURE VALLEY TEMPLE
QUEEN'S PYRAMIDS
SOUTHEAST CORNERS ALL ALIGNED

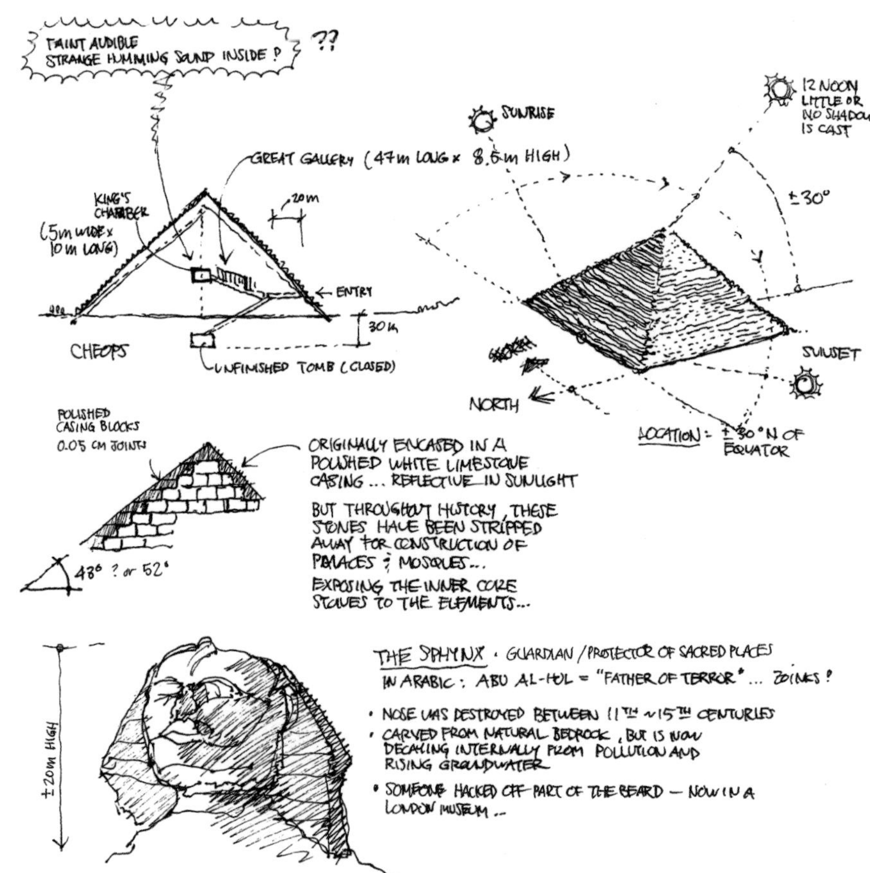

FAINT AUDIBLE STRANGE HUMMING SOUND INSIDE ? ??
GREAT GALLERY (47m LONG x 8.5m HIGH)
KING'S CHAMBER (5m WIDE x 10m LONG)
20 m
CHEOPS
ENTRY
UNFINISHED TOMB (CLOSED)
30 m
SUNRISE
12 NOON LITTLE OR NO SHADOW IS CAST
± 30°
NORTH
SUNSET
LOCATION: ± 30° N OF EQUATOR
POLISHED CASING BLOCKS 0.05 CM JOINTS
ORIGINALLY ENCASED IN A POLISHED WHITE LIMESTONE CASING ... REFLECTIVE IN SUNLIGHT
BUT THROUGHOUT HISTORY, THESE STONES HAVE BEEN STRIPPED AWAY FOR CONSTRUCTION OF PALACES & MOSQUES...
EXPOSING THE INNER CORE STONES TO THE ELEMENTS...
48° ? or 52°
THE SPHYNX · GUARDIAN/PROTECTOR OF SACRED PLACES
IN ARABIC: ABU AL-HOL = "FATHER OF TERROR" ... ZEUS?
· NOSE WAS DESTROYED BETWEEN 11TH ~15TH CENTURIES
· CARVED FROM NATURAL BEDROCK, BUT IS NOW DECAYING INTERNALLY FROM POLLUTION AND RISING GROUNDWATER
· SOMEONE HACKED OFF PART OF THE BEARD — NOW IN A LONDON MUSEUM ..
± 20 m HIGH

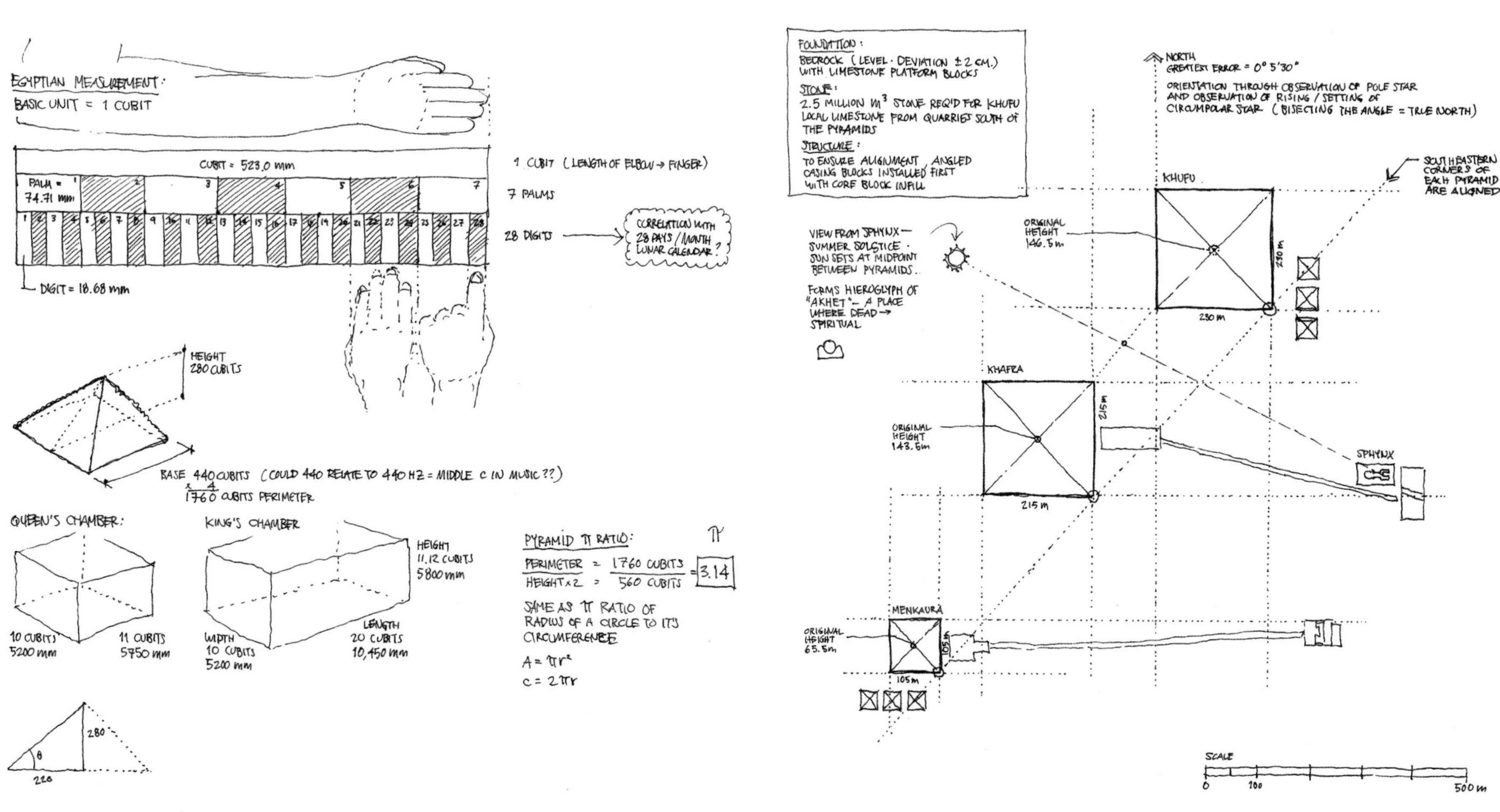

Cairo, Egypt: The Giza Plateau is home to some of the world's greatest architectural, astronomical, and mathematical mysteries. The more one learns, the more questions crop up!

TEMPLE OF PHILAE 9 OCT 2002

ASWAN, EGYPT

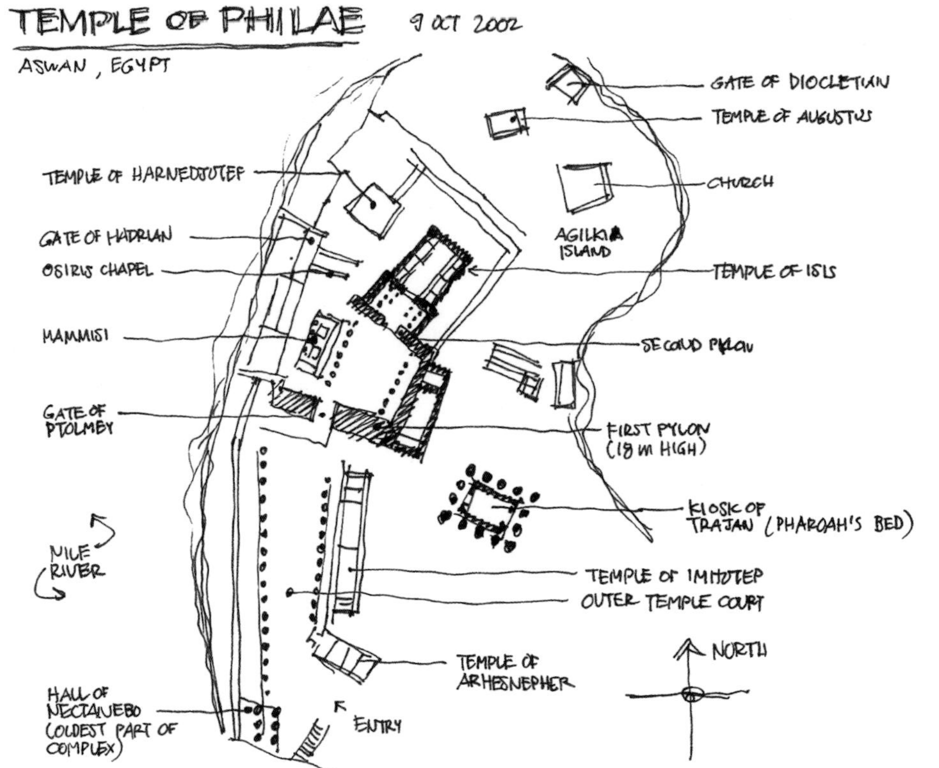

SAQQARA SITE PLAN

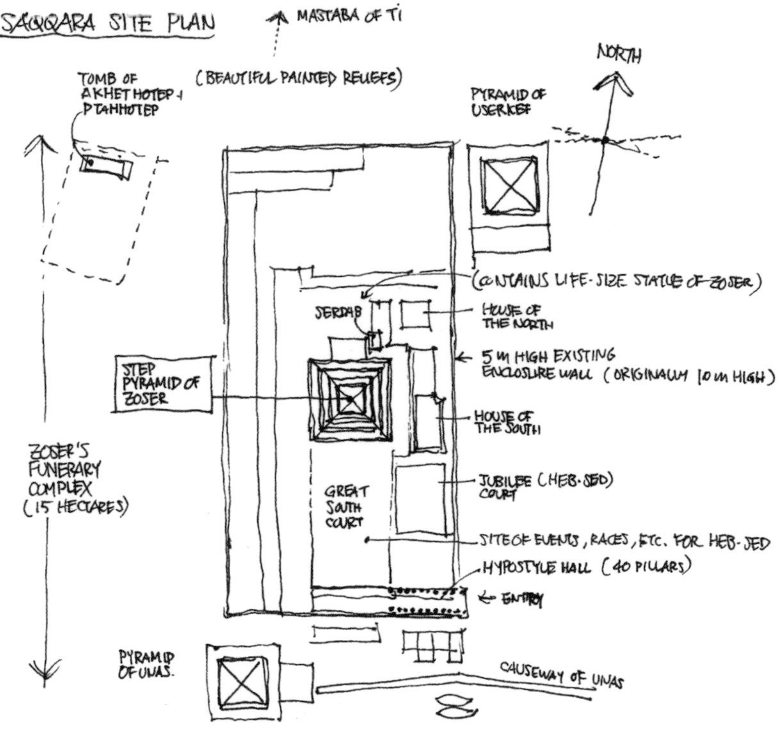

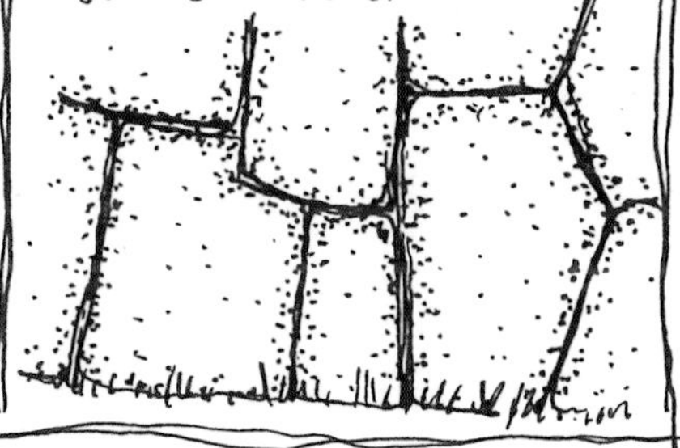

Cusco, Peru: Intricately carved Incan stonework has stood the test of time and continues to boggle the minds of visitors from around the world. How were these 300-ton stones fitted together so perfectly more than 500 years ago?

A MORNING AT CHAN-CHAN...

The first ruin we visited was LA HUACA ARCO IRIS
(a.k.a. the rainbow temple) - Chimu temple

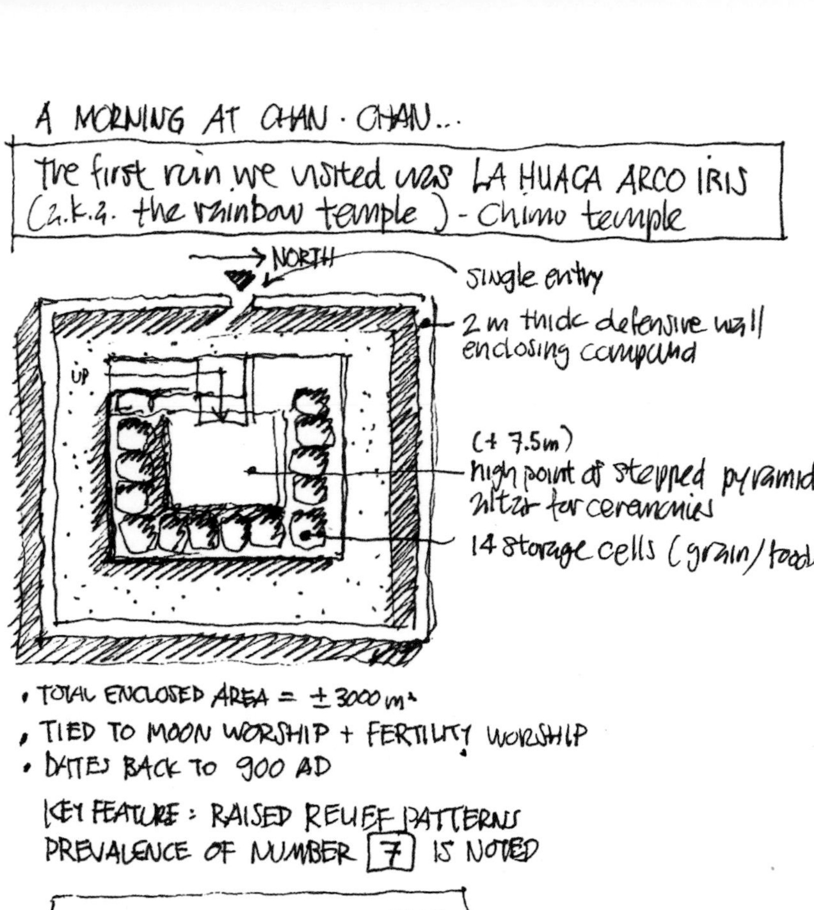

- TOTAL ENCLOSED AREA = ± 3000 m²
- TIED TO MOON WORSHIP + FERTILITY WORSHIP
- DATES BACK TO 900 AD

KEY FEATURE: RAISED RELIEF PATTERNS
PREVALENCE OF NUMBER 7 IS NOTED

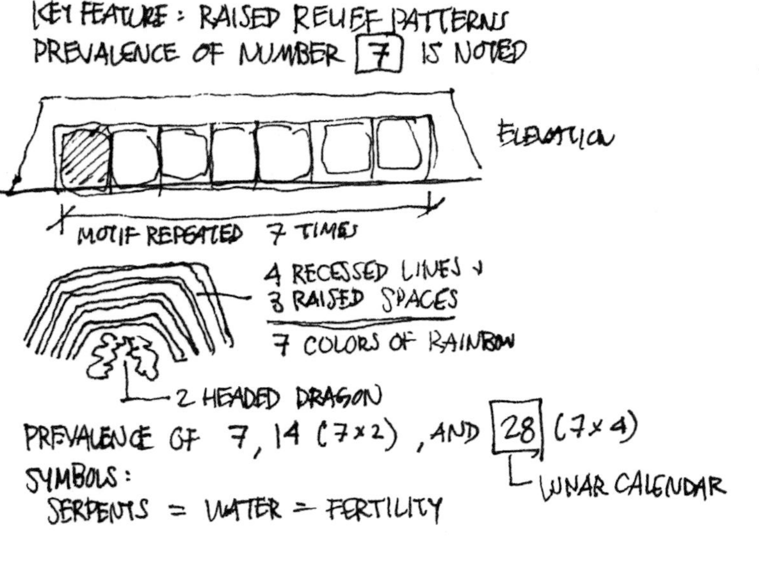

PREVALENCE OF 7, 14 (7×2), AND 28 (7×4)
LUNAR CALENDAR
SYMBOLS:
SERPENTS = WATER = FERTILITY

CHAN CHAN / TSCHUDI COMPLEX

CHAN = SUN
CHAN = SUN

○ BIGGEST "MUD CITY" IN THE WORLD (UNESCO SITE)
○ BUILT 12TH CENTURY, 20 KM² IN AREA, 250,000 RESIDENTS
○ WAS CAPITOL OF REINO CHIMU ALONG PACIFIC COAST
○ MARINE ICONOGRAPHY - SEA WAVES, BIRDS, FISH, FISHING NETS

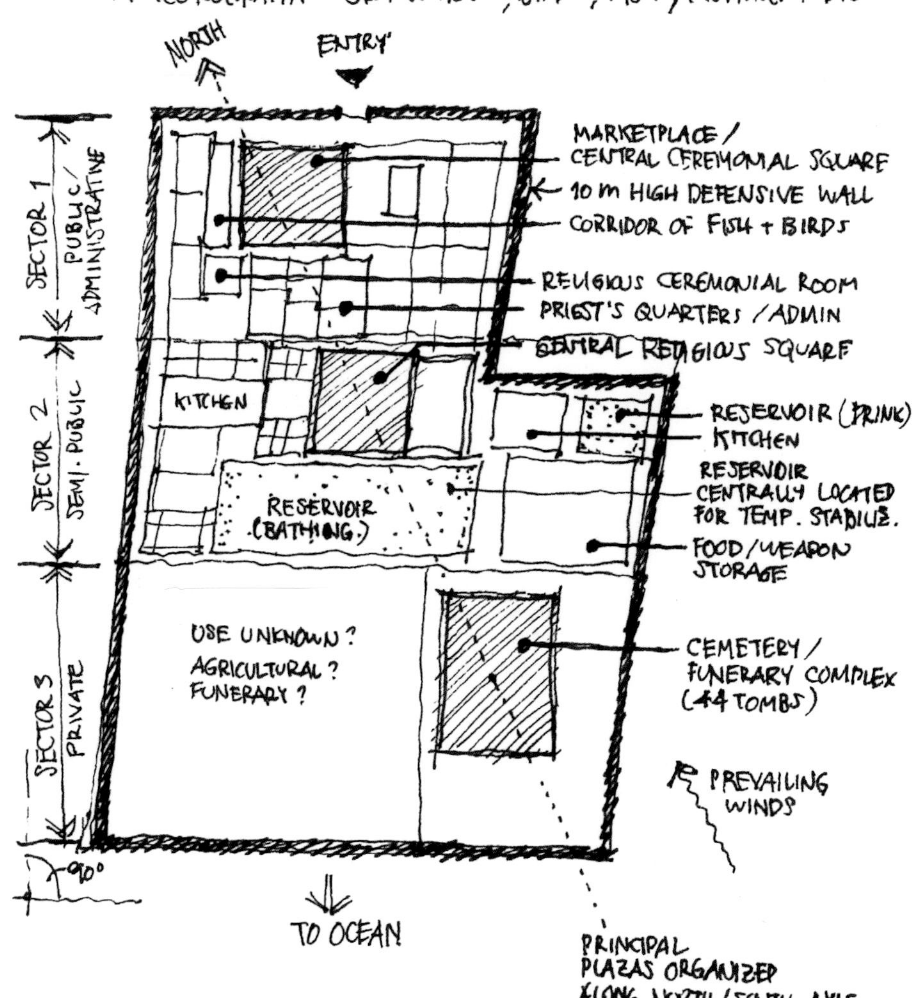

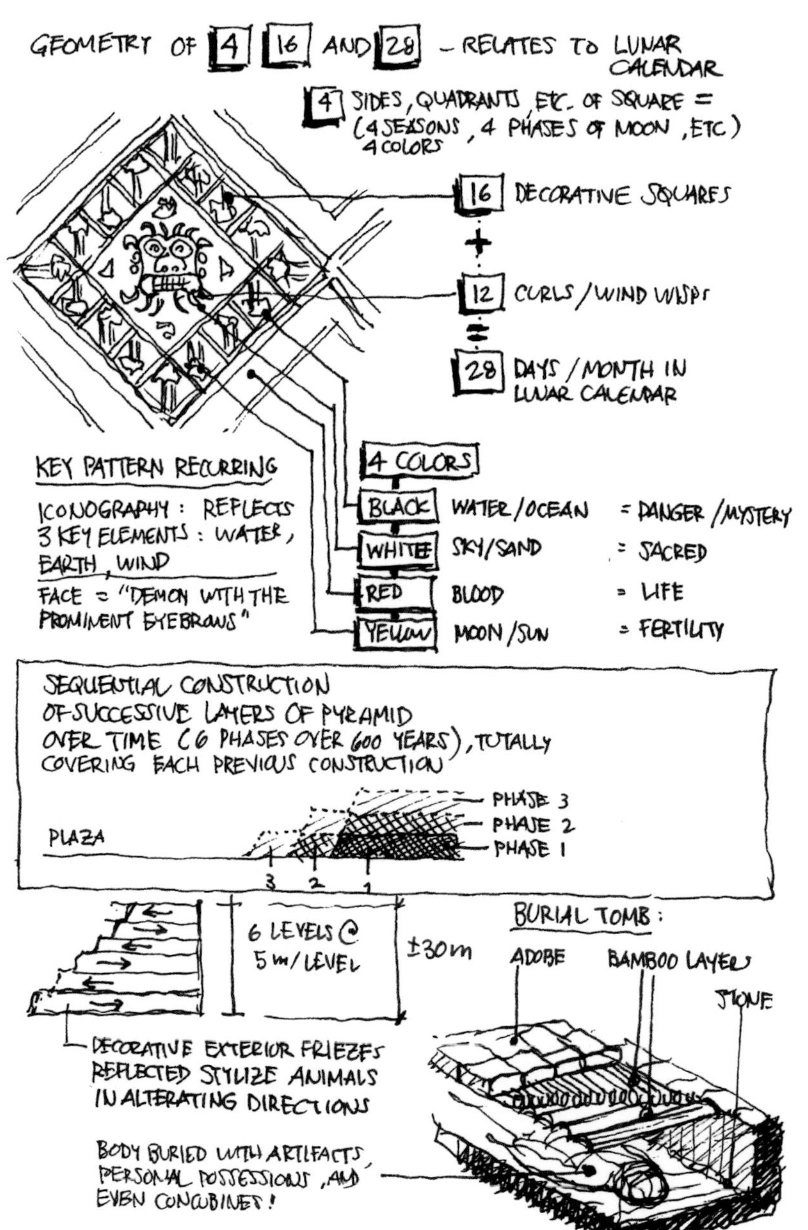

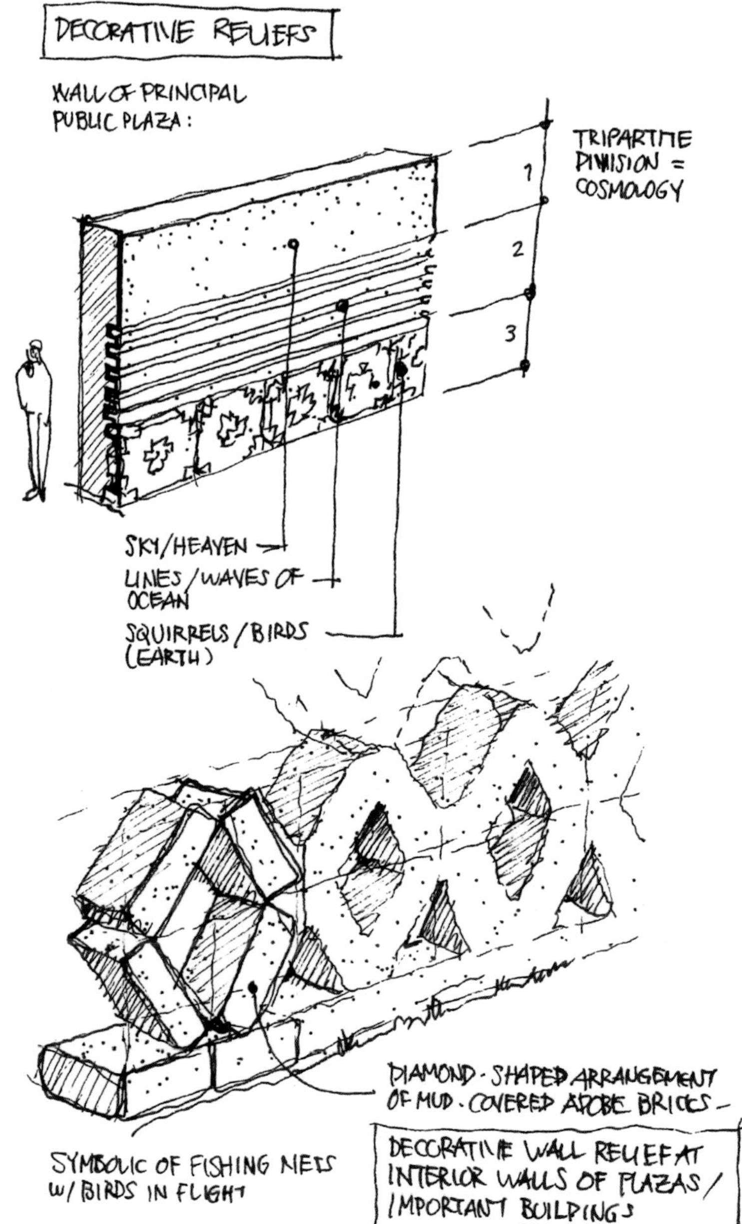

Trujillo, Peru: The pre-Columbian archaeological sites of Chan Chan and the Temple of the Moon are so rich in numerology that depictions of construction systems using in-situ materials soon filled my sketchbooks.

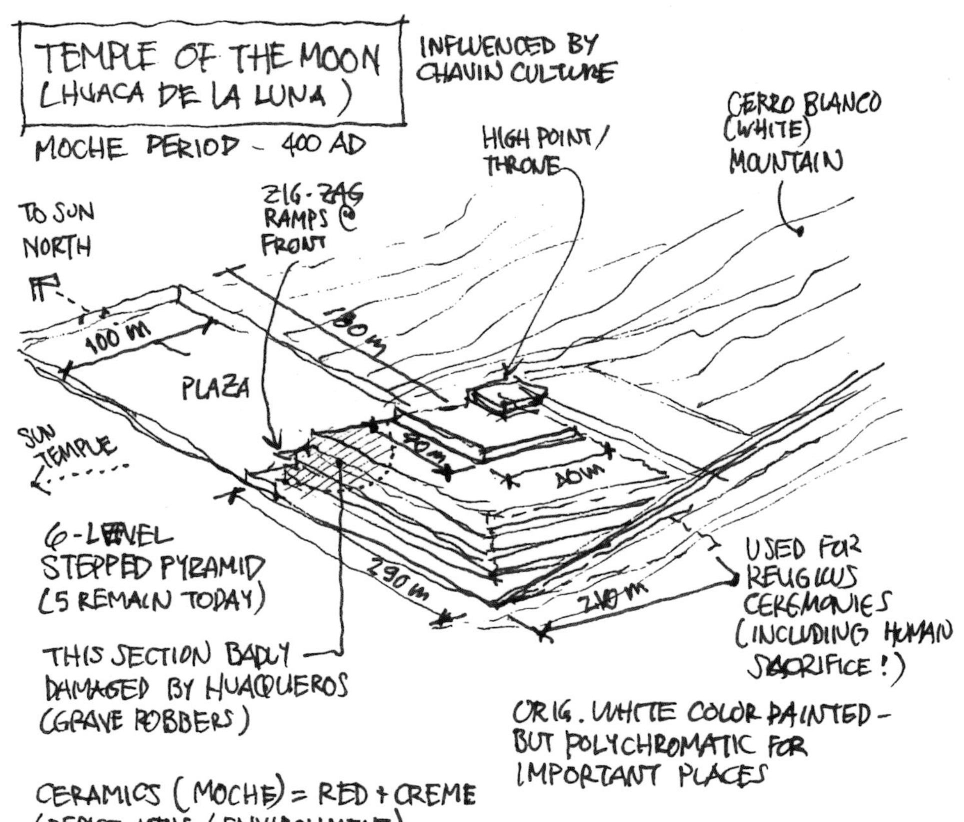

TEMPLE OF THE MOON
(HUACA DE LA LUNA)
MOCHE PERIOD - 400 AD
INFLUENCED BY CHAVIN CULTURE
HIGH POINT / THRONE
CERRO BLANCO (WHITE) MOUNTAIN
TO SUN NORTH
ZIG-ZAG RAMPS @ FRONT
100 M
130 M
PLAZA
SUN TEMPLE
32 M
60 M
290 M
210 M
6-LEVEL STEPPED PYRAMID (5 REMAIN TODAY)
THIS SECTION BADLY DAMAGED BY HUAQUEROS (GRAVE ROBBERS)
USED FOR RELIGIOUS CEREMONIES (INCLUDING HUMAN SACRIFICE!)
ORIG. WHITE COLOR PAINTED - BUT POLYCHROMATIC FOR IMPORTANT PLACES
CERAMICS (MOCHE) = RED + CREME (DEPICT MTNS / ENVIRONMENT)

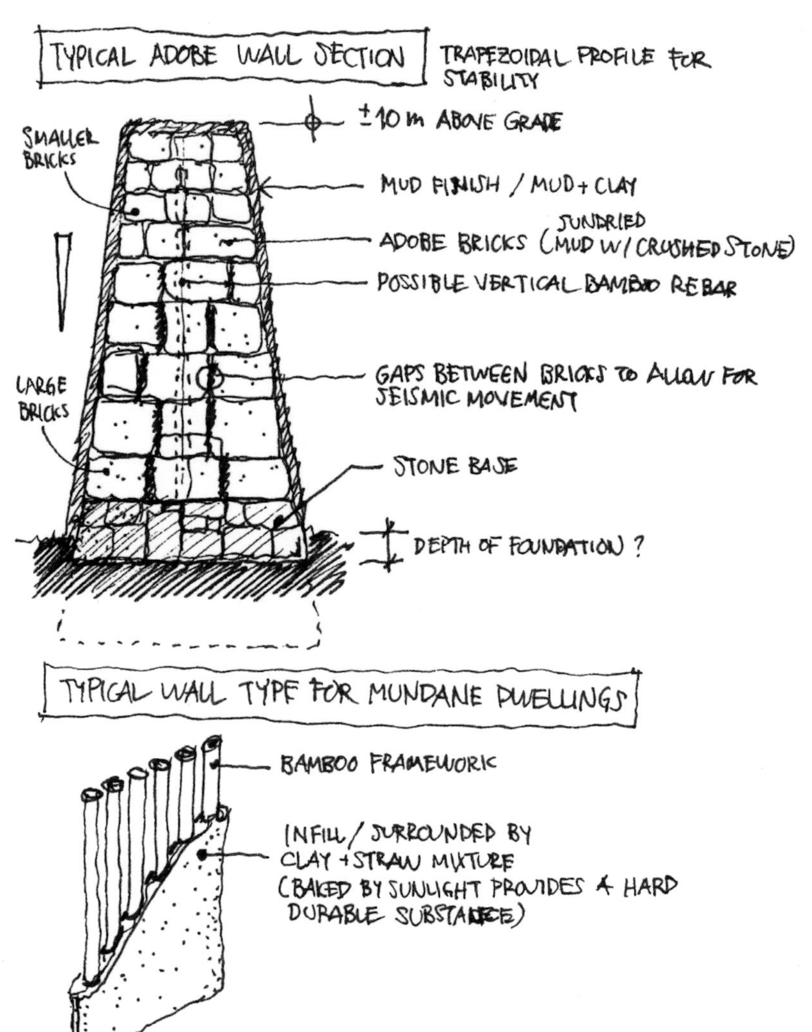

TYPICAL ADOBE WALL SECTION
TRAPEZOIDAL PROFILE FOR STABILITY
± 10 m ABOVE GRADE
SMALLER BRICKS
MUD FINISH / MUD + CLAY
ADOBE BRICKS (MUD W/ CRUSHED STONE) SUNDRIED
POSSIBLE VERTICAL BAMBOO REBAR
LARGE BRICKS
GAPS BETWEEN BRICKS TO ALLOW FOR SEISMIC MOVEMENT
STONE BASE
DEPTH OF FOUNDATION ?
TYPICAL WALL TYPE FOR MUNDANE DWELLINGS
BAMBOO FRAMEWORK
INFILL / SURROUNDED BY CLAY + STRAW MIXTURE (BAKED BY SUNLIGHT PROVIDES A HARD DURABLE SUBSTANCE)

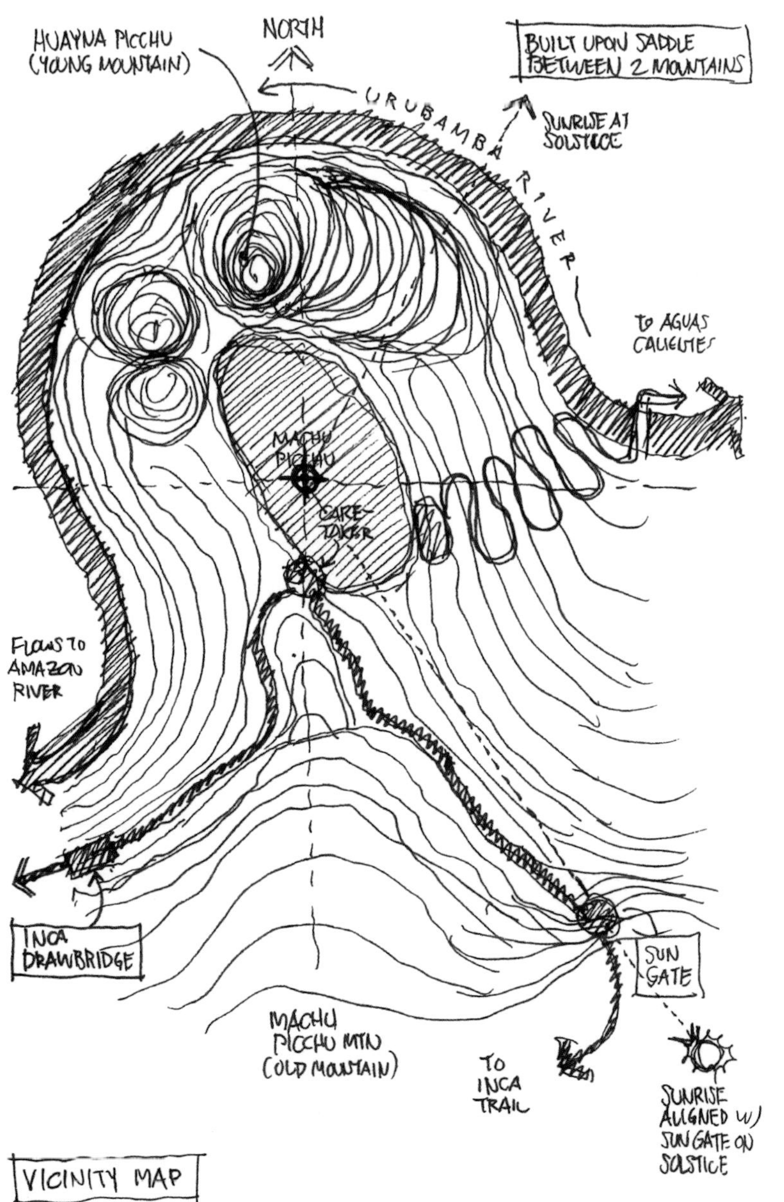

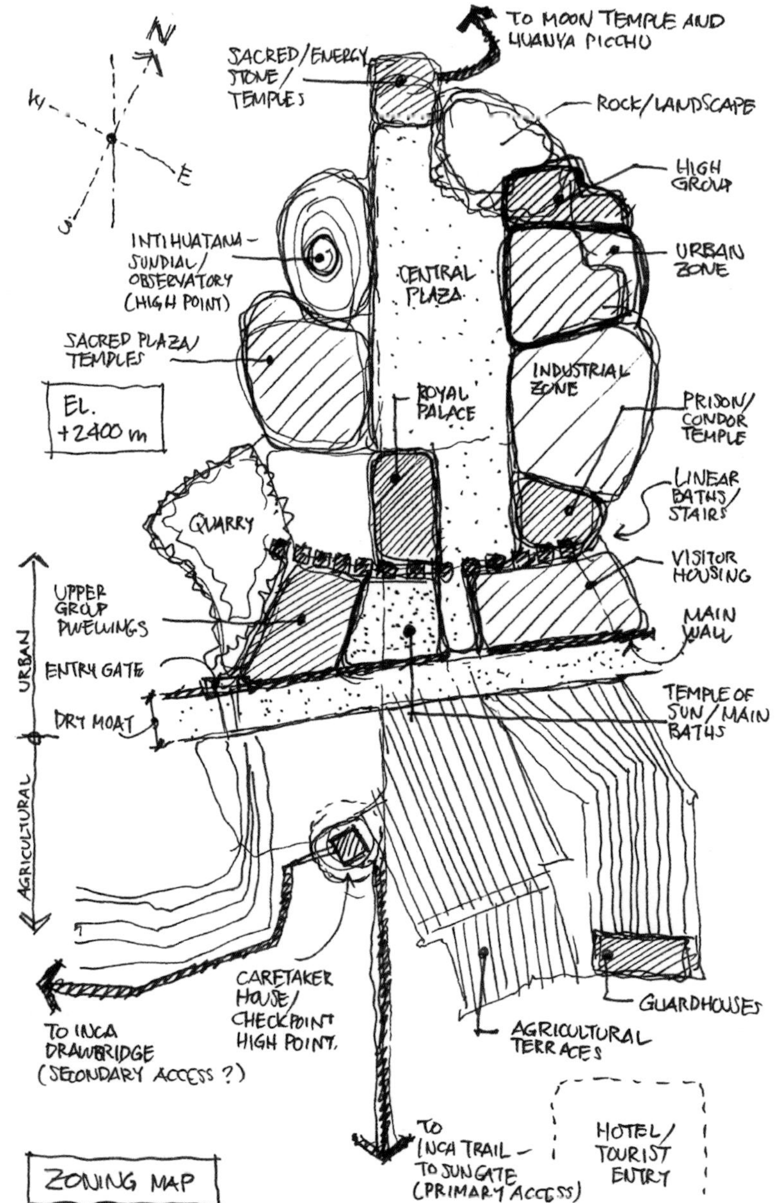

Machu Picchu, Peru: The picturesque 15th century Incan citadel tops the bucket list for many travellers. The siting and construction of this architectural feat is best appreciated at sunrise after completing the arduous 3-day trek along the Inca Trail.

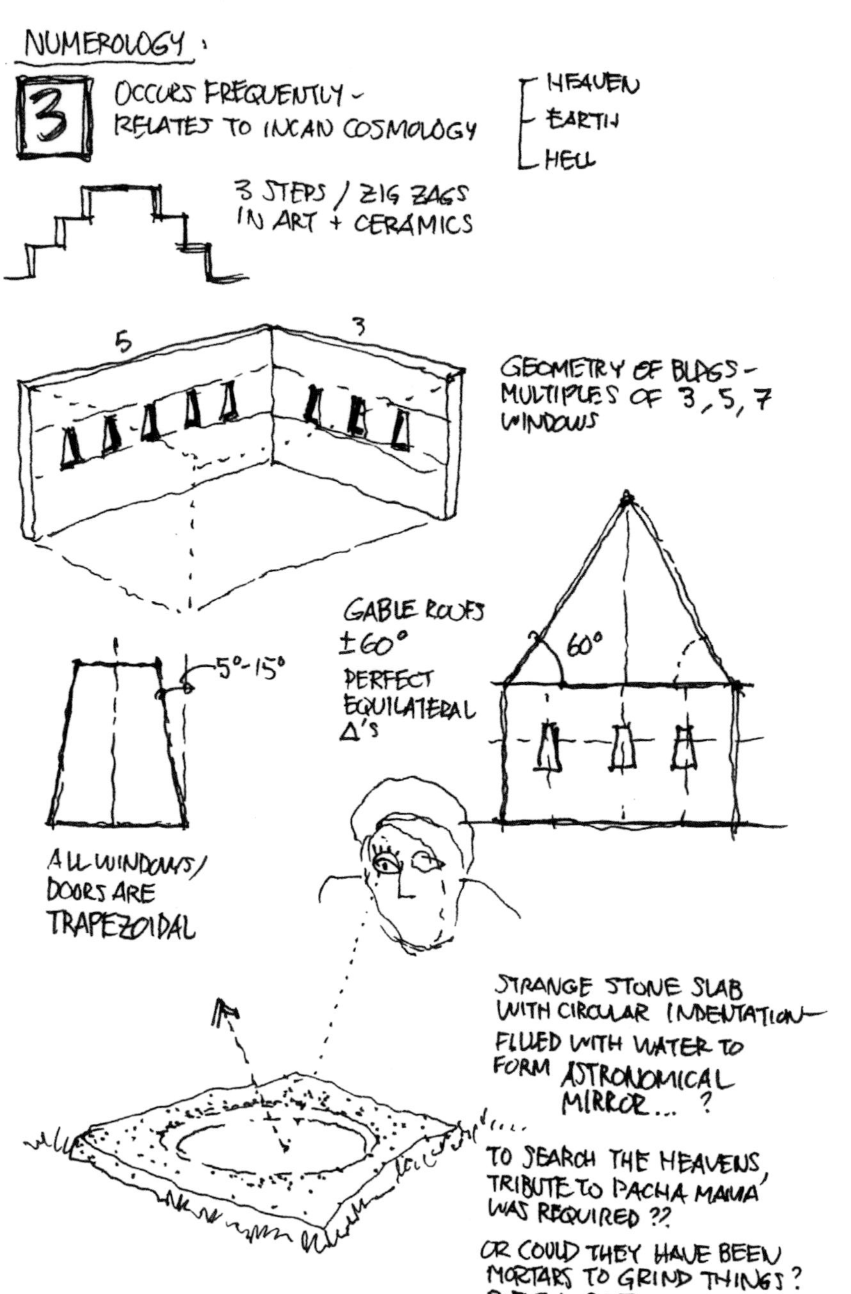

NUMEROLOGY:
3
OCCURS FREQUENTLY - RELATES TO INCAN COSMOLOGY
HEAVEN
EARTH
HELL
3 STEPS / ZIG ZAGS IN ART + CERAMICS
5
3
GEOMETRY OF BLDGS - MULTIPLES OF 3, 5, 7 WINDOWS
5° - 15°
GABLE ROOFS ± 60° PERFECT EQUILATERAL △'s
60°
ALL WINDOWS / DOORS ARE TRAPEZOIDAL
STRANGE STONE SLAB WITH CIRCULAR INDENTATION FILLED WITH WATER TO FORM ASTRONOMICAL MIRROR...?
TO SEARCH THE HEAVENS, TRIBUTE TO PACHA MAMA WAS REQUIRED ??
OR COULD THEY HAVE BEEN MORTARS TO GRIND THINGS? BUT FLAT BOTTOM... UNLIKELY.

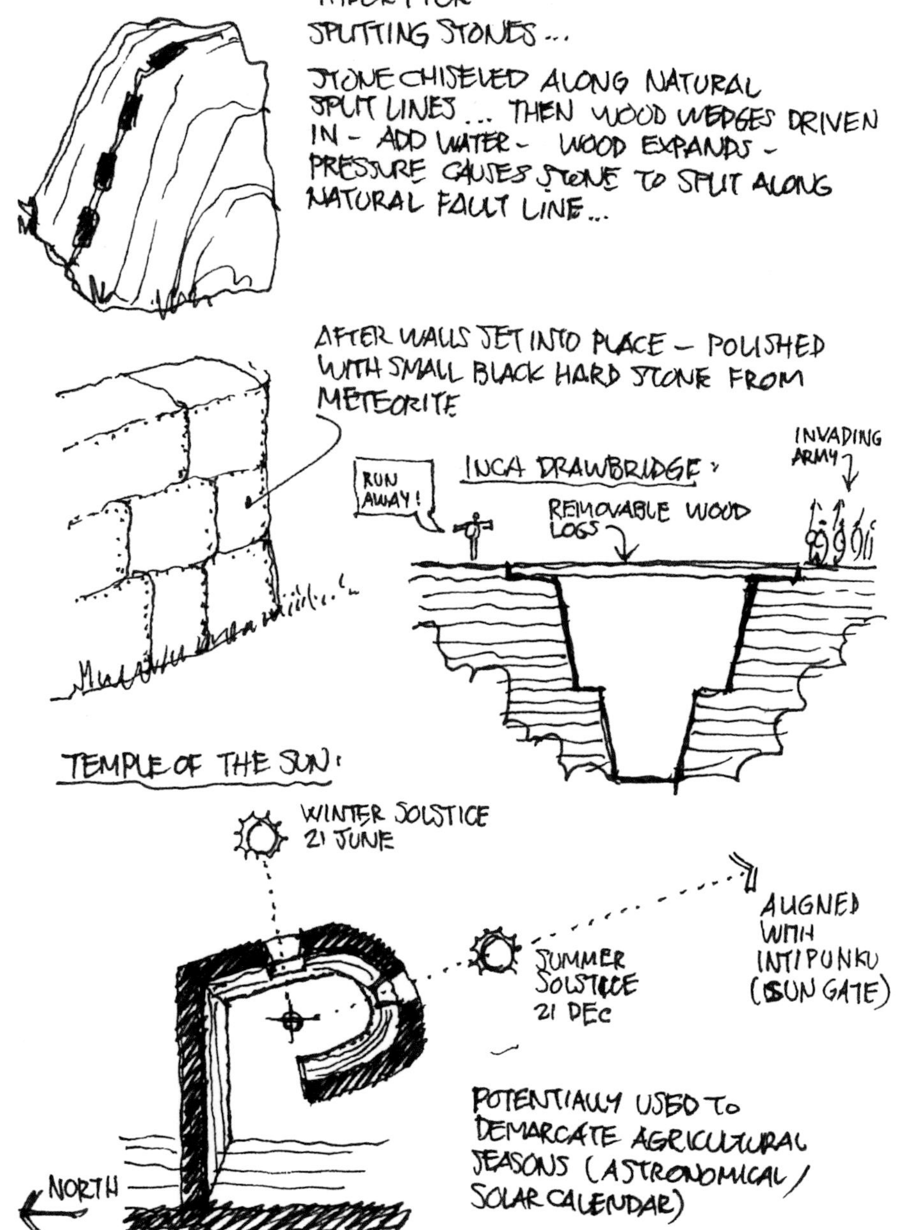

THEORY FOR SPLITTING STONES...
STONE CHISELED ALONG NATURAL SPLIT LINES... THEN WOOD WEDGES DRIVEN IN - ADD WATER - WOOD EXPANDS - PRESSURE CAUSES STONE TO SPLIT ALONG NATURAL FAULT LINE...
AFTER WALLS SET INTO PLACE - POLISHED WITH SMALL BLACK HARD STONE FROM METEORITE
INCA DRAWBRIDGE:
RUN AWAY!
INVADING ARMY
REMOVABLE WOOD LOGS
TEMPLE OF THE SUN:
WINTER SOLSTICE 21 JUNE
SUMMER SOLSTICE 21 DEC
ALIGNED WITH INTIPUNKU (SUN GATE)
NORTH
POTENTIALLY USED TO DEMARCATE AGRICULTURAL SEASONS (ASTRONOMICAL / SOLAR CALENDAR)

RECONSTRUCTED ROOF SYSTEMS (THEORY)

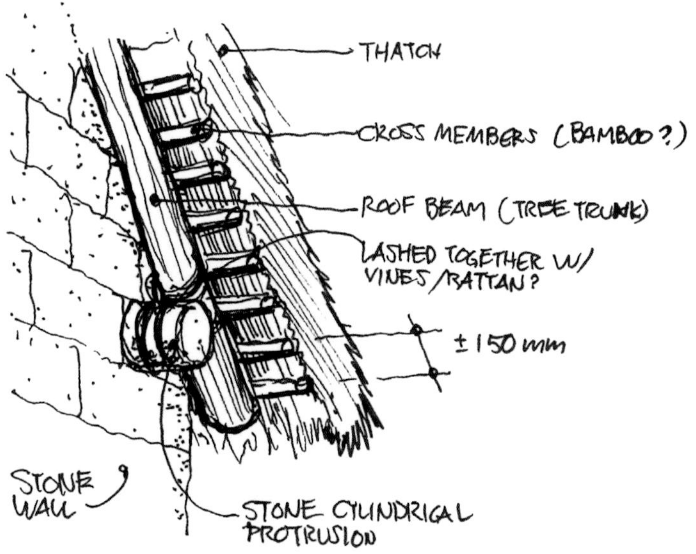

AGRICULTURAL TERRACES

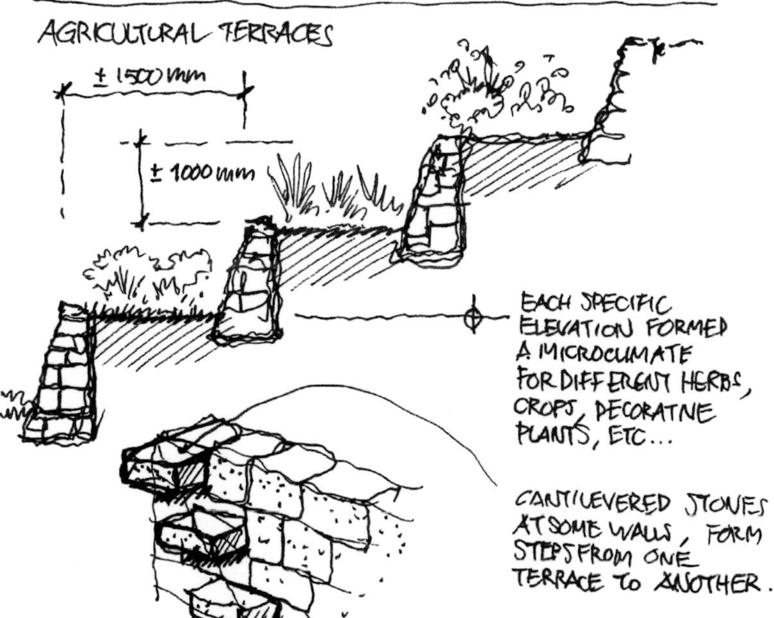

EACH SPECIFIC ELEVATION FORMED A MICROCLIMATE FOR DIFFERENT HERBS, CROPS, DECORATIVE PLANTS, ETC...

CANTILEVERED STONES AT SOME WALLS, FORM STEPS FROM ONE TERRACE TO ANOTHER...

SOUTHERN CROSS ROCK...

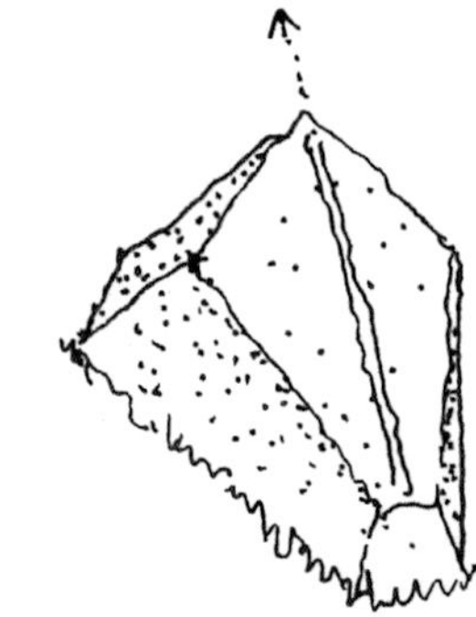

SOUTHERN-CROSS SHAPED RHOMBOID CARVED ROCK POINTS DIRECTLY TOWARD SOUTHERN CROSS CONSTELLATION

RELIGIOUS OR ASTRONOMICAL FUNCTION?

SACRIFICIAL TABLES...

CARVED ROCK...

NEXT TO CARETAKERS HUT — SHAPE AND SIZE SIMILAR TO OPERATING TABLE — USED FOR HUMAN/ANIMAL SACRIFICES... OR MUMMIFYING BODIES...

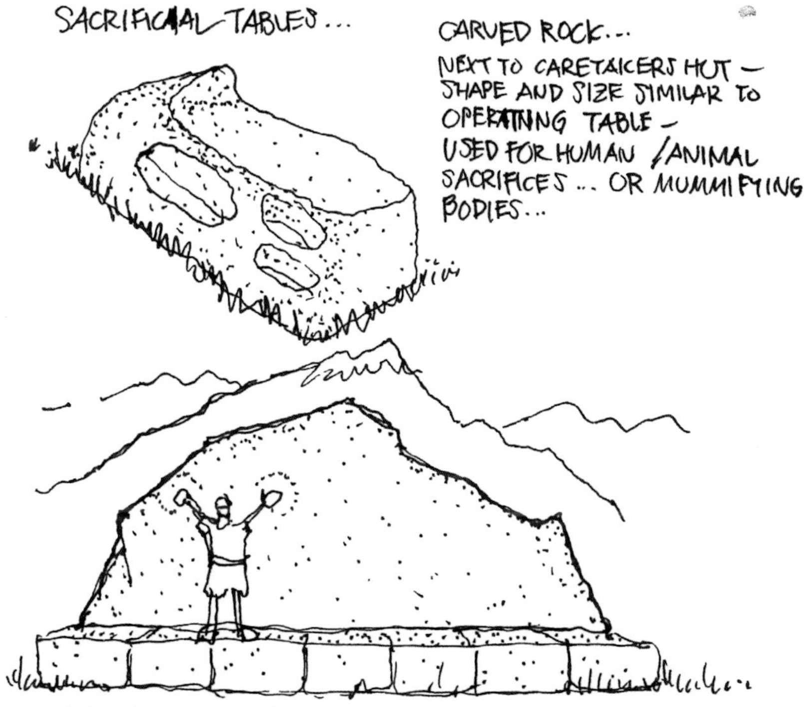

SACRED ROCK: (A.K.A. ECHO ROCK)

PROFILE MATCHES PROFILE OF MOUNTAIN RANGE BEYOND... SAID TO BE 50% QUARTZ AND CONCENTRATED WITH SPIRITUAL ENERGY... STANDING WITH BOTH HANDS ON THIS FLAT SURFACED ROCK WILL GIVE YOU A CHARGE OF POSITIVE ENERGY...

THE
SIWAN
WINDOW
INSECT SCREEN
DATE PALMS AND OLIVE TREES...
NATURAL WATER SPRINGS
FIXED WOOD FRAME
HINGED WINDOW WITH FIXED GLASS PANEL
GLASS
HINGED WOOD COVER WITH SLIDING WOOD LATCH (SHADING DOORS)
INTERIOR
ADOBE WALL (SALT CHIPS + SILT + CLAY SUN BAKED)
DEEP RECESS
EXTERIOR
SIWAN WINDOWS (INTERIOR VIEW)
OUTER INSECT SCREEN
OPEN
POSITION
CLOSED
ALL DOORS CLOSED — BLACKOUT MODE...
LIGHT DOORS OPEN REVEALING FIXED GLASS PANES — ADMITS LIGHT ONLY
SECONDARY DOORS OPEN ALLOWING VENTILATION
VISUAL NOTES

HOW DOES IT WORK?

I have always been a very curious person, and my architecture studies reinforced frequent acts of observation and analysis by recording "visual notes" in my sketchbook.

Even the most complex assemblies can be studied, dissected, enlarged and visually explained in order to gain a deeper understanding of how things work, how they fit together, and how they were created.

I often add annotations to my sketches to indicate building materials, estimated dimensions and other design features to help me remember various aspects of whatever I am drawing at the time. Sometimes I will draw 3D cutaway sections of buildings or walls to better recollect a particular design element or construction detail.

I also document smaller items that I find interesting or unique -- whether it is a handicraft, a local musical instrument, or even a unique hand-carved item that is used in everyday life.

With the deluge of information we are assaulted with on a daily basis, I find that if I don't take these visual notes as and when I experience things, I will inevitably forget what I've seen.

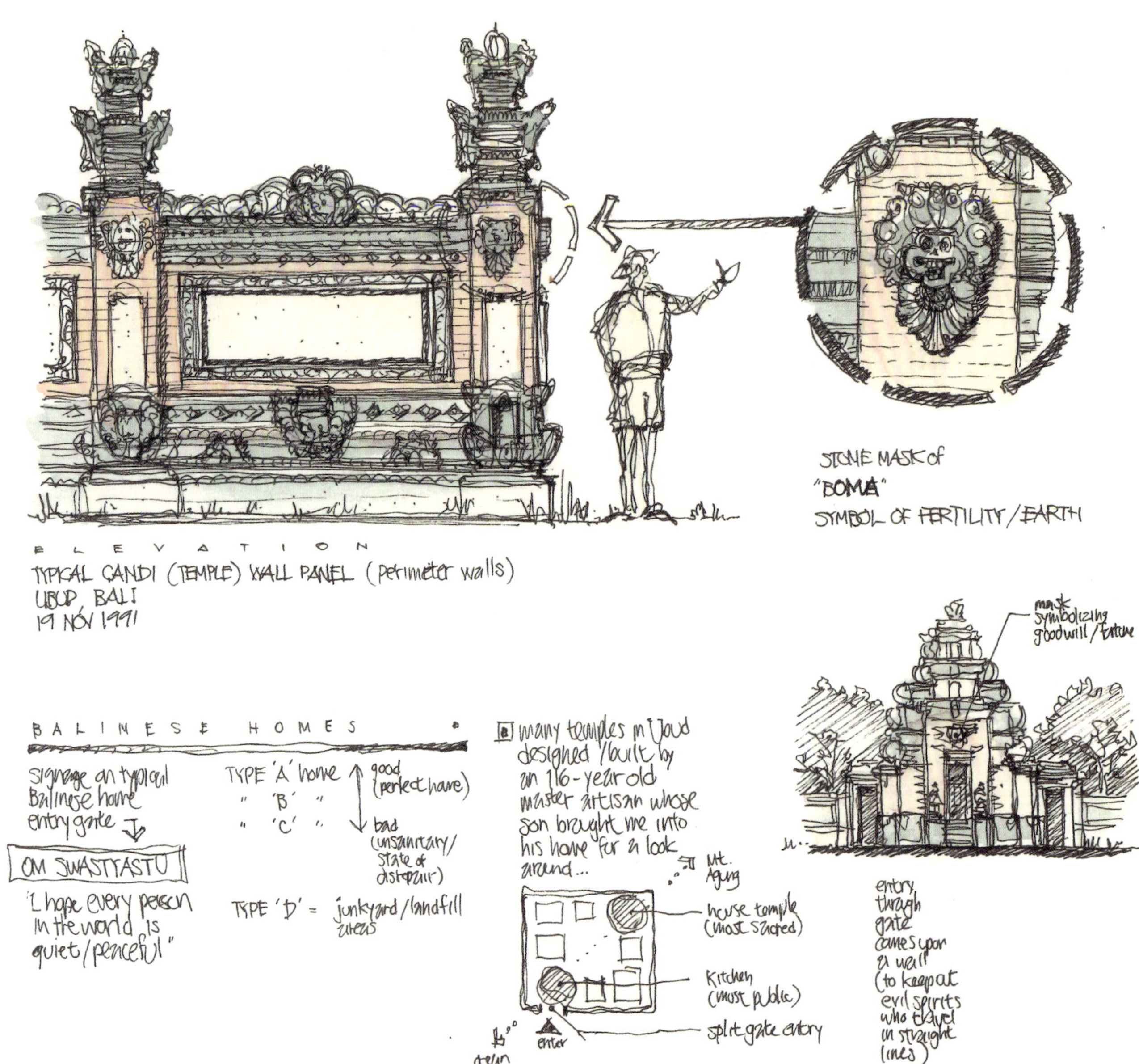

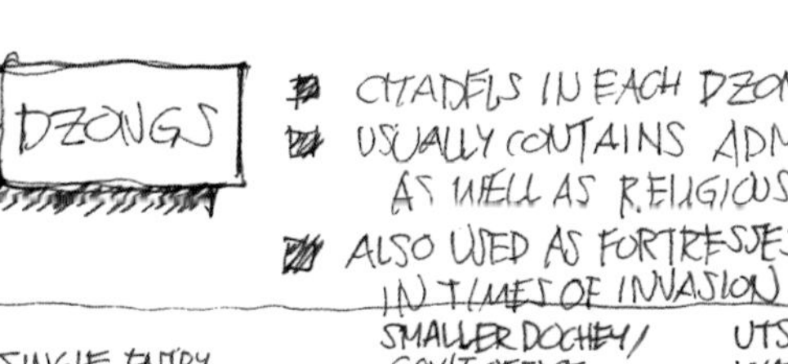

- CITADELS IN EACH DZONGKHAG (DISTRICT)
- USUALLY CONTAINS ADMINISTRATIVE HEADQUARTERS AS WELL AS RELIGIOUS AUTHORITIES. (2 COURTYARDS)
- ALSO USED AS FORTRESSES TO PROTECT VILLAGERS IN TIMES OF INVASION

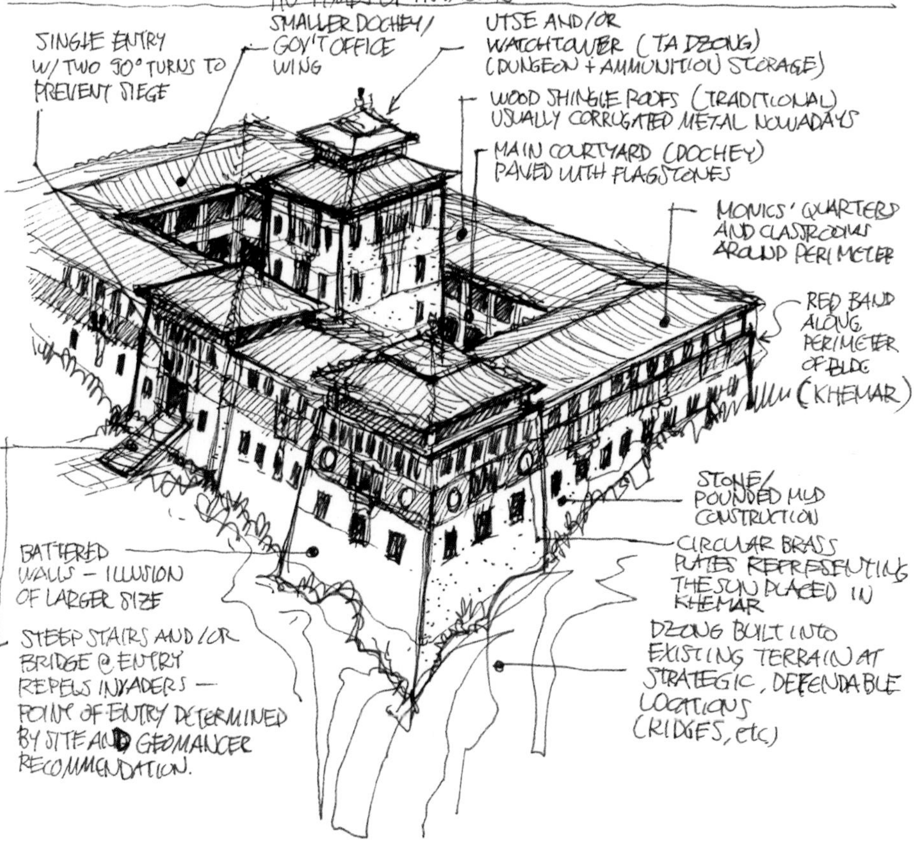

- NO NAILS USED IN CONSTRUCTION
- ARCHITECTS DON'T USE PLANS / DRAWINGS — ONLY MENTAL CONCEPT
- TWO MAIN WINGS (ONE FOR GOV'T OFFICES AND ONE FOR MONASTERY
- SEPARATE WATCHTOWER OFTEN PROVIDED
- UTSE USUALLY HAS SERIES OF CHAPELS ON UPPER FLOORS — LOWER FLOOR HAS "LHAKHANG"
- MASSIVE CYPRESS (?) TREE USUALLY PLANTED DIRECTLY OUTSIDE OF ENTRY
- CIRCULATION WITHIN DZONG / AROUND PRAYER WHEELS / THROUGH LHAKHANGS ALWAYS IN A CLOCKWISE PROGRESSION...
- RESIDENT MONK IS CALLED "RABDEY"

Bhutan: One of the more untouched, fascinating and friendly places I've had the privilege of visiting.

GOEMBAS & LHAKHANGS

- OWNED BY THE STATE AS WELL AS PRIVATELY HELD.
- EACH DESIGNED PER WISHES OF FOUNDERS, ARCHITECTS, OR SPONSORS

GOEMBA = MONASTERY

- LOCATION OFTEN ISOLATED SO MONKS HAVE PEACE / SOLITUDE (ROCKY CRAGS, REMOTE HILLSIDES, ETC.)
- SOMETIMES LOCATED AT SACRED CAVES USED FOR MEDITATION
- SELF-CONTAINED COMMUNITIES W/ CENTRAL LHAKHANG AND SLEEPING QUARTERS
- LHAKHANG LOCATED AT CENTER OF DOCHEY (COURTYARD) — USED AS DANCE ARENA DURING FESTIVALS.

LHAKHANG = PRIMARY CHAPEL (BUT ALSO MEANS ENTIRE BLDG. SOMETIMES)

- HAS CUPOLA + BALL SHAPED ORNAMENT (SERTO) ON ROOF
- PAVED PATH AROUND PERIMETER WITH RACKS OF PRAYER WHEELS

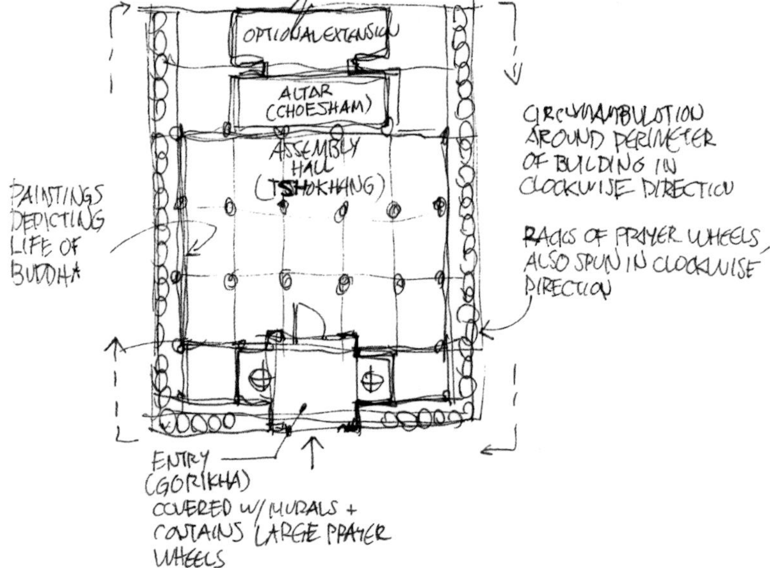

CHORTEN

- RECEPTACLE FOR OFFERINGS
- SITUATED IN UNLUCKY LOCATIONS TO WARD OFF EVIL (OFTEN RIVER JUNCTIONS, CROSSROADS, MOUNTAIN PASSES, BRIDGES, ETC.)
- SHAPE BASED ON CLASSIC INDIAN STUPA

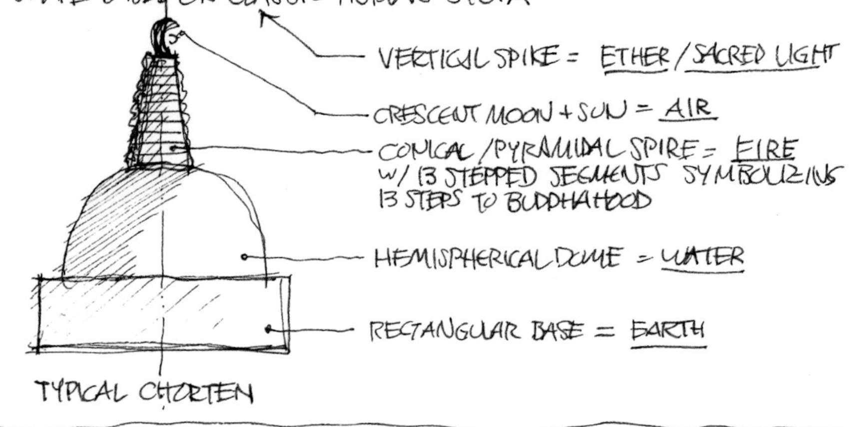

3 TYPES OF CHORTEN IN BHUTAN:

BHUTANESE	NEPALESE	TIBETAN
REDUCED FORM OF CLASSIC STUPA W/ SQUARE STONE PILLAR (KHEMAR) NEAR TOP	BASED ON CLASSIC STUPA	SHAPE SIMILAR TO STUPA, BUT ROUNDED PART FLARES OUTWARD (INSTEAD OF DOME SHAPE)
SOME CHORTENS HAVE BALL/CRESCENT AT TOP SYMBOLIZING SUN + MOON	4 SIDES OF TOWER PAINTED W/ SET OF EYES	THIMPHU NAT'L MEMORIAL CHORTEN EXEMPLIFIES THIS STYLE
	CHENDEBJI CHORTEN EXEMPLIFIES THIS STYLE	

the upper level is allocated to family quarters, with an open-air attic as a general purpose storage area for hay, dried meat, and a multitude of other household items.

UPPER LEVEL PLAN:

LOWER LEVEL:
- LIVESTOCK STORAGE

LOG STAIR UP TO ATTIC

CONCRETE / OVEN STOVE.

STOR

TOILET

ADDITION

WC

DW

KIT / LIVING

TV

STOR

STOR

ALTAR

BED.

PRAYER

"CHOESUM" (CHAPEL) LOCATION DETERMINED BY ASTROLOGER ON CASE-BY-CASE BASIS

DRIED CHILI PEPPERS

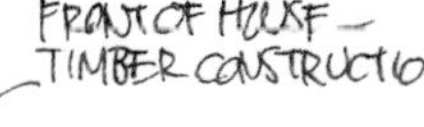

METAL CORRUGATED ROOFING

HANGING PHALLUS @ EACH CORNER OF ROOF
OPEN-AIR ATTIC —
HAY STORAGE
WOOD "
DRIED MEATS / CHILIS

FRONT ELEVATION

SECTION

FAMILY

LIVESTOCK

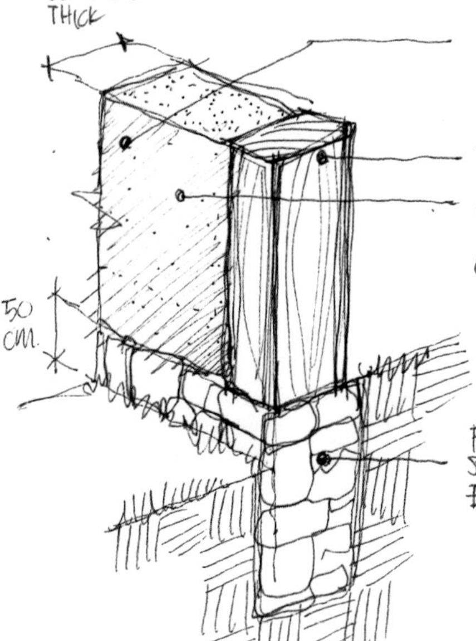

HOUSES

80 - 100 CM THICK

■ STYLE DEPENDS UPON LOCATION / ELEVATION
■ NO NAILS USED IN TRADITIONAL STRUCTURES! ALL WOOD JOINERY...

TYPICAL WHITE-WASHED FINISH

TIMBER FRAME

STONE INFILL (CENTRAL / EASTERN BHUTAN)
OR
COMPACTED EARTH (WEST BHUTAN)
(DAMP MUD FILLED INTO FORMS THEN COMPACTED / POUNDED BY WOODEN POLES BY GROUPS OF WOMEN)

50 CM.

FOUNDATION —
STONES PLACED IN TRENCH, EXTEND 500mm ABOVE GRADE

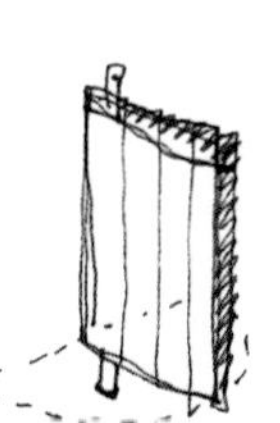

TRADITIONAL DOOR —
TONGUE + GROOVE WITH ROUND PEG HINGES @ TOP + BOTTOM

FRONT OF HOUSE — TIMBER CONSTRUCTION

HOLES FOR WOODEN BEAMS — UPPER FLOOR SUPPORTED BY BEAMS AND CENTRAL COLUMNS BELOW

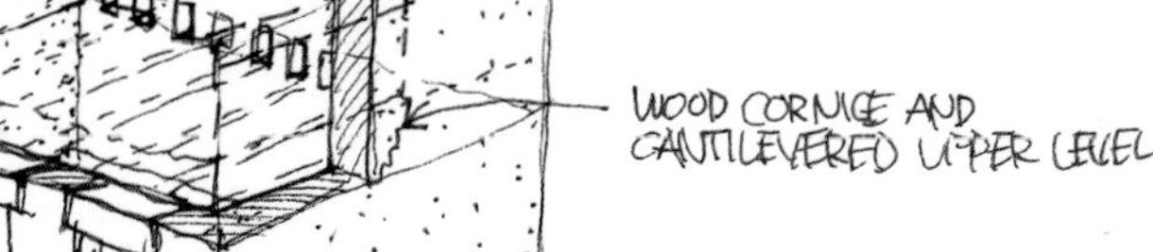

WOOD CORNICE AND CANTILEVERED UPPER LEVEL

INTERNAL PARTITIONS:
TIMBER FRAME WITH WOVEN BAMBOO INFILL PLASTERED WITH MUD
("SHADDAM" OR WEAVE MUD)

FACES SOUTH

scaled the series of planks leading up the hillside to a ramshackle collection of wooden buildings around the longhouse itself. Removed our footwear and climbed a few steps onto a wide verandah that ran the entire length of the longhouse where a group of small children stood and cast uncertain stares. Passed an old man hunched over squatting near the railing with a bony outstretched arm prodding interloping chickens with a long branch. The chickens would occasionally prance over to steal a few pieces of grain/seeds that were drying on grass mats in the sunshine. The man was thoroughly tattooed with a greenish-black ink on his forearms and feet — his mouth contained the red mush of a betel nut wrapped in a leaf that he crushed with gleaming orangy-copper metallic teeth ... he too had the eerie droopy ear lobes ...

... soon we were on our third bottle when the old woman of the house produced a brass oil lamp of some kind that resembled a large candlestick ... she lit the wick ... soon the faces of these people of Borneo took on surreal qualities in the flickering candlelight ... another woman joined our circle on the floor of this room devoid of furniture and began gossiping with the first as they simultaneously prepared a dose of betel nut with robot-like motions. As they smacked away with their metallic teeth (perhaps another government subsidized benefit?), John began conveying the inner workings and laws of his longhouse ... actually — really communal and village-like. The chief of the village acts as a mediator in family conflicts as well as the obvious role of "leader" of the longhouse ... important decisions regarding life in the longhouse are determined by lengthy secret meetings by the longhouse elders ... lots of intricate customs that could never be ascertained in one visit ...

After: The final illustration in Bumbling Through Borneo, based upon the sketchbook entry on the preceding page.

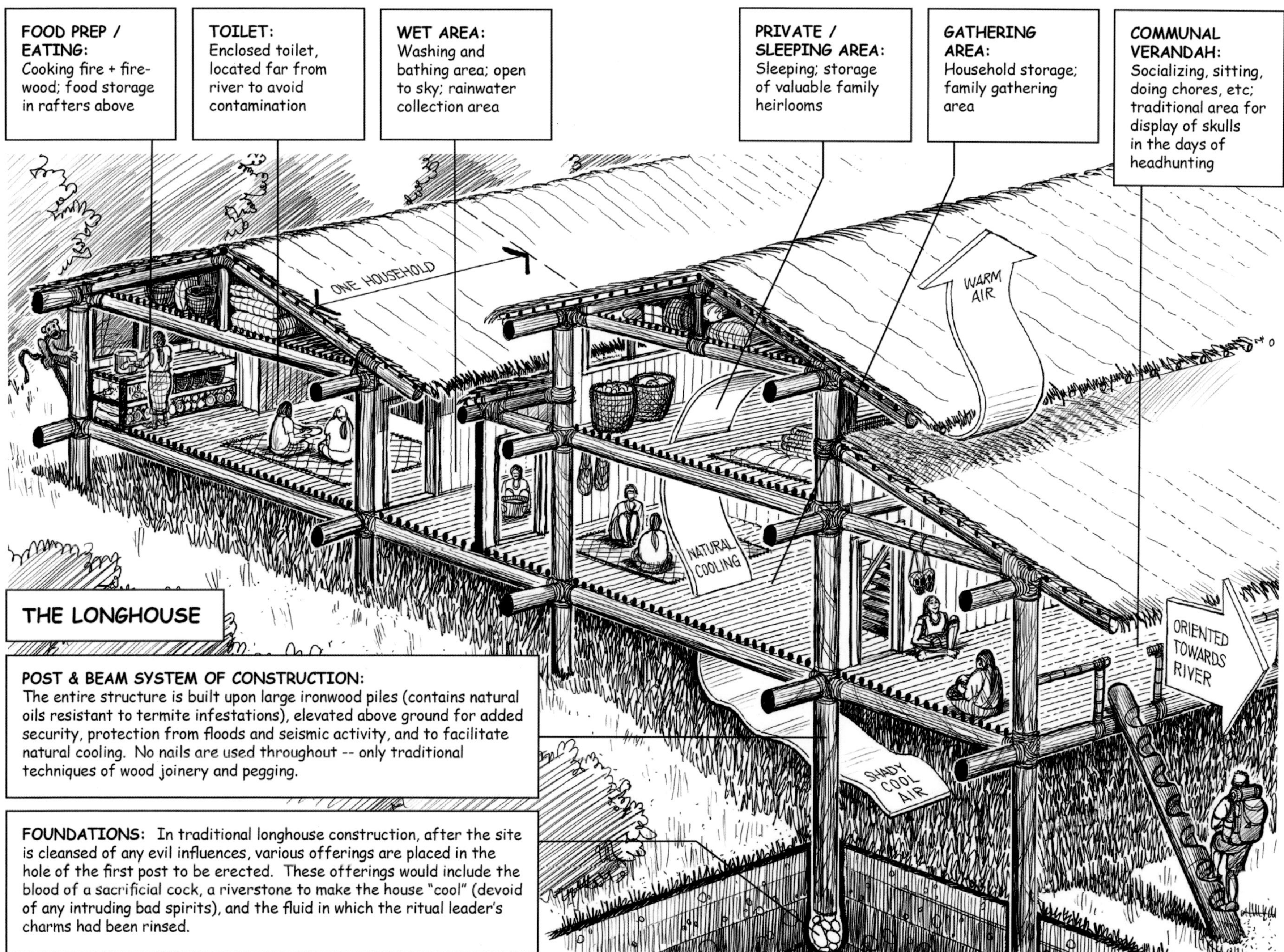

FOOD PREP / EATING:
Cooking fire + firewood; food storage in rafters above

TOILET:
Enclosed toilet, located far from river to avoid contamination

WET AREA:
Washing and bathing area; open to sky; rainwater collection area

PRIVATE / SLEEPING AREA:
Sleeping; storage of valuable family heirlooms

GATHERING AREA:
Household storage; family gathering area

COMMUNAL VERANDAH:
Socializing, sitting, doing chores, etc; traditional area for display of skulls in the days of headhunting

ONE HOUSEHOLD

WARM AIR

NATURAL COOLING

ORIENTED TOWARDS RIVER

SHADY COOL AIR

THE LONGHOUSE

POST & BEAM SYSTEM OF CONSTRUCTION:
The entire structure is built upon large ironwood piles (contains natural oils resistant to termite infestations), elevated above ground for added security, protection from floods and seismic activity, and to facilitate natural cooling. No nails are used throughout -- only traditional techniques of wood joinery and pegging.

FOUNDATIONS: In traditional longhouse construction, after the site is cleansed of any evil influences, various offerings are placed in the hole of the first post to be erected. These offerings would include the blood of a sacrificial cock, a riverstone to make the house "cool" (devoid of any intruding bad spirits), and the fluid in which the ritual leader's charms had been rinsed.

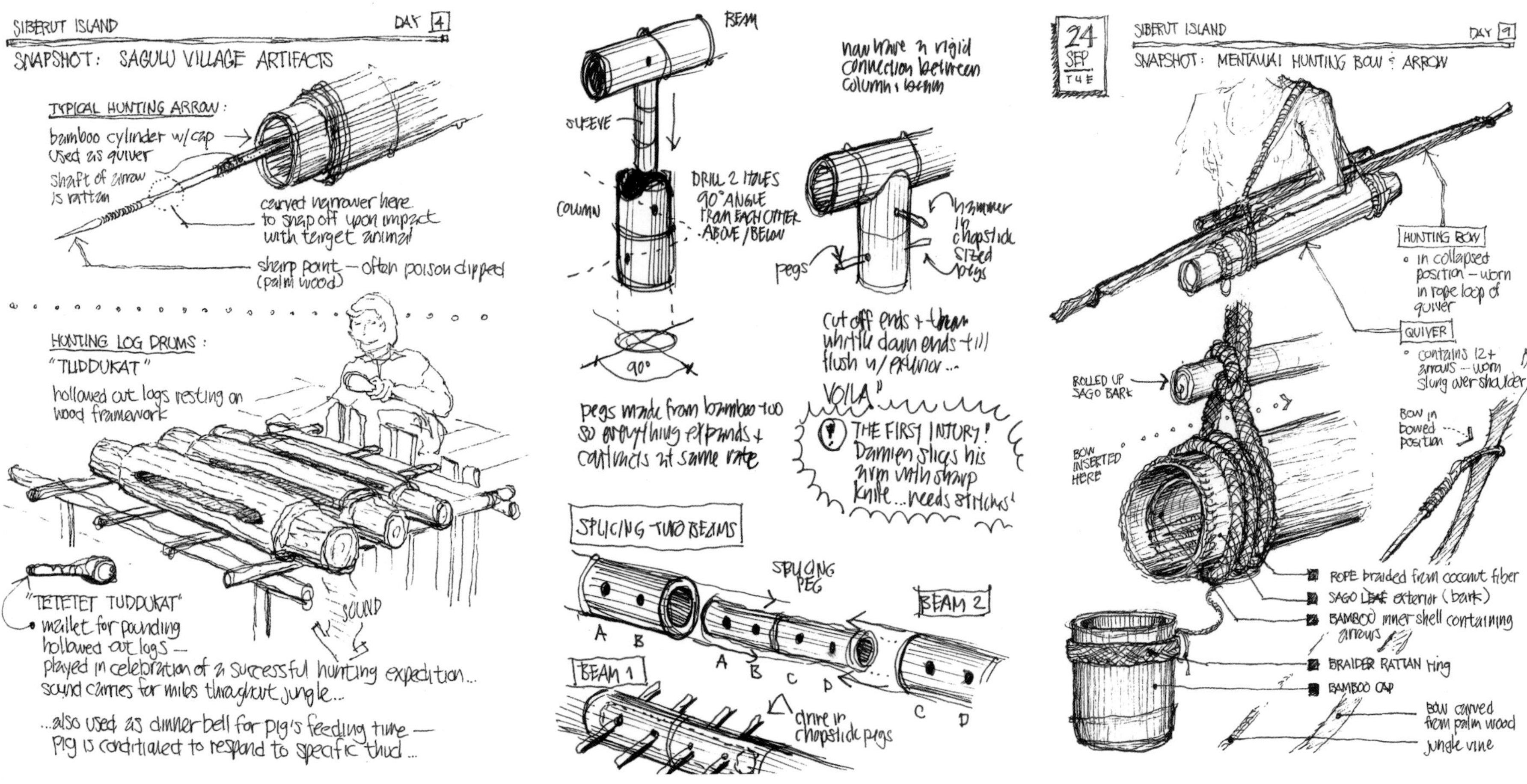

Bamboo: This fast-growing grass is one of the most sustainable and versatile gifts from nature; bamboo can be used for constructing everything from buildings and household items, to musical instruments and weapons.

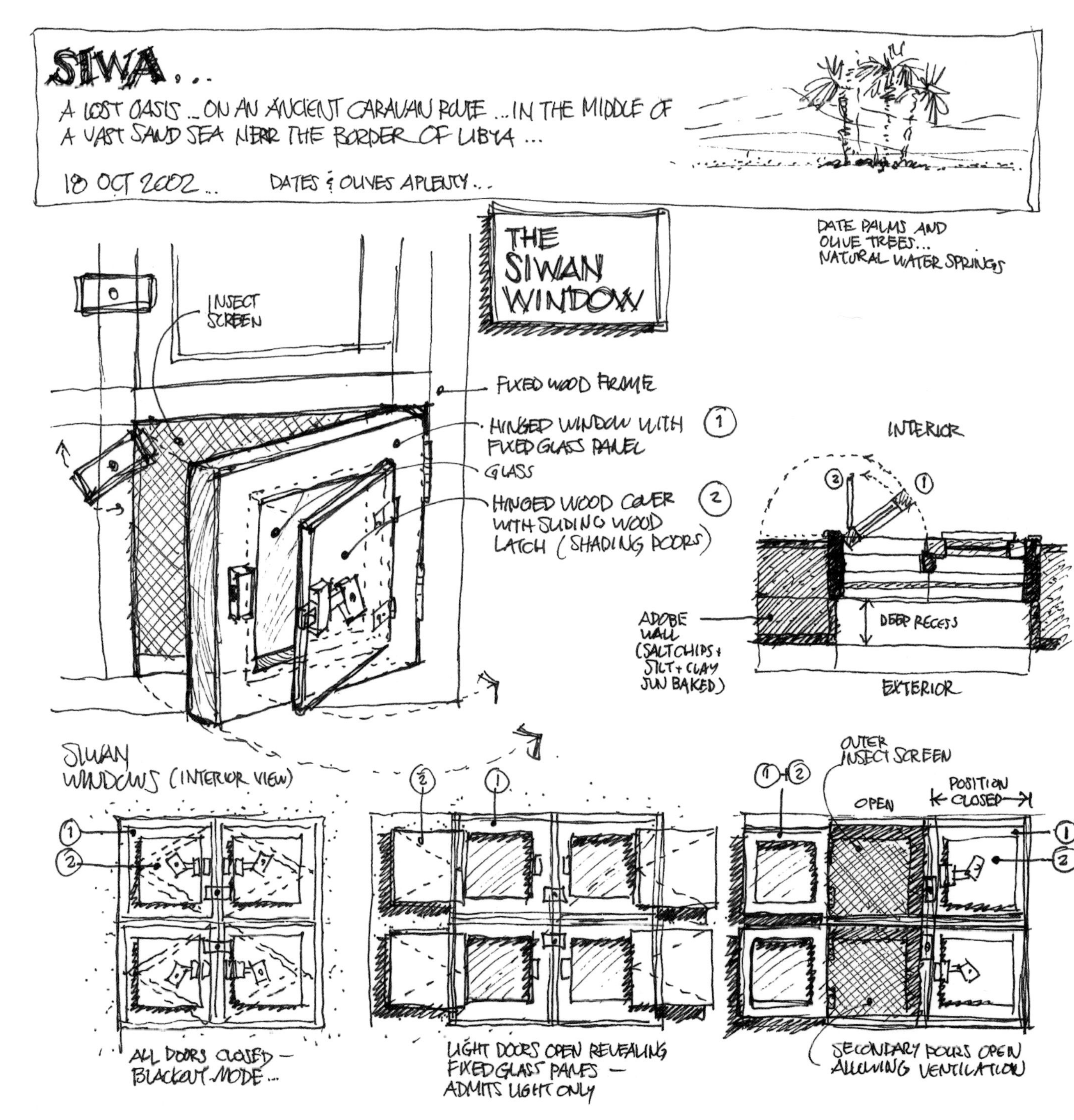

SIWA...
A LOST OASIS ... ON AN ANCIENT CARAVAN ROUTE ... IN THE MIDDLE OF
A VAST SAND SEA NEAR THE BORDER OF LIBYA ...
18 OCT 2002 ...   DATES & OLIVES APLENTY ...
DATE PALMS AND
OLIVE TREES ...
NATURAL WATER SPRINGS
THE SIWAN WINDOW
INSECT SCREEN
FIXED WOOD FRAME
HINGED WINDOW WITH FIXED GLASS PANEL   1
GLASS
HINGED WOOD COVER WITH SLIDING WOOD LATCH (SHADING DOORS)   2
INTERIOR
2   1
ADOBE WALL (SALT CHIPS + SILT + CLAY SUN BAKED)
DEEP RECESS
EXTERIOR
SIWAN WINDOWS (INTERIOR VIEW)
1
2
ALL DOORS CLOSED — BLACKOUT MODE ...
2   1
LIGHT DOORS OPEN REVEALING FIXED GLASS PANES — ADMITS LIGHT ONLY
1   2
OUTER INSECT SCREEN
OPEN
POSITION CLOSED
1
2
SECONDARY DOORS OPEN ALLOWING VENTILATION

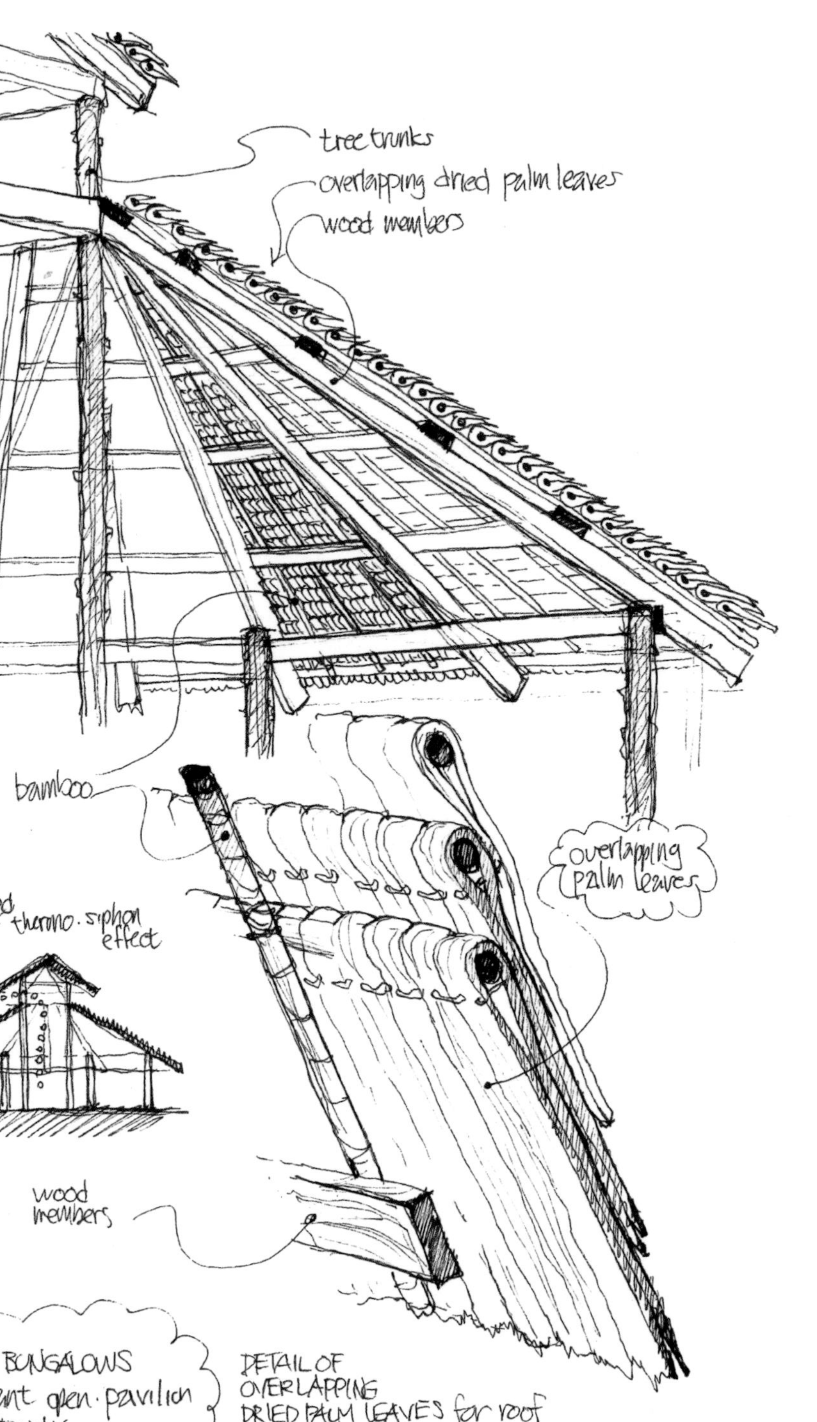

SNAPSHOT: ROGDOG VILLAGE HOUSE

☑ PUBLIC:
- communal verandah … evening gatherings with other villagers

☑ SEMI-PRIVATE:
- multiple families share communal bamboo-floored sleeping / eating area … can be closed in from elements / outside verandah by 2 top-hung doors covering entry
- cooking fire on back wall

☑ PRIVATE:
- small intimate family living quarters (sleeping … keep place of possessions) flanking interior eating area ..

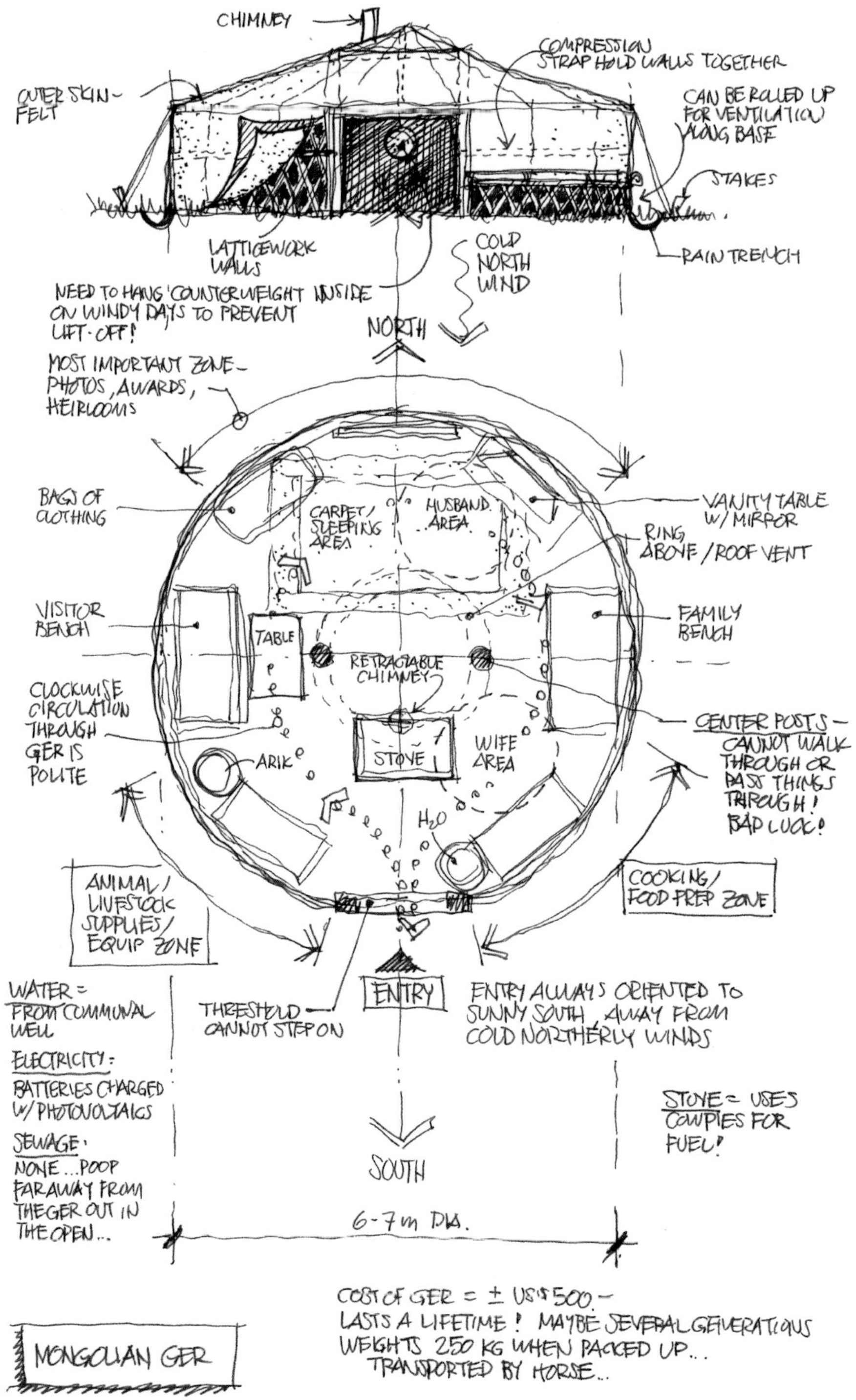

MONGOLIAN GER

CHIMNEY

OUTER SKIN — FELT

COMPRESSION STRAP HOLD WALLS TOGETHER

CAN BE ROLLED UP FOR VENTILATION ALONG BASE

STAKES

RAIN TRENCH

LATTICEWORK WALLS

COLD NORTH WIND

NORTH

NEED TO HANG 'COUNTERWEIGHT' INSIDE ON WINDY DAYS TO PREVENT LIFT·OFF!

MOST IMPORTANT ZONE — PHOTOS, AWARDS, HEIRLOOMS

BAGS OF CLOTHING

CARPET / SLEEPING AREA

HUSBAND AREA

VANITY TABLE W/ MIRROR

RING ABOVE / ROOF VENT

FAMILY BENCH

VISITOR BENCH

TABLE

RETRACTABLE CHIMNEY?

CLOCKWISE CIRCULATION THROUGH GER IS POLITE

ARIK

STOVE

WIFE AREA

CENTER POSTS — CANNOT WALK THROUGH OR PASS THINGS THROUGH! BAD LUCK!

H₂O

ANIMAL / LIVESTOCK SUPPLIES / EQUIP ZONE

COOKING / FOOD PREP ZONE

WATER = FROM COMMUNAL WELL

ELECTRICITY: BATTERIES CHARGED W/ PHOTOVOLTAICS

SEWAGE: NONE … POOP FAR AWAY FROM THE GER OUT IN THE OPEN …

THRESHOLD CANNOT STEP ON

ENTRY

ENTRY ALWAYS ORIENTED TO SUNNY SOUTH, AWAY FROM COLD NORTHERLY WINDS

STOVE = USES COWPIES FOR FUEL!

SOUTH

6-7 m DIA.

COST OF GER = ± US$500 — LASTS A LIFETIME! MAYBE SEVERAL GENERATIONS. WEIGHS 250 KG WHEN PACKED UP … TRANSPORTED BY HORSE …

YAK HERDER'S TENT

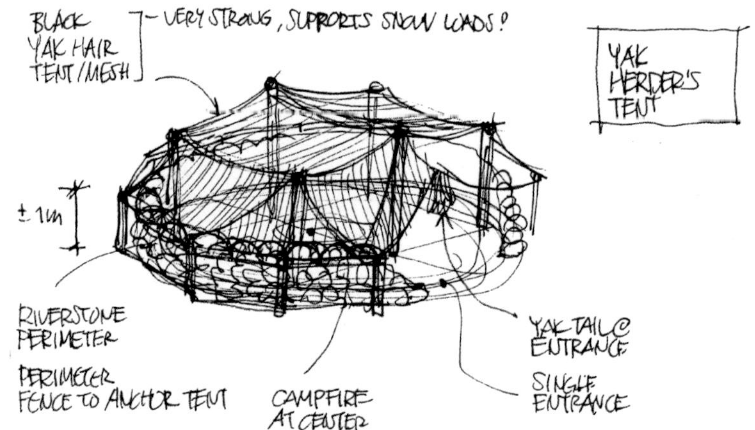

BLACK YAK HAIR TENT / MESH — VERY STRONG, SUPPORTS SNOW LOADS!

± 1 m

RIVERSTONE PERIMETER

PERIMETER FENCE TO ANCHOR TENT

CAMPFIRE AT CENTER

YAK TAIL @ ENTRANCE

SINGLE ENTRANCE

- FOUND USUALLY AT HIGHER ELEVATIONS
- DISMANTLED / MOVED EVERY 2-3 MONTHS TO "GREENER PASTURES" TO INSURE YAK'S HAVE FOOD
- CENTRAL FIRE PIT SURROUNDED BY YAK SKINS / BLANKETS FOR SLEEPING
- DRIED MEAT, etc. HANGS FROM UNDERSIDE OF TENT
- ALSO CONTAINS MILK / BUTTER CHURNING CONTAINER
- KNOWN AS THE "100 PEG TENT"
- BJA IS SEASONAL HOME OF BJOBS (SEMI·NOMADIC TRIBE AT BHUTAN'S HIGHER ELEVATIONS)
- BJOBS LIVE IN BJA FOR 6 MONTHS / YEAR
- WEAVING A BJA :
  * COLLECTION OF 160 SANG (3 SANGS = 1 KG) OR 53 KG. OF COMPLETELY BLACK YAK HAIR
  * AFTER COLLECTING WOOL, CONSULT A "TSIB" (ASTROLOGER) TO FIX DATE TO COMMENCE WEAVING WOOL → FELT.
  * FOR DURABILITY, NEED THE LONGEST + MOST COARSE WOOL FROM OLDER, MATURED YAKS (SOFT WOOL IS NOT DURABLE) … WHITE WOOL IS THOUGHT TO WEAKEN STRENGTH!
- BJOBS SPEND MUCH FREE TIME SPINNING / TWINING YAK HAIR → YARN FOR WEAVING YAK SADDLE BAGS, ROPES, BLANKETS, CLOTHING
- NOWADAYS, PEOPLE WEAVING BJAS ARE DECLINING

Rustic Structures: People who live off the land typically construct shelter with whatever is readily available -- whether this is animal hides, mud bricks, or timber and bamboo from a nearby forest. Today's sustainable design is all about getting back to the basics our ancestors once mastered.

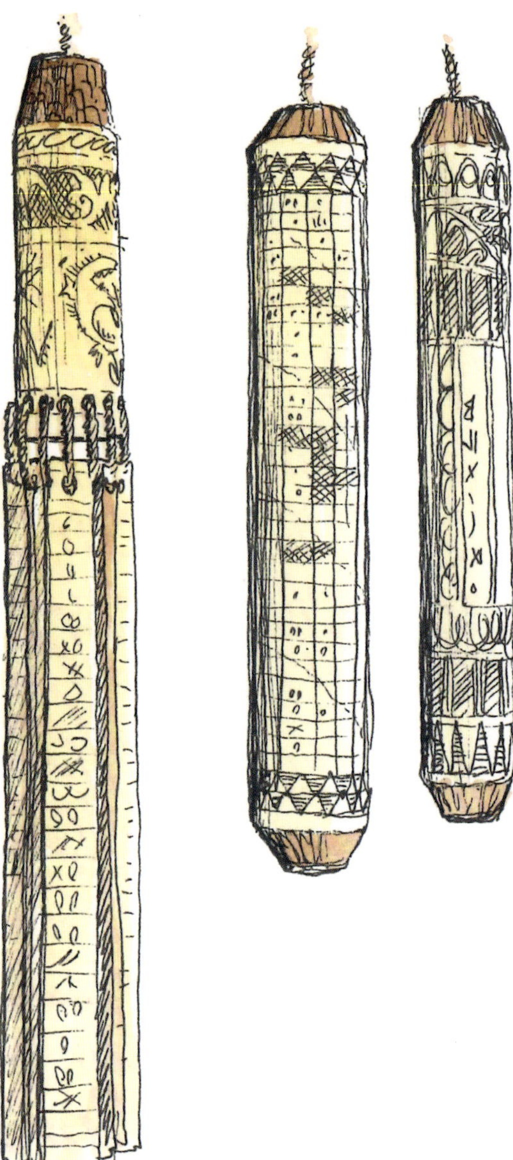

BATAK "PORHALAAN" (divining calendars)

- calendars etched in bamboo of 30 days and 12 months — used to determine auspicious days on which to embark on activities such as marriage or planting of the fields... (see following pages :)

Handmade Treasures: Sketching is a great way to document handmade items you encounter during your travels, as well as the stories behind them.

MAIZE (CORN) -
used as animal feed for pigs and chickens

also used in making whiskey

RICE -
primary food staple in highland villages

OPIUM -
used in small quantities for medicinal purposes

important cash crop (used as currency) in bartering for other food and consumer goods

OIL -
opium poppy oil and sesame oil used for cooking and fuel for lamp light

HERBS / SPICES -
used in cooking and as condiments

SUPPLEMENTARY CROPS -
yams, taro, cocoyam, and potatoes grown in case rice crop fails

FRUIT -
papaya, pineapple, melons, and banana eaten - also used for animal feed

TEA -
medicinal beverage

BAMBOO - over 13 different varieties grown

used extensively in construction of dwellings

used as water / food containers and as cooking utensils

SOAP NUT -
used as soap & shampoo

SMOOTH LOOFAH -
used as scrubber

COSMETIC HERBS -
leaf scrapings worn as rouge by women

FIBER PLANTS - used in weaving, clothing, and making containers

cotton used in clothing

hemp used as thread

wheat straw used in decorative clothing

bottle gourds - used as utensil receptacles, water containers; small gourds worn as ornamental jewelry

COCONUT PALM -
substems used for broom handles

fronds used as roof and wall thatch

RELIGIOUS CROPS -
certain crops grown to protect field from bad spirits that may bring farmer bad luck

From there, went to the "Duomo" - focal element (cathedral) of Florence
designed by Brunelleschi - climbed between the double-shell dome to the top
which opens up to a fantastic view to the city...

...walking between the 2 domes is very
bizarre, walking through strange non-
perpendicular spaces makes you lose your
balance walking at an
angle

...now sitting on a hilltop(looking
at the Duomo) inside Belvedere
fortress (Florence)...

I have discovered that Italy is the
land of deception - hidden costs everywhere,
but still beautiful nonetheless...

construction begun 1299 ...→

...bridge stretching across
river with shops / dwellings
built on over time
[Ponte Rialto ?]

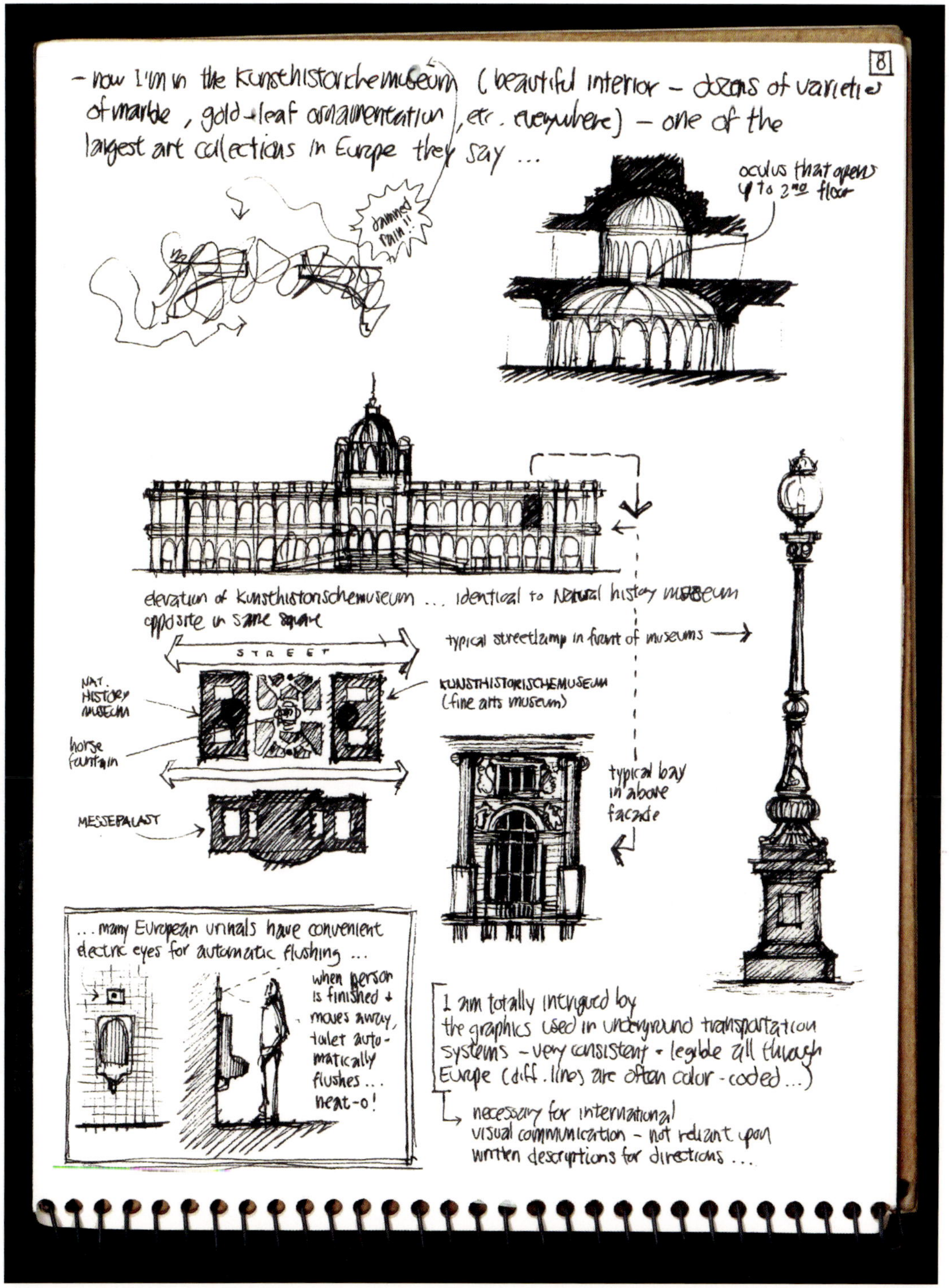

8
- now I'm in the Kunsthistorischemuseum (beautiful interior - dozens of varieties of marble, gold-leaf ornamentation, etc. everywhere) - one of the largest art collections in Europe they say ...
damned rain!!
oculus that opens up to 2nd floor
elevation of Kunsthistorischemuseum ... identical to Natural history museum opposite in same square
typical streetlamp in front of museums
STREET
NAT. HISTORY MUSEUM
KUNSTHISTORISCHEMUSEUM (fine arts museum)
horse fountain
MESSEPALAST
typical bay in above facade
... many European urinals have convenient electric eyes for automatic flushing ...
when person is finished + moves away, toilet automatically flushes ... neat-o!
I am totally intrigued by the graphics used in underground transportation systems - very consistent + legible all through Europe (diff. lines are often color-coded ...)
necessary for international visual communication - not reliant upon written descriptions for directions ...

A Visual Journal: While some people travel with a sketchbook used just for their drawings, I typically employ a journal that combines a travel diary with travel sketches -- and is also a repository for beer labels, ticket stubs, and other odds and ends I collect along the way.

Sketchbooks with spiral bindings should be avoided as the coils are usually so large that they interfere with the sketching process *and* tend to shred the inside of your backpack. Live and learn.

GREAT THEATRE
built into hillside (like Epidauros)
Originally constructed in Hellenistic period - seats 25,000 people
STAGE
ORCHESTRA PIT
SEATING FOR:
- magistrates/well-to-do
- lower/middle class
- women and low class
- poor and slaves (standing room only)
THEATRE RESTORATION - leaves certain sectors unrestored to show aging of past restorations and original structure
NEWLY RESTORED
RESTORED IN PAST ERAS
ORIGINAL

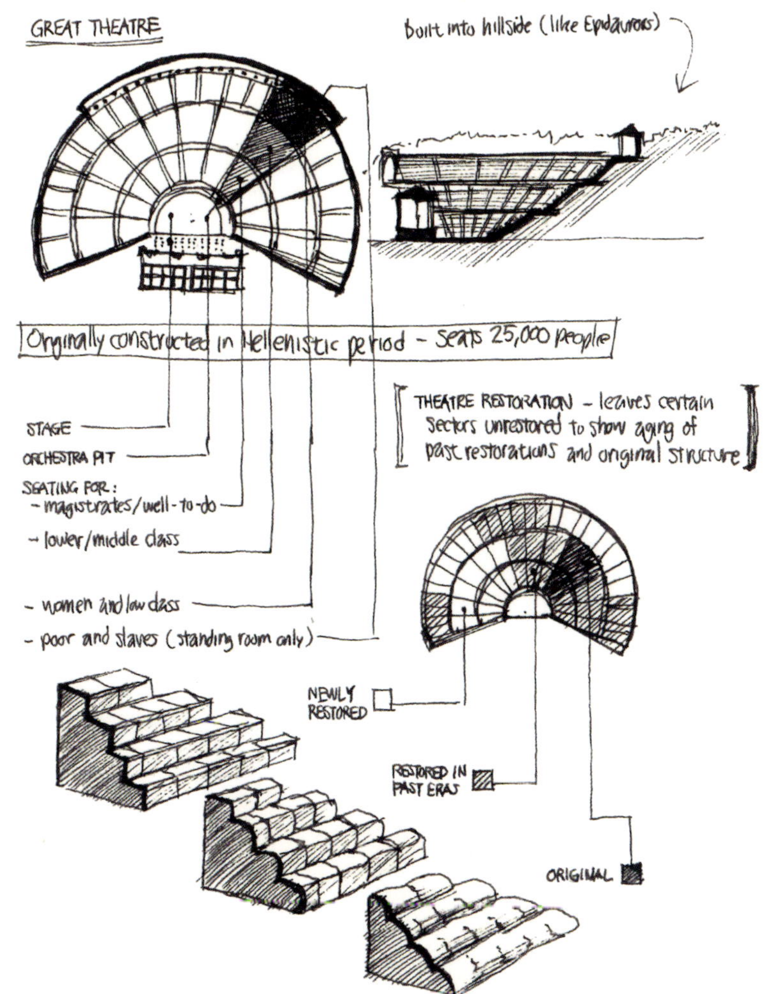

VENICE FACTOIDS:

6 DISTRICTS:
— (SESTIERI)

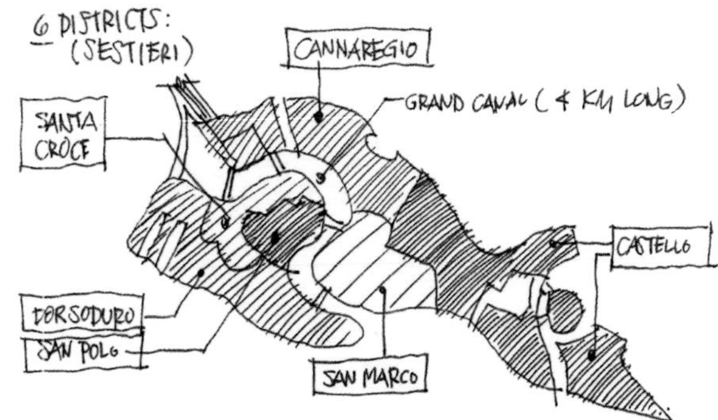

ORIG. BLDGS. BUILT UPON TIMBER PILES AND HORIZONTAL TIMBER MEMBERS ON SWAMP LAND — SHORELINES REINFORCED BY TIMBER POSTS

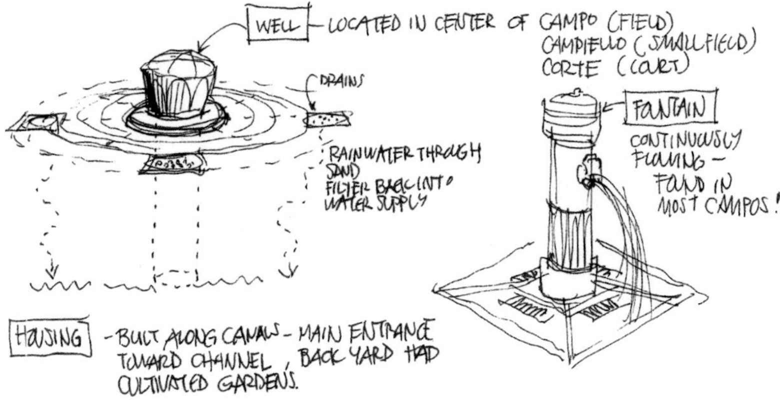

HOUSING — BUILT ALONG CANALS — MAIN ENTRANCE TOWARD CHANNEL, BACK YARD HAD CULTIVATED GARDENS.

CANALS — 150 TOTAL CANALS
— FLUSHED OUT EVERY 6 HOURS DUE TO TIDAL FLUCTUATION

VAPORETTO — BUSES ALONG CANALS — USED IF IN A HURRY... MOST PEOPLE WALK...

BRIDGES — ORIGINALLY BUILT WITHOUT RAILINGS — RAILS ADDED MID 1800'S

DISTRICTS

CASTELLO	CANNAREGIO	DORSODURO	SAN POLO	SAN CROCE	SAN MARCO
- MOST POPULATED - SHIPYARDS - LOTS OF GARDENS	- LINK TO MAINLAND - "GHETTO" HEBREW QUARTER WITH TALL HOUSES (8 STORIES) - HOME TO JEWISH COMMUNITY	- SPECIAL STONY GROUND - SCHOOLS	- HEART OF VENICE - MAZE-LIKE STREETS	- SIMILAR TO SAN POLO	- CENTER OF ART, HISTORY, CULTURE - PALACES, GOV'T BLDGS - PIAZZA SAN MARCO - BASILICA SAN MARCO - CLOCK TOWER (LARGEST ASTRONICAL CLOCK) - DOGE PALACE

VENICE FLOODING:

SIRENS GO OFF IF WATER LEVEL RISES ABOVE 1100 MM ABOVE SEA LEVEL (AUTUMN MONTHS) — CAN GO AS HIGH AS 1300 - 1400 MM — DUE TO PHASE OF MOON, LOW PRESSURE, AND SOUTHERLY WINDS ... TIDE CLIMBS FOR 6 HOURS, THEN RECEDES

RESIDENTS MUST BLOCK ENTRANCES WITH STEEL BULKHEADS!

CAMPOS — DOUBLE AS KID'S PLAYGROUNDS, FOUNTAINS USED FOR WATER BALLOONS, KIDS DRAW ON PAVEMENT W/ COLORED CHALK, ROLLER BLADE, RUN AROUND

BOATS —

GONDOLA

climbed hundreds of stairs to the top of the Scott Monument

ascend through spiral staircases to top spire

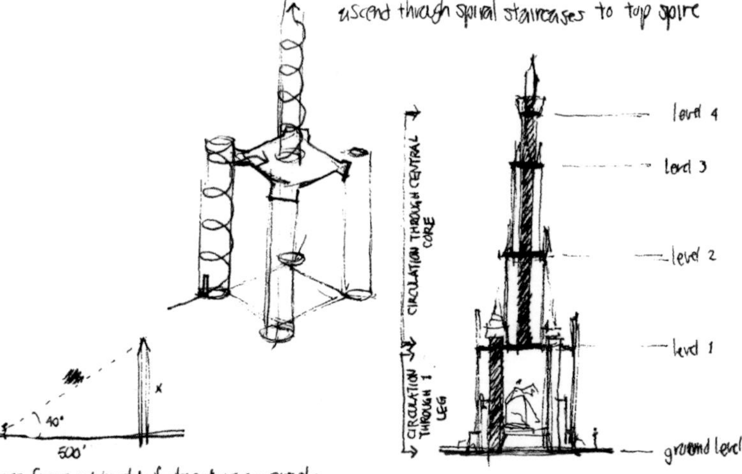

can figure out height of object using simple trignometry SOHCAHTOA

$\tan \theta = \dfrac{O}{A}$

$\tan \theta° = \dfrac{X}{dist}$

40°

500'

$dist (\tan \theta) = $ height of object

height of object = distance away from object × degrees off horizon

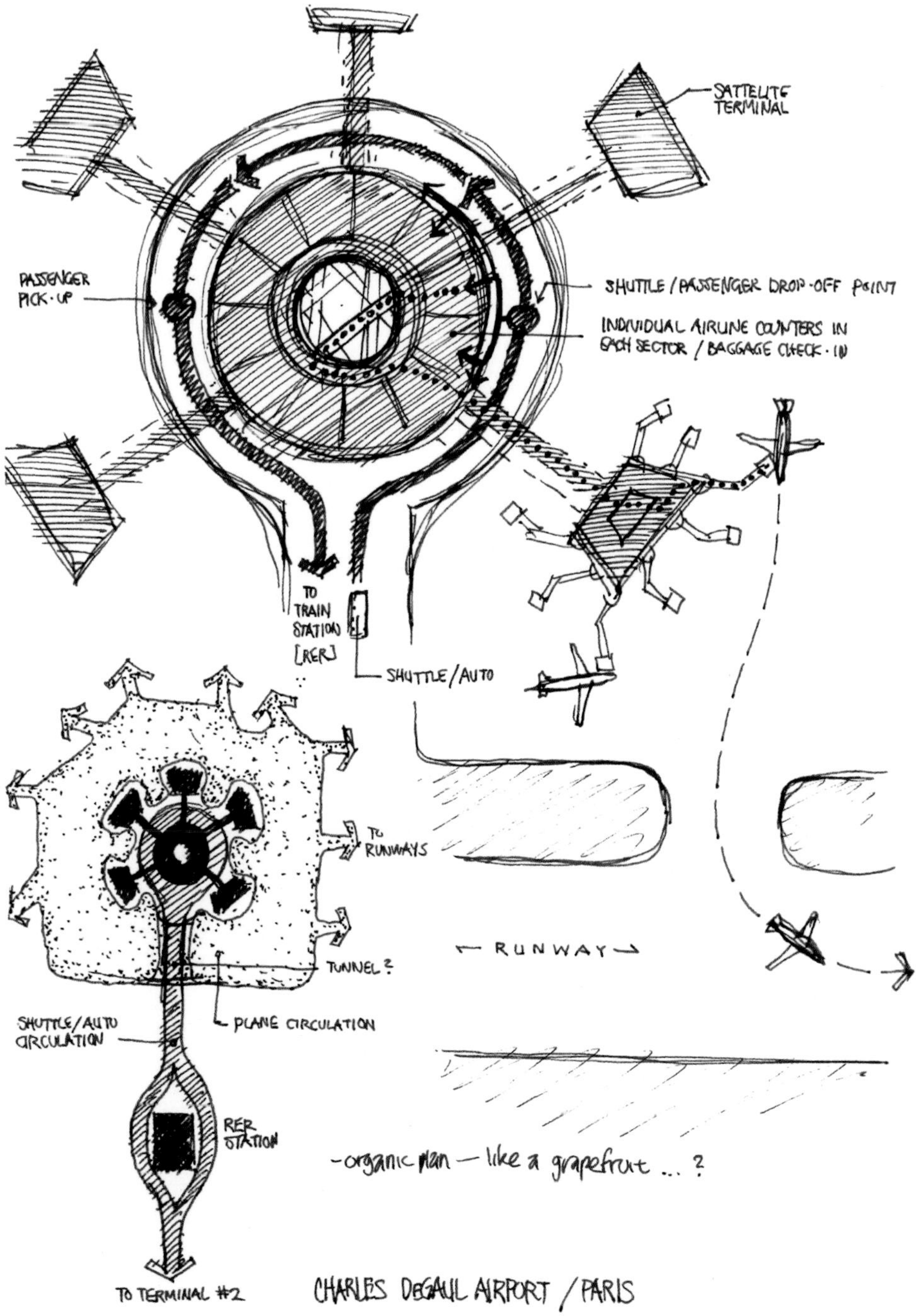

→ degrees of horizon (a fist held at arm's length ≅ 10°)

- organic plan - like a grapefruit ...?

CHARLES DEGAUL AIRPORT / PARIS

Toledo, home of the painter El Greco, has it's old city situated high atop a hilltop within medieval fortress walls...

explored and attempted to understand the design of the magnificent "Cathedral" (gothic style) here in Toledo:

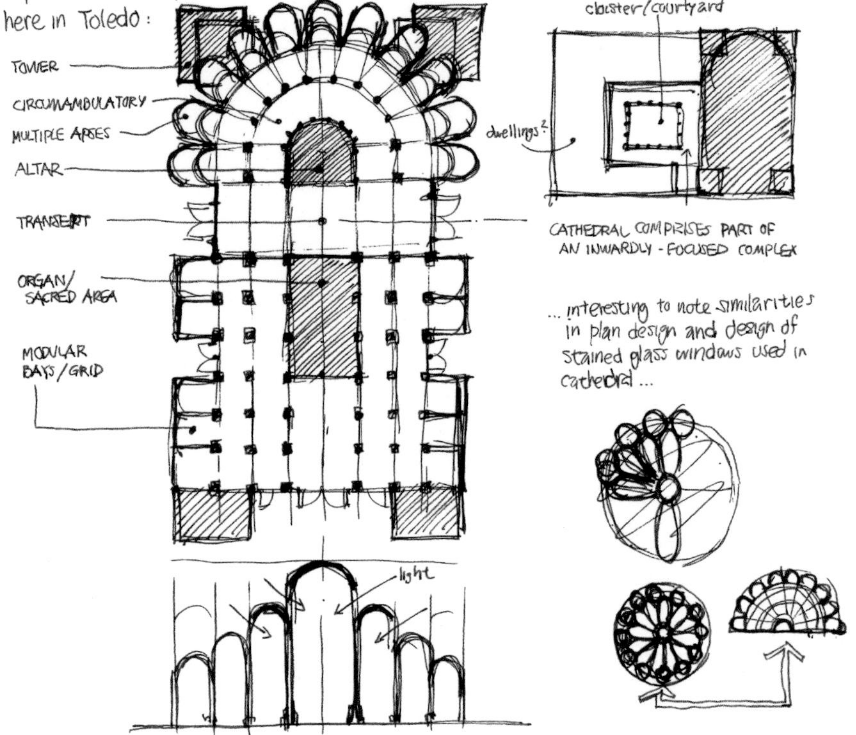

...interesting to note similarities in plan design and design of stained glass windows used in cathedral...

The Musée d'Orsay was once one of Paris' railway stations — now converted into an art gallery /museum

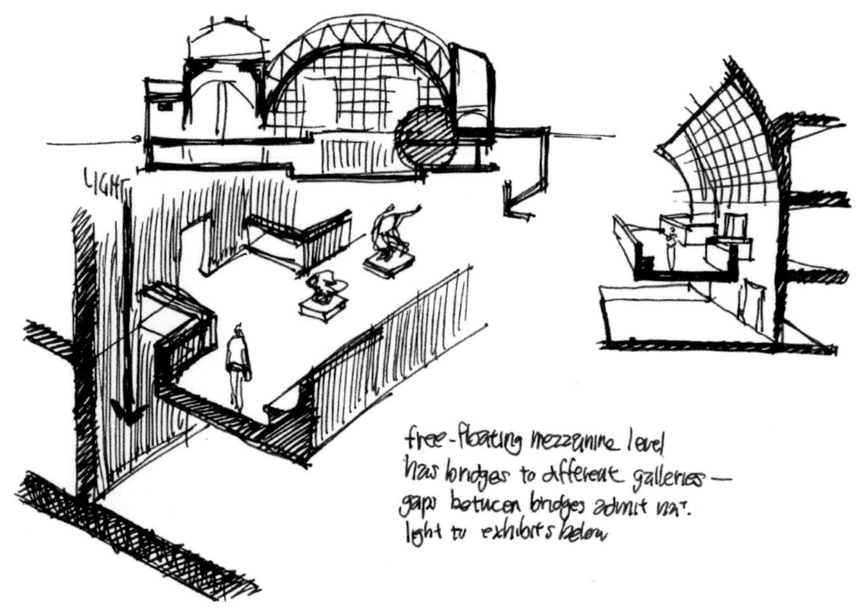

free-floating mezzanine level has bridges to different galleries — gaps between bridges admit nat. light to exhibits below

the interior architecture is a magnificent juxtaposition of cubic and planar forms against the curvilinear arches that already exist — most galleries revolve around the grand central space which serves as a point of reference

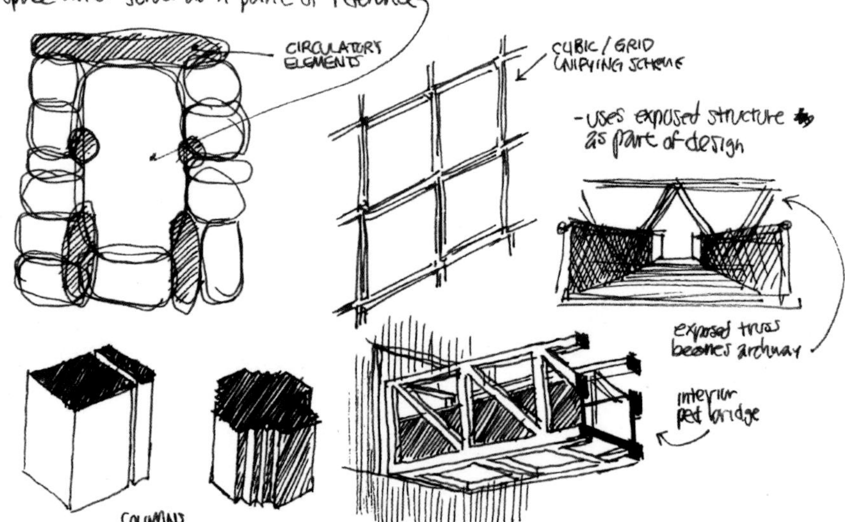

SEVILLA , SPAIN

29 NOV 1988 — I am in a complete daze this morning ... yesterday got a haircut and last night shaved select portions of my beard off — photographically documenting the whole process — while consuming a bottle of extremely cheap wine ... I have the worst wine hangover I've had in a very long time ...

I am now sitting in "Plaza de España" sketching and watching people pass in horse-buggies...

this would be a great idea for stationery [image along left-hand margin and writing here ...]

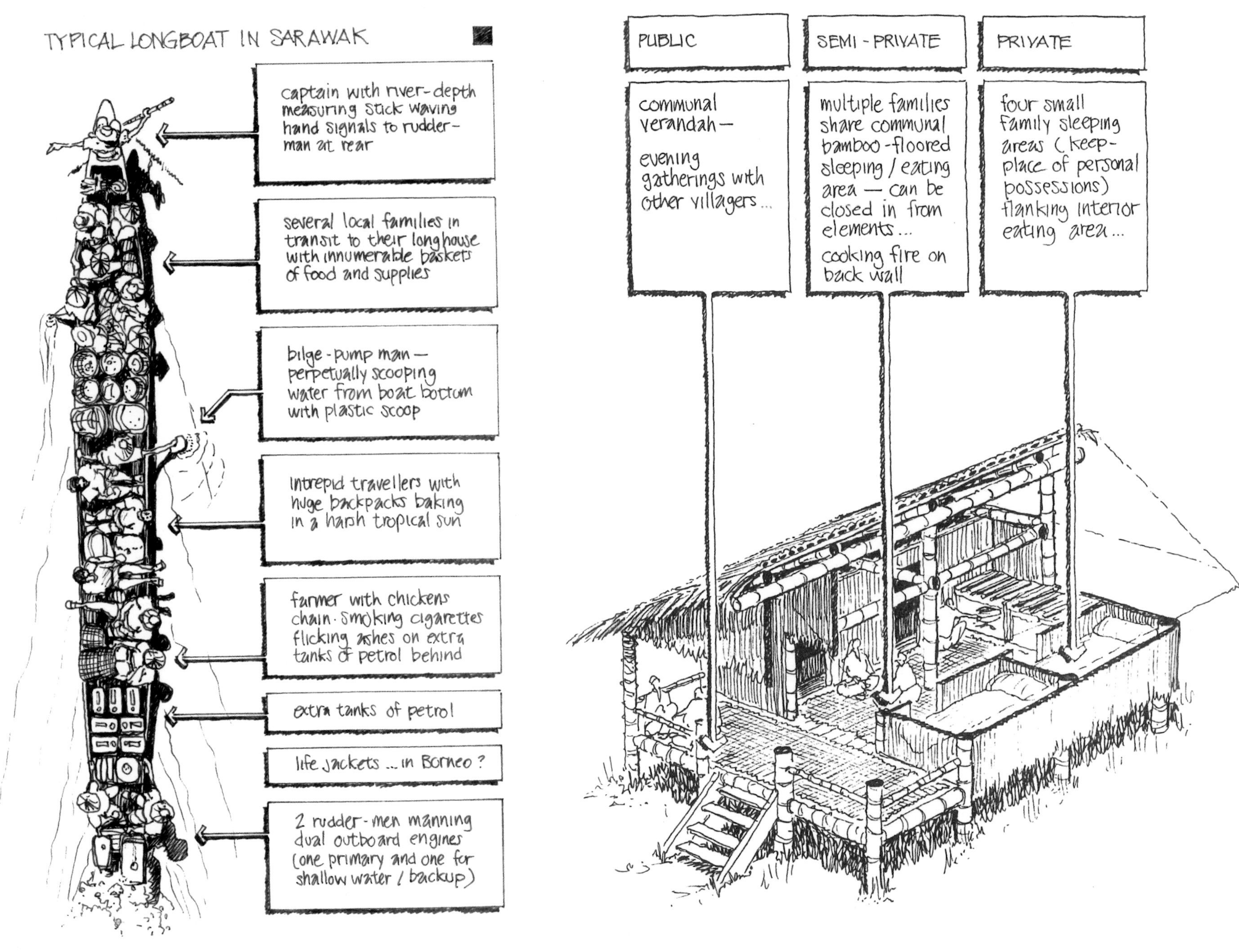

TYPICAL LONGBOAT IN SARAWAK

captain with river-depth measuring stick waving hand signals to rudder-man at rear

several local families in transit to their longhouse with innumerable baskets of food and supplies

bilge-pump man — perpetually scooping water from boat bottom with plastic scoop

intrepid travellers with huge backpacks baking in a harsh tropical sun

farmer with chickens chain-smoking cigarettes flicking ashes on extra tanks of petrol behind

extra tanks of petrol

life jackets ... in Borneo ?

2 rudder-men manning dual outboard engines (one primary and one for shallow water / backup)

PUBLIC

communal verandah —

evening gatherings with other villagers ...

SEMI-PRIVATE

multiple families share communal bamboo-floored sleeping / eating area — can be closed in from elements ...

cooking fire on back wall

PRIVATE

four small family sleeping areas (keep-place of personal possessions) flanking interior eating area ...

Singapore: To this day, the venerable Raffles Hotel is both a source of architectural inspiration and a cool oasis on a hot and sticky summer afternoon.

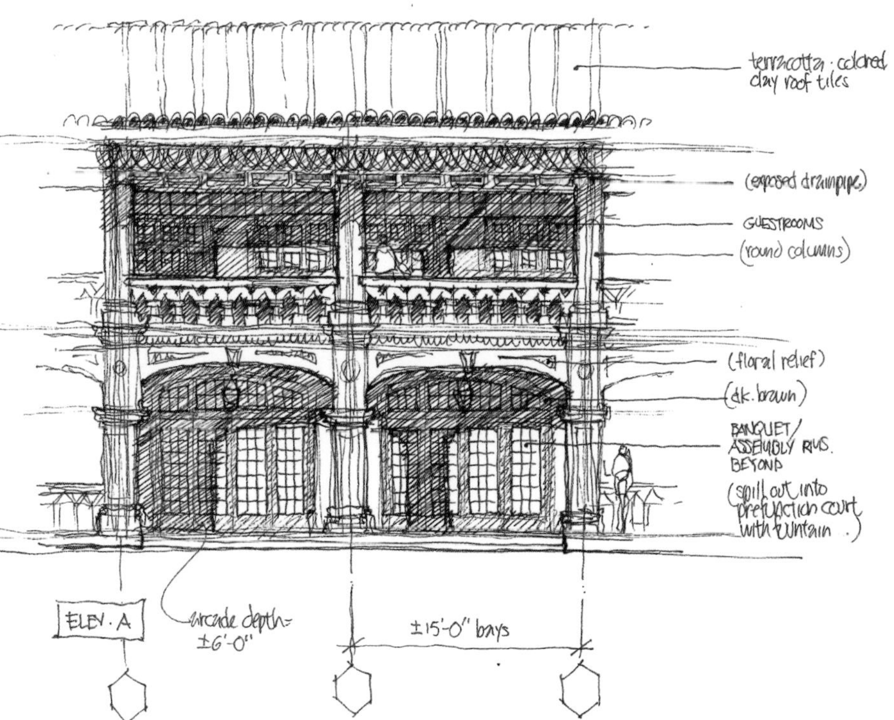

terracotta - colored clay roof tiles
(exposed drainpipe)
GUESTROOMS
(round columns)
(floral relief)
(dk. brown)
BANQUET / ASSEMBLY RMS. BEYOND
(spill out into prefunction court with fountain)
ELEV. A
arcade depth = ±6'-0"
±15'-0" bays

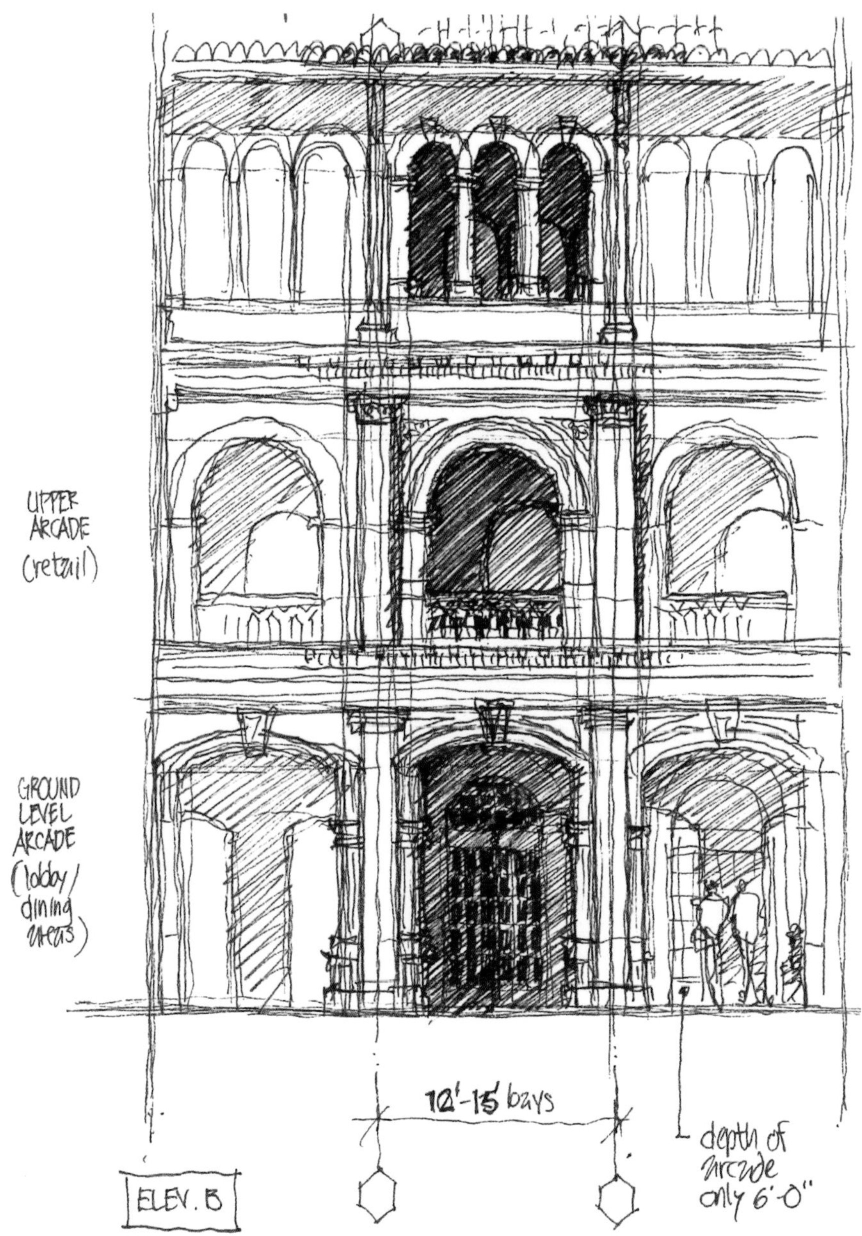

UPPER ARCADE (retail)
GROUND LEVEL ARCADE (lobby / dining areas)
12'-15' bays
depth of arcade only 6'-0"
ELEV. B

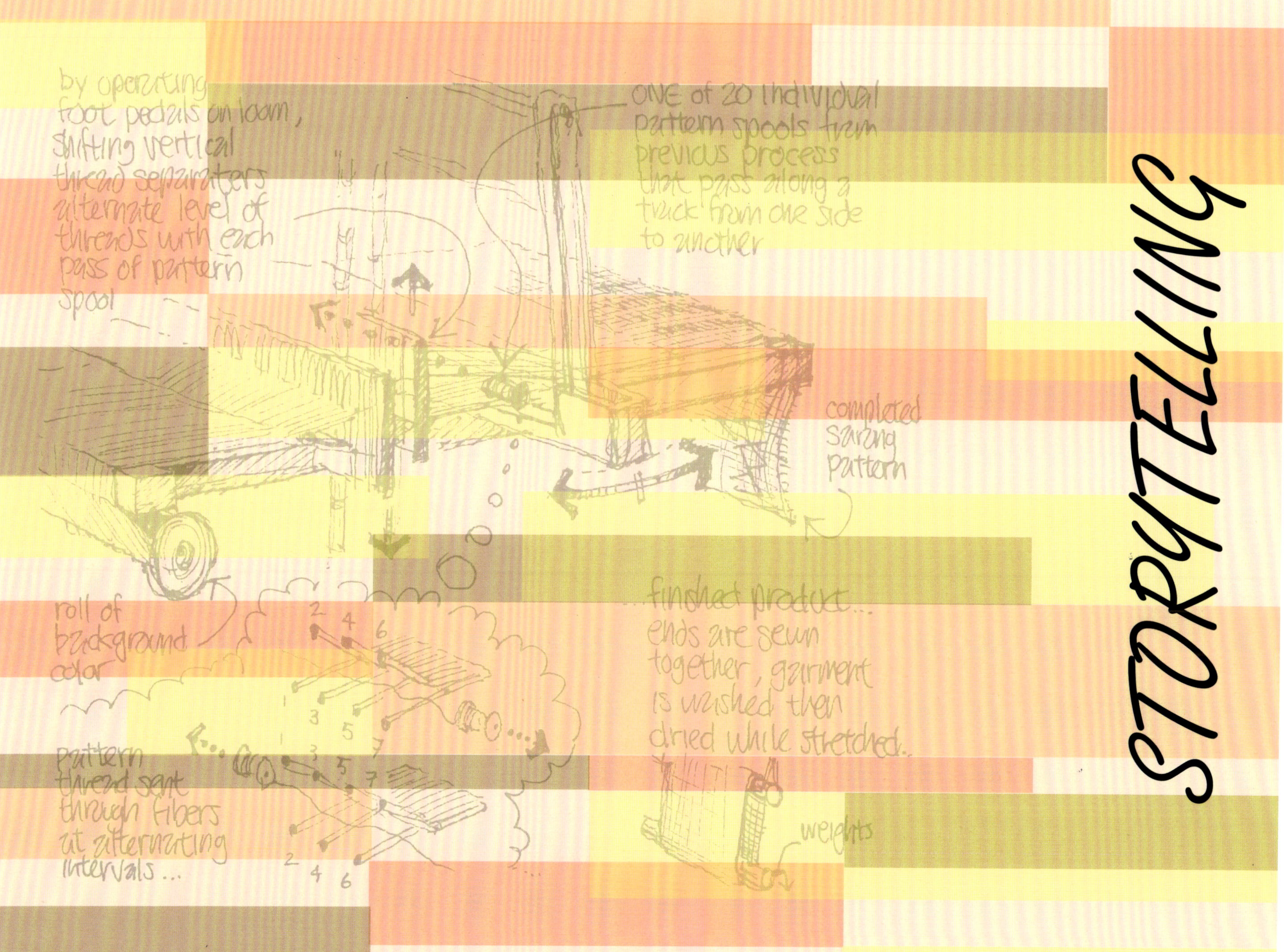
by operating
foot pedals on loom,
shifting vertical
thread separators
alternate level of
threads with each
pass of pattern
spool
one of 20 individual
pattern spools from
previous process
that pass along a
track from one side
to another
completed
sarong
pattern
roll of
background
color
finished product...
ends are sewn
together, garment
is washed then
dried while stretched.
pattern
thread sent
through fibers
at alternating
intervals...
weights
STORYTELLING

AND THEN WHAT HAPPENED?

Travel sketching can also be used to communicate stories or a particular sequence of events. In addition to architectural sketches, I often keep detailed written travel journals, interspersed with small vignettes to illustrate a specific event in a day. Sometimes these sequentially arranged sketches end up as "storyboards" highlighting key activities, or a portion of my journey.

When visiting a place for an extended period of time, I like to take short, educational day-trips or tours that visit multiple places. These locally-guided excursions often provide valuable insights into the handicrafts, economics, and other resources of an area -- and take you off the beaten path.

As a solo traveller, you may occasionally be thrown into an ad hoc tour group, together with a motley crew of other curious travellers, all of whom contribute to the experience.

While I take copious, often illegible notes during such an excursion, I will typically do a "brain dump" before the end of each day -- while the story is still fresh in my mind -- and create a visual storyboard to depict what transpired, along with pertinent information from my notes.

Some of these storyboards ultimately became the seeds for my *Bumbling Traveller Adventure Series* of educational graphic novels.

WARUNG BARU
BICYCLE TOUR AROUND
SOLO

A cycling foursome ...
two Swedish girls named
Eva and Ulrika, Johan
and myself ... and of course,
our guide for the day ...
AGUS ... from the Warung
Baru restaurant ...

Plunged into the morning
swarm of becaks and
motorcycles and headed
out into the countryside...

BATIK FACTORY

Our first stop was at the BATIK KERIS factory...
employing over 8000 workers, and supplying over 70%
of all Yogya's batiks, this factory boasted to be
the largest in Indonesia, if not the world...

After cotton material (imported) is boiled to
remove the oils, it is then dried, cut, then
hammered with huge wooden mallets producing a
flat, soft cloth...

FOUR METHODS OF BATIK:

SCREEN PRINTING	STAMPED WAX PATTERN	HAND-DRAWN WAX PATTERN	COMBO HAND/STAMP

SCREEN PRINTING:

3-4 DIFFERENT SCREENS (one per color)
SYSTEMATICALLY PRINTED DOWN LENGTH OF
35 meter piece of fabric

STAMPED WAX PATTERN PROCESS:

...only male employees

repetitive pattern is stamped on one side, then other side...must have perfect registration, otherwise piece is rejected...

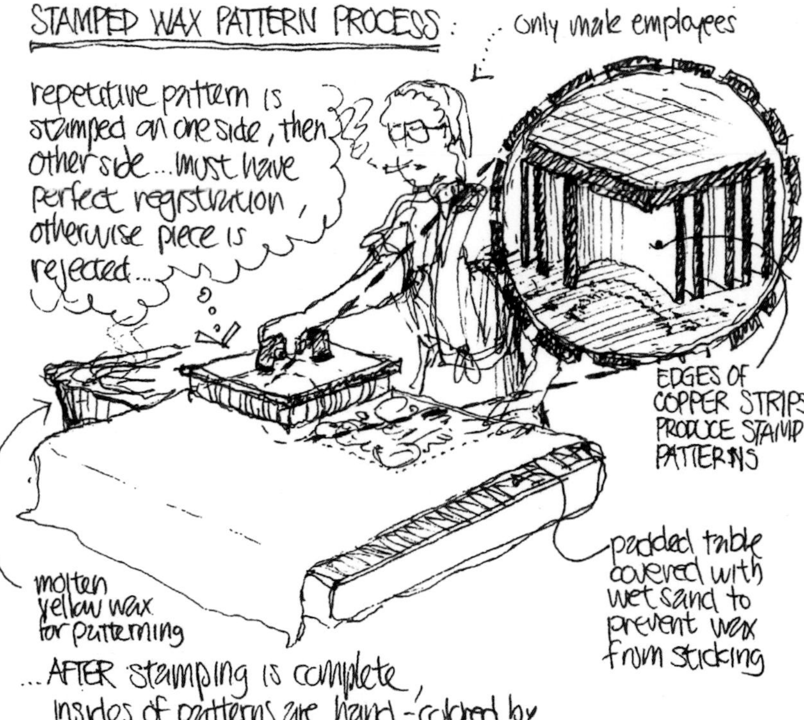

...AFTER stamping is complete, insides of patterns are hand-colored by a room full of female employees...using stalks of rattan as paintbrushes...

...then fabric is plunged into a vat of diluted H_2SO_4 (sulfuric acid) to bring out true colors of dyes...

...handpainted pattern colors are then "blocked" out with a stronger brown wax to protect colors when whole piece is later dipped into vat of the background color

RED, BROWN, YELLOW — traditional natural batik colors

BATIK FACTORY

BATIK DYE PROCESS:

stamped batik pieces are then brought to a large room of concrete vats containing bubbling dyes...

BACKGROUND COLOR... 2 men alternate pulling piece around a bar in a trench containing a specific dye...

All pieces are dyed yellow as a base, then other colors later...

piece is then rinsed then plunged into BOILING WATER to remove wax...

...final piece immersed in starch bath for color-fastness, then dried...

WAX PROCESSING:

recycled wax is boiled...impurities sink to bottom...top layer is skimmed and poured into molds dusted with tapioca flour (to prevent sticking).

Wax is boiled again, then mixed with other ingredients (beeswax, parrafin, animal fat, gum, and resin) to bring composition to quality of batik printing...

brown wax (for blocking) — composed of more gum (stronger) and parrafin...

yellow wax (for patterning) — composed of more white parrafin...

We next pedalled to a darkened warehouse filled with clattering hand-powered looms ...

...first, an amazing hand-powered machine for combining threads into bundles of 40 strands each...

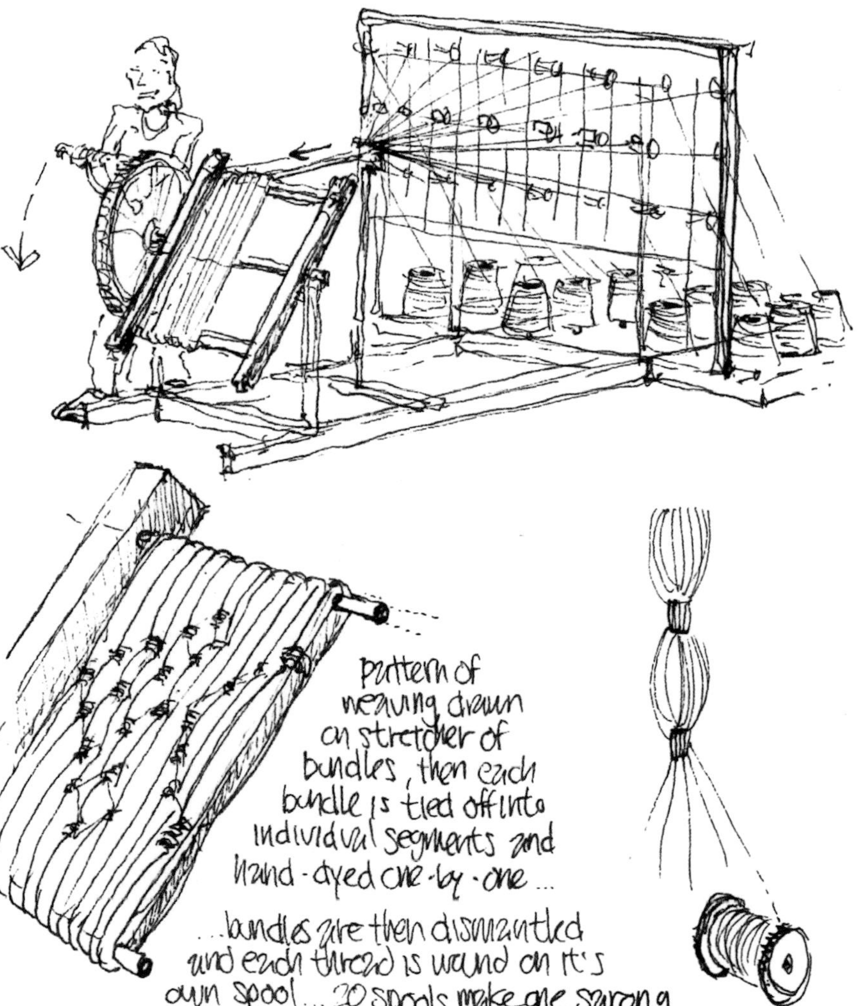

pattern of weaving drawn on stretcher of bundles, then each bundle is tied off into individual segments and hand-dyed one-by-one ...

...bundles are then dismantled and each thread is wound on it's own spool ...20 spools make one sarong

by operating foot pedals on loom, shifting vertical thread separators alternate level of threads with each pass of pattern spool

ONE of 20 individual pattern spools from previous process that pass along a track from one side to another

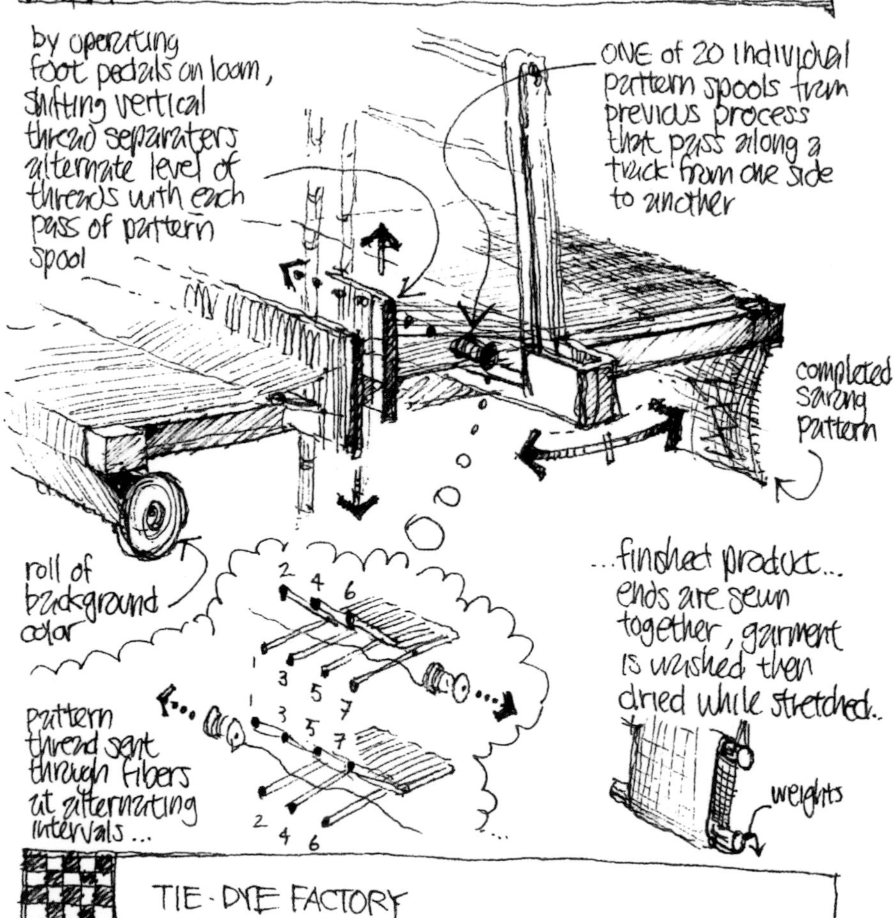

completed sarong pattern

roll of background color

pattern thread sent through fibers at alternating intervals ...

...finished product... ends are sewn together, garment is washed then dried while stretched.

weights

TIE-DYE FACTORY

A quick stroll across the road revealed a small tie-dye factory

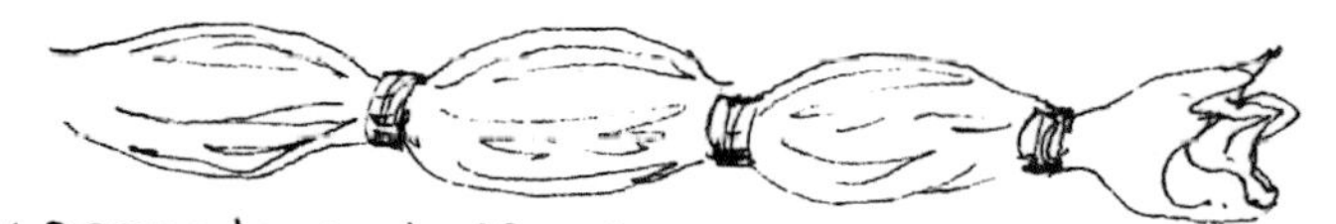

indiv. segments tied off with strings then indiv. dyed

LUNCH AT A COUNTRYSIDE WARUNG

Detailed down a straight dirt road to a small warung at a small intersection... had a mixture of local vegetables and tofu and a spicy fruit salad...

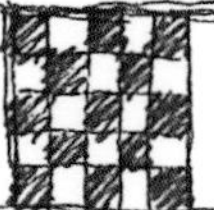

GAMELAN · MAKING

After a quality meal at only 400 rps (2 servings @ 200) we were off to our next destination: a small gamelan instrument · making operation where black-smiths forge huge gongs and other bronze components for this series of instruments

60-70 million rps for complete 30 instr. Gamelan set...

4 men pumping bellows by hand to produce heat to bring bronze to a malleable state... then they spring into action when bronze is removed and begin hammering...

2 men turning bronze gong with stalks of fire-retardant young banana tree

Zillions of red-hot sparks shoot up the chimney ceiling of this structure — sometimes setting the rafters ablaze...

GAMELAN · MAKING

GONG-FORGING PROCESS:

WEIGH QUANTITIES OF COPPER (CU) and TIN (Sn)...

DETERMINE CORRECT PROPORTION OF EACH [USUALLY 1:3 (CU : Sn)] MELT IN CLAY MELTING POT...

BRONZE MIXTURE POURED INTO MOLD... LATER POUNDED WITH LARGE WOODEN MALLETS INTO SPECIFIC GONG SHAPE... REPEATEDLY REHEATED and REPOUNDED FOR 2-3 DAYS UNTIL PERFECT CONFIGURATION IS ACHIEVED...

GONG IS THEN FILED FOR EXACT CURVILINEAR FORMS BY AN ANTI-SOCIAL HUNCHED-OVER CHARACTER

PITCH OF EACH GAMELAN INSTRUMENT VARIES WITH SIZE and CONFIGURATION

FINALLY, GONG IS SANDED AND POLISHED GIVING THE BRONZE A SHIMMERING GOLDEN LUSTRE...

TOFU · MAKING ... in _six_ easy · to · follow steps ..

COUNTRY BAKERY

Made a unplanned stop at our guide's family's house ... a small country bakery ... sampled some piping hot fresh-baked rolls and banana bread... mass quantities were being handwrapped and transported via bicycle basket for sale in Solo ...

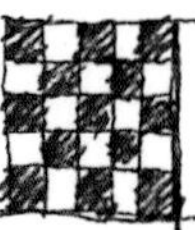

RICE CRACKER PRODUCTION

Our squeaking mountain-bikes rolled up to a small house that produces nothing but rice crackers for the entire region ... trays of small crackers drying outside in the sun ... it was time to investigate:

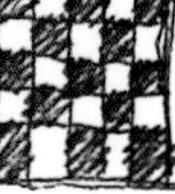

ARAK DISTILLERY

Ended our bicycle tour around Solo with a visit to the Arak-brewing village of Sentul ...

A mystery blend of water, sugarcane, molasses, yeast and badek (residue of previous distillation) is allowed to ferment for 3-4 days...

solution is boiled... evaporated steam is collected in a chamber surrounded by cold water — thus condensing steam into liquid

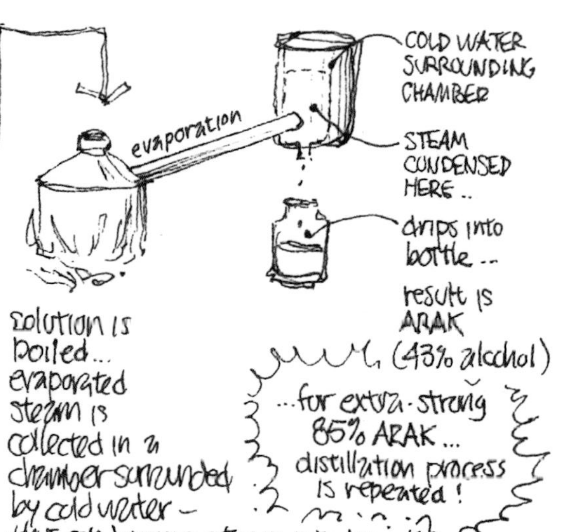

village well-known for traditional weaving & woodcarving

Pandai Sikat = "good weavers"

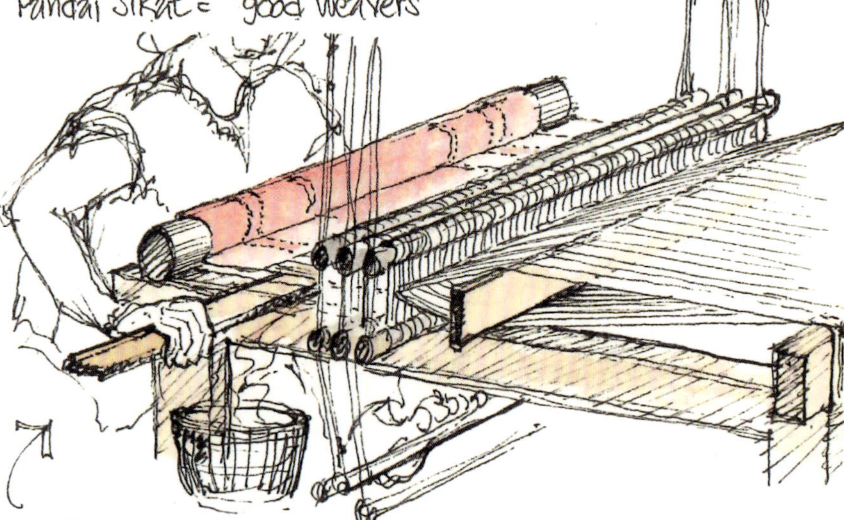

master weavers
create colorful <u>songket</u> cloths interwoven
with gold & silver threads...

... a cassette tape of Dire Straits filled the
morning air as our adventure van skidded
to a halt alongside a vast valley of rice padis...

terraced planting fields
allow controlled irrigation — water originates
from mountains ... specific planting plateaus
can be drained or dammed up to hold water
depending on the crop / life-cycle it contains...

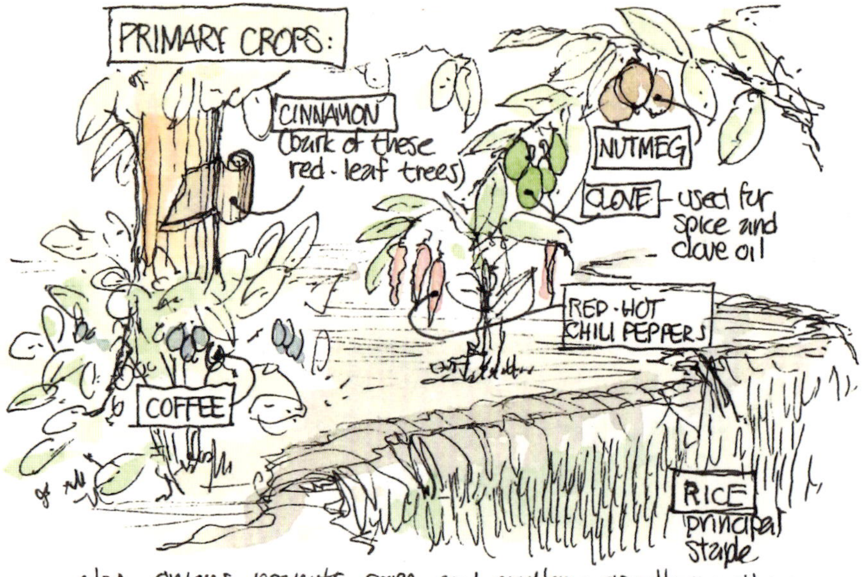

...also...onions, peanuts, corn, and anything else that will grow...

"center of Minangkabau culture..."

...Ironically, ~~and~~ short of time, we sped through this town containing several features unique to the Minangkabau culture:

...On the way to Pegaruyang, stopped by a group of women planting rice in the fields... even though one woman owns her own field, they collectively plant each other's fields... making the act of planting more of a social occasion...

"KING'S PALACE" – example of trad. Minangkabau arch.

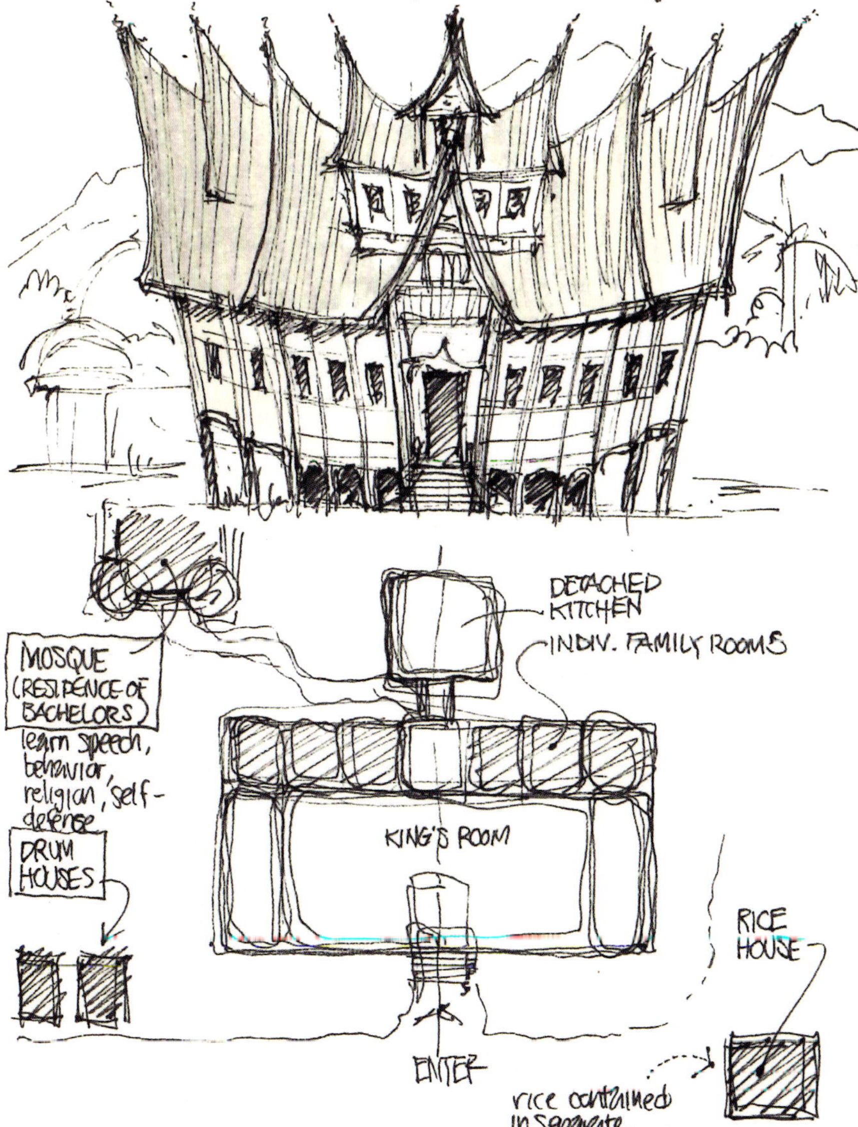

SECTION

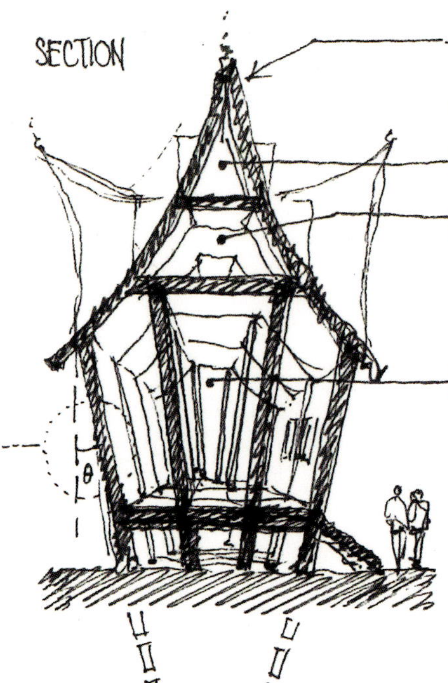

ROOF IS SYMBOLIC OF TRYING TO GET "CLOSE TO GOD..."

FLOOR

3 MEETING AREA OF CLAN LEADERS

2 RESIDENCE OF KING'S UNMARRIED DAUGHTER
— learns customs, religion, weaving, etc.

1 KING'S ROOM (gathering area for special events)

also RESIDENCE OF KING'S MARRIED CHILDREN

SPIRITUAL EARTHQUAKE PROTECTION

[belief that pillars formed converging lines before the center of the earth to insure protection against earthquakes]

• all pillars slanted from vertical — resembles the wood construction of ships ...

DRUM HOUSE :
• used to signal Muslim prayer time
• alarm / emergency
• death / mourning
• post-Ramadan festival

...pulled into a restaurant coincidentally owned by Jimmy's "uncle"... the seven of us feasted on spicy Padang food presented in small individual bowls... you pay for how many plates you eat...

...another sight that was passed at warp 9... stones etched with ancient Sanskrit writing...

Historic village containing a 300-year old traditional Minangkabau house...

<u>ALL-WOOD CONSTRUCTION</u>
<u>FLOOR FRAMING DETAIL</u>

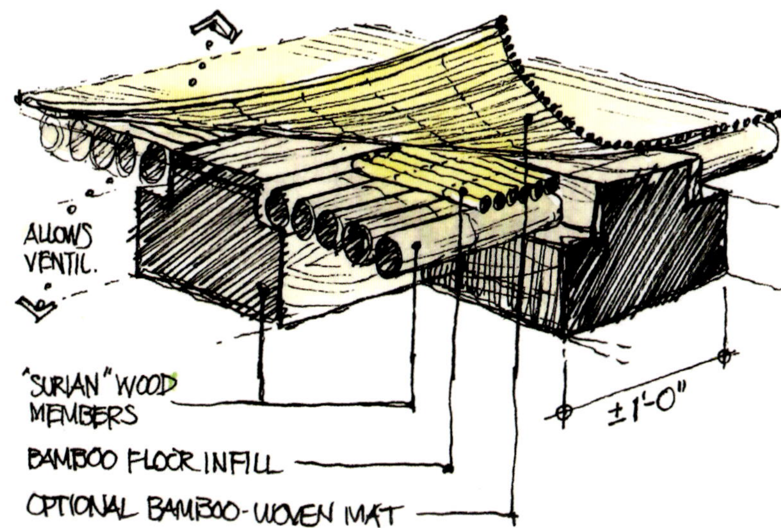

<u>MINANGKABAU MARRIAGE CUSTOMS:</u>
- cannot marry someone of the same "clan"
- husband moves into wife's mother's house upon marriage...
- If a man marries and has children — those children will be of his wife's clan (MATRILINEAL CULTURE)
- If a family has no daughters to carry on clan, and all sons marry wives of other clans, then family clan is lost...
- In some towns, woman is required to pay man's family upon marriage (2-3 gold coins, livestock, etc.)

Continuing on in our magical Karaoke Bus, paused for a few minutes at a canyon below Lake Singkarek... a place where tapioca and sweet potatoes are grown...

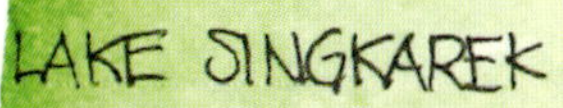

We were scheduled for a short swim in one of Sumatra's largest lakes... several of the Dutch people took a quick dip... I opted to entertain our guide, Jimmy, and our driver with video game impressions...

...forgot my camera... so... SKETCHY IMPRESSIONS:

GRHADIKA YOGYA PARIWISATA
RAMAYANA BALLET
PERFORMANCE at
"Dalem Pujokusoman"

graceful blend of pantomime and dancing... beautiful dancer!

"GONG AGENG"

SOME GAMELAN ENSEMBLE MUSICIANS

perfect robot-like movements

gold-colored pots

violet costume

BONANG player

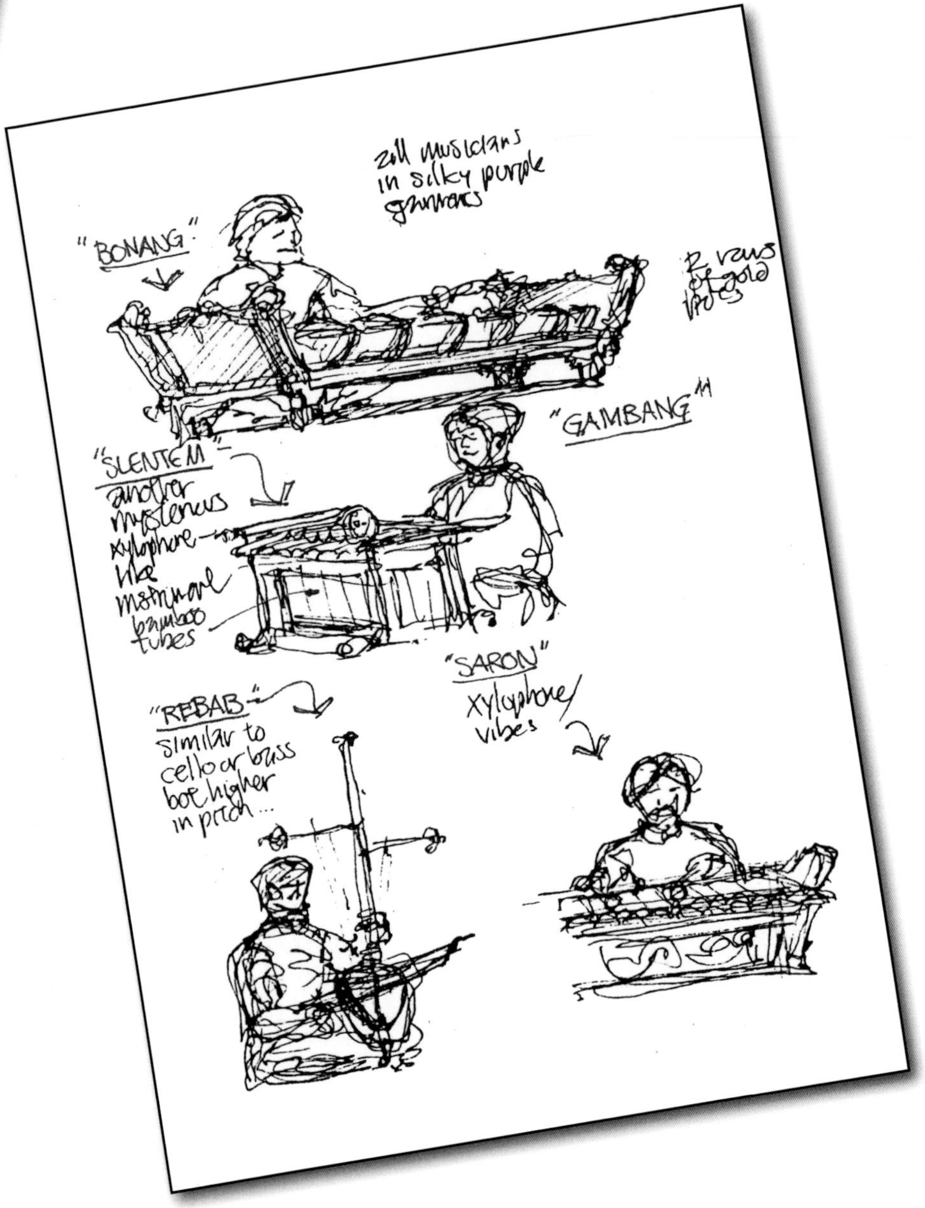

all musicians in silky purple garments

"BONANG"

2 rows of gold pots

"SLENTEM" another mysterious xylophone-like instrument bamboo tubes

"GAMBANG"

"REBAB" similar to cello or bass but higher in pitch...

"SARON" xylophone/vibes

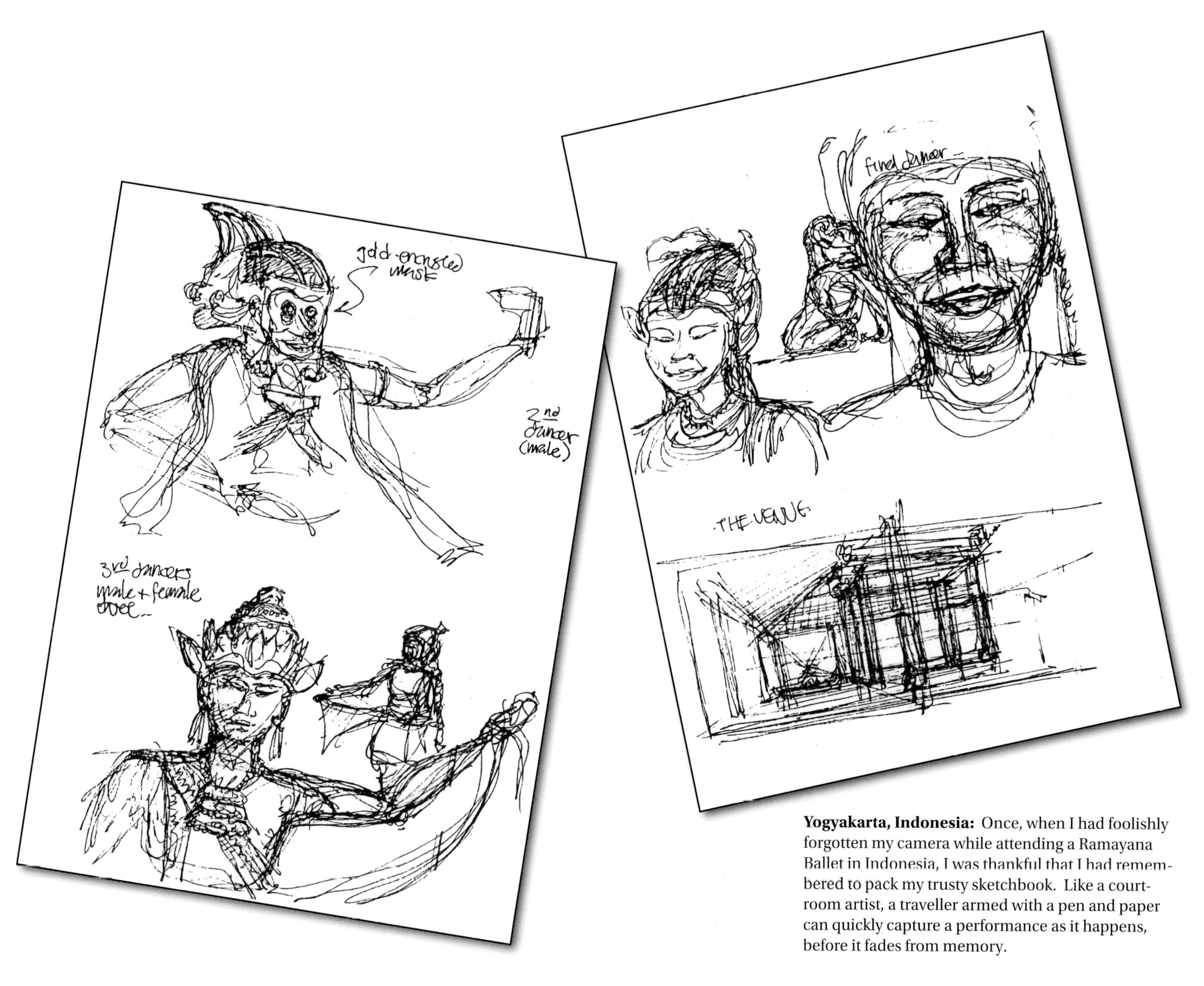

Yogyakarta, Indonesia: Once, when I had foolishly forgotten my camera while attending a Ramayana Ballet in Indonesia, I was thankful that I had remembered to pack my trusty sketchbook. Like a courtroom artist, a traveller armed with a pen and paper can quickly capture a performance as it happens, before it fades from memory.

PEOPLE

HEY! WHO WAS THAT GUY?

The world is filled with people, and people are almost always part of the travel experience ... for better or for worse.

As a solo traveller, I've always found it very entertaining to sit at a street cafe and "people watch." While an unsolicited photograph of a stranger might be too intrusive and provoke an unfriendly reaction, quietly capturing someone's essence in a sketchbook is both fun and less invasive.

William Shakespeare observed that, *"All the world's a stage, and all the men and women merely players ..."*

There is drama happening all around us each and every day. From the hysterically funny to the heartbreaking, hand sketching will help you capture the human condition as you travel the world.

Like the proverbial fly on the wall, I've always enjoyed watching strangers from afar, postulating where they might be from, what languages they speak, what professions they have, and imagining what their personalities may be. Sometimes this results in the creation of a silly mini-comic strip starring the hapless stranger.

People Everywhere:
With billions of people going about their
business across the planet, people provide
an endless source of entertainment for the
solo traveller.

<u>INDONESIAN SCHOOLCHILDREN:</u>

PRIMARY
SCHOOL
UNIFORM

(RED/WHITE)

JR. HIGH
SCHOOL
UNIFORM

(WHITE/BLUE)

SR. HIGH
SCHOOL
UNIFORM

(WHITE/GREY)

SATURDAY
COMMUNITY SERVICE
UNIFORM

(BROWN/ORANGE)

The evening began with a hungry visit to the night market before getting dressed up in the traditional Balinese outfit to attend yet another ceremony at the riverside temple here in Ubud ... tonight's ceremony: Perembon Bon (unmasked dance/opera) by the Panca Arta dance troupe ... the kind women here at Sukadana's homestay outfitted us in perfect Balinese attire.

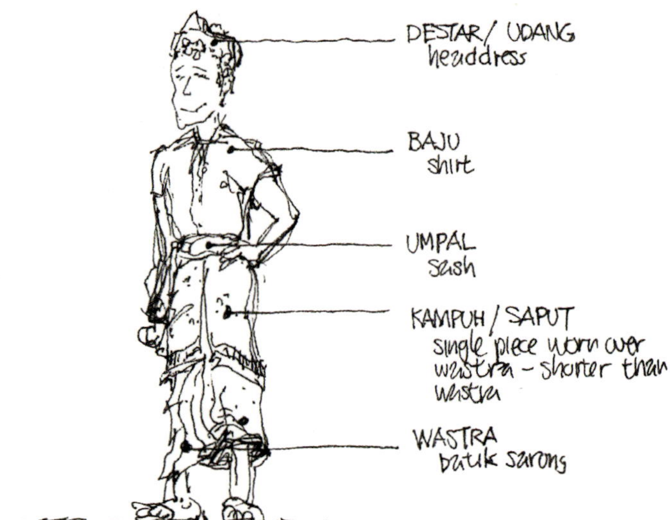

Dressing Up: Clothing often reflects a society's culture and values -- as a visitor, you sometimes need to dress for the occasion.

BALINESE BALANCING ACTS
BEYOND BELIEF. . .

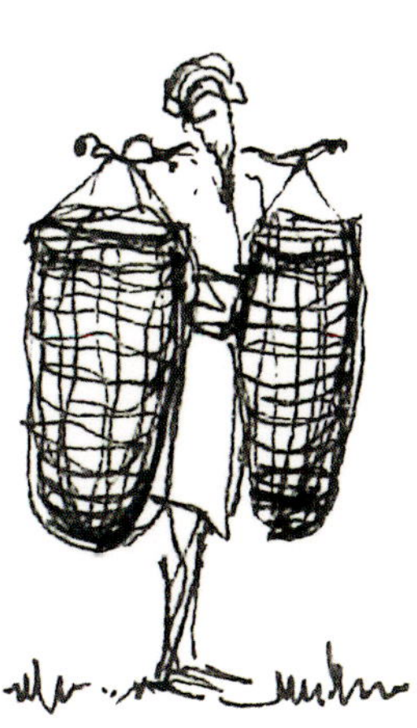

Distant Cousins: Orangutans share 97% of our DNA, and are definitely more well behaved than some of the travellers I've met!

Street Vendors: The vibrancy of a place can often be attributed to the colorful characters who sell food and other wares on the street or in alleys, accosting passers-by hoping to make a sale, and chattering endlessly as they go about their business.

WANDA ... the fashion rebel
head waitress at an obscure
cafe in the central United States ...

1 DEC 91 / 1.0

WHAT ARE PSYCHO MATH TEACHERS IN HIGH SCHOOL?

INDONESIAN DISCO COWBOY GUY
on GILI TRAWANGAN

... perpetually consuming magic mushroom tea dancing wildly to western tunes at Trawangan's nightly rotating party...

Star of the Show: Sometimes I like to extrapolate my observations of the people I sketch and incorporate them into drawings of absurd and comical situations.

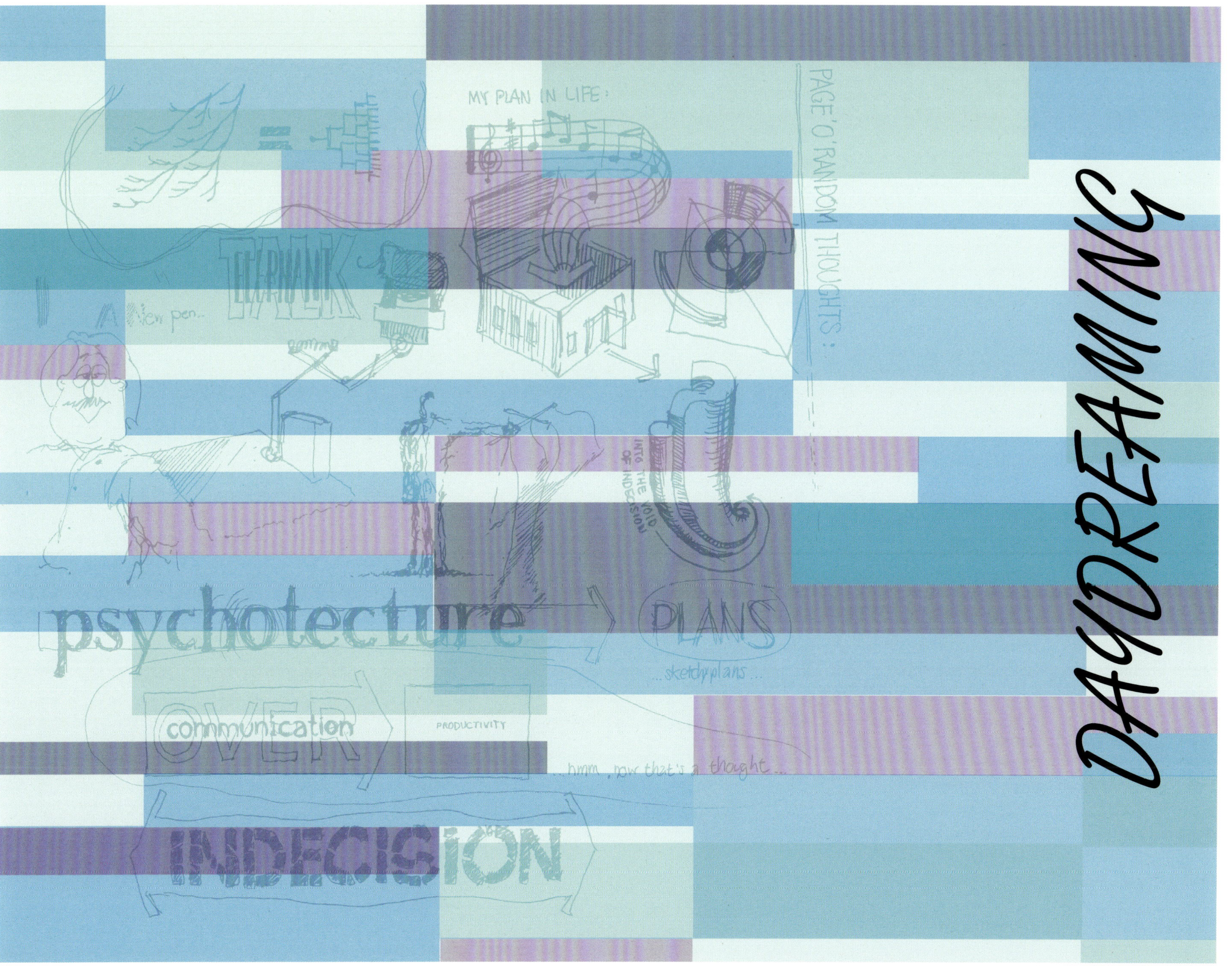
MY PLAN IN LIFE:
PAGE 'O' RANDOM THOUGHTS:
DAYDREAMING
TELEPHONE TALK
A New pen...
psychotecture
PLANS
...sketchy plans...
INTO THE VOID OF INDECISION
OVER
communication
PRODUCTIVITY
...hmm...now that's a thought...
INDECISION

HAVE YOU LOST YOUR MIND?

Travelling solo has its pros and cons.

It can be completely liberating, allowing you to go with the flow and enjoy a maximum degree of spontaneity at a moment's notice.

However, it can also be lonely and, sometimes, depressing. During these solitary times, writing in a journal or doodling in a sketchbook may be "just what the doctor ordered."

These periods of introspection, or daydreaming, may culminate in your pondering the meaning of life. You might begin to wonder how your brain works, or how dreams are stored and accessed from your memory. Or, like me, perhaps you'll wonder whether time travel is in fact possible, after experiencing a sudden feeling of déjà vu when visiting a place for the very first time. Or how time seems to bend when you travel: You might feel like you've been travelling for years, while no time seems to have elapsed for your friends when you return home.

A solo traveller has the time and space to ponder the big existential questions that have perplexed humankind for centuries. Without consciously thinking, creative, silly and strange thoughts often emerge on paper as you put your brain on auto-pilot and daydream.

So get that pen out and dream away!

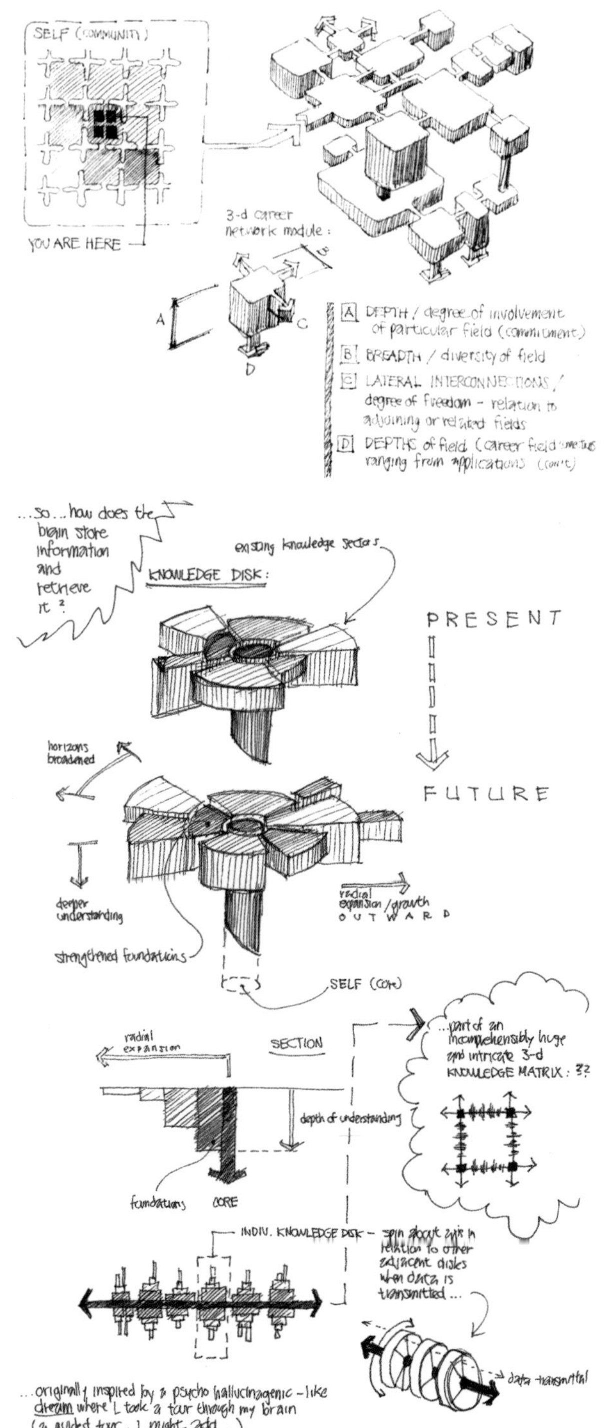

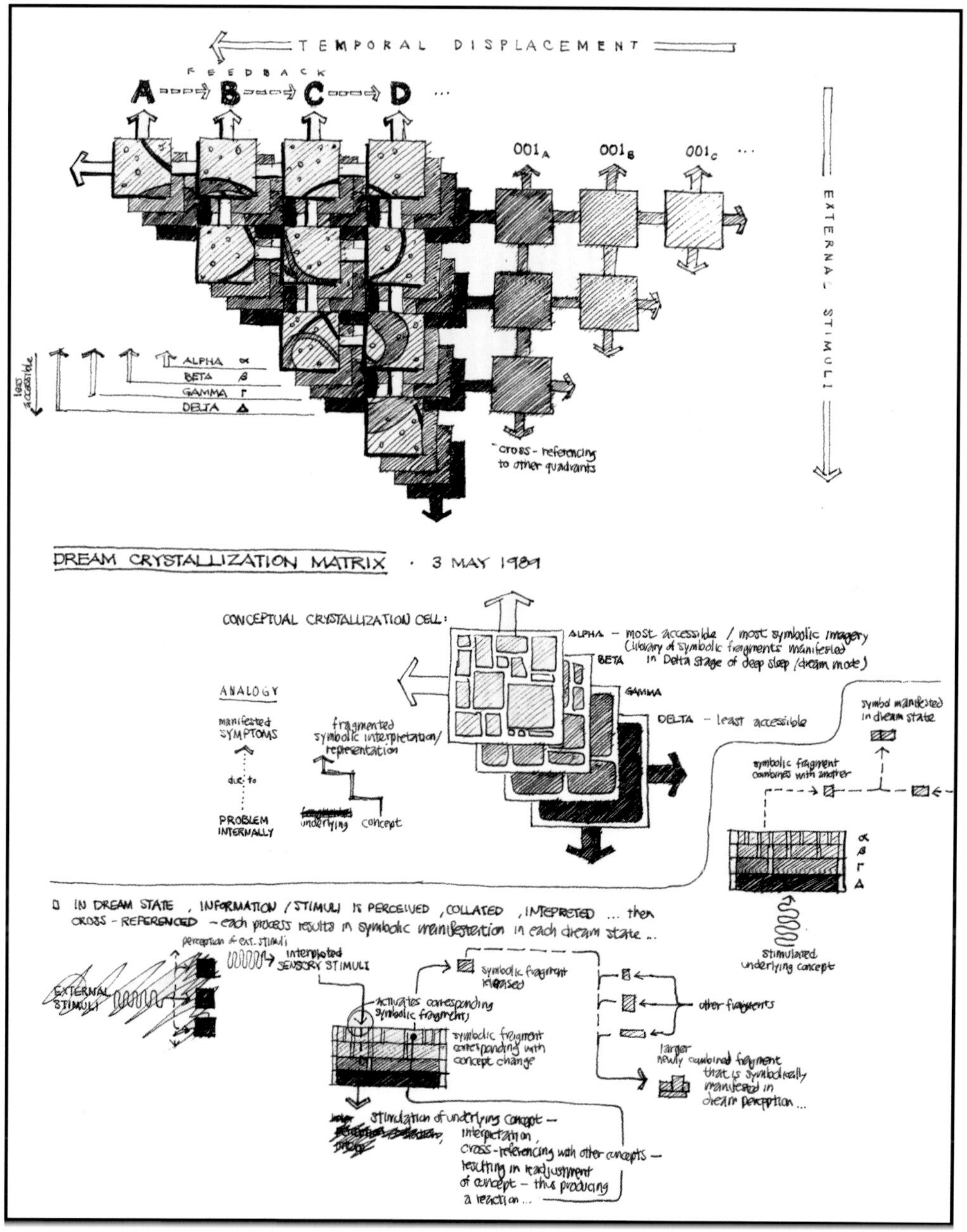

The Mind's Eye: Pondering how the human brain stores information and knowledge, and how that might be depicted graphically.

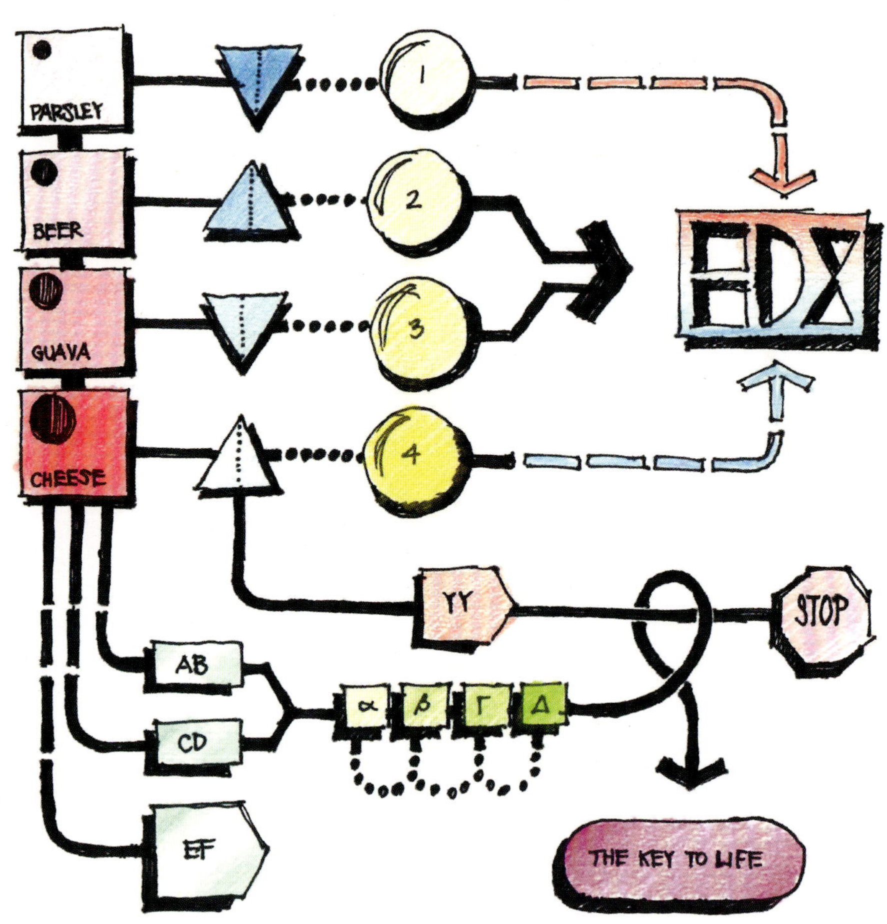

A POTENTIAL PLAN TO FIND THE "KEY TO LIFE"..

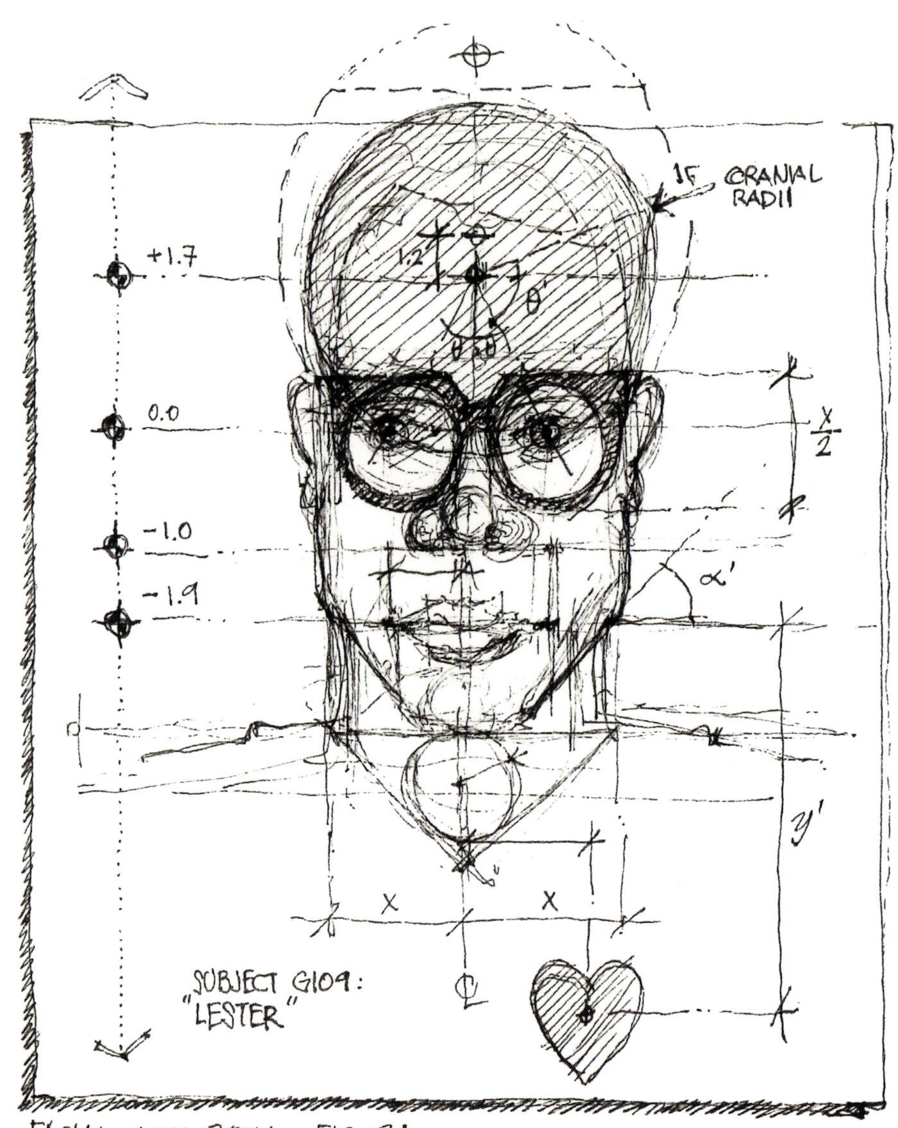

FACIAL GEOMETRY   FIG. 3A

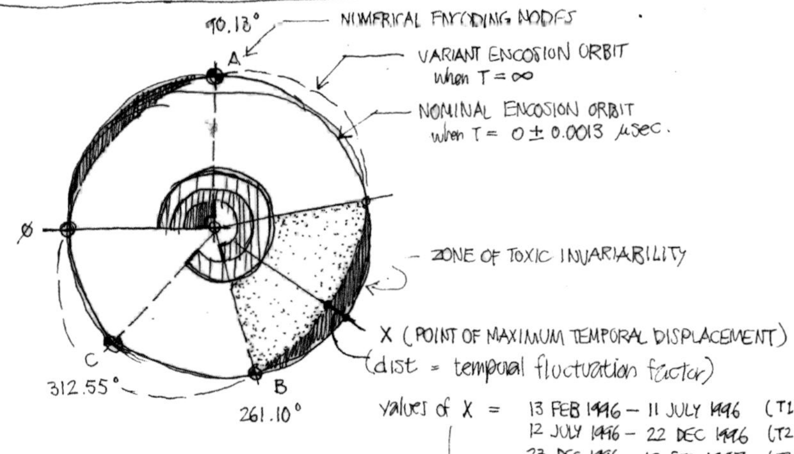

X (POINT OF MAXIMUM TEMPORAL DISPLACEMENT)
(dist = temporal fluctuation factor)

values of X =
13 FEB 1996 — 11 JULY 1996	(T1)
12 JULY 1996 — 22 DEC 1996	(T2)
23 DEC 1996 — 12 FEB 1997	(T3)

$T1 = 221.7316° \pm 0.0003°$ mean radians
$T2 = 221.6491° \pm 0.0003°$ "   "
$T3 = 221.8113° \pm 0.0003°$ "   "

<u>PREVIOUS STUDY DATA :</u>

▫ MEAN DISTORTIONAL FACTOR due to IONOSPHERIC INTERFERENCE :

$$\overline{ION}_{int} = 0.372 \times 10^{-91} \text{ mrev/sec}$$
$$\pm 0.001 \times 10^{-91} \text{ mrev/sec}$$

▫ DAYS OF MINIMUM $\overline{ION}_{int}$ WITHIN T2 SEASON :

	TOXIC INVAR. QUOTIENT	
25 AUG 1996	0	→ A
29 AUG 1996	1	
03 SEP 1996	1	
01 NOV 1996	0	→ B
20 DEC 1996	1	

TARGET DATE :	25 AUG 1996
SECONDARY DATE :	01 NOV 1996

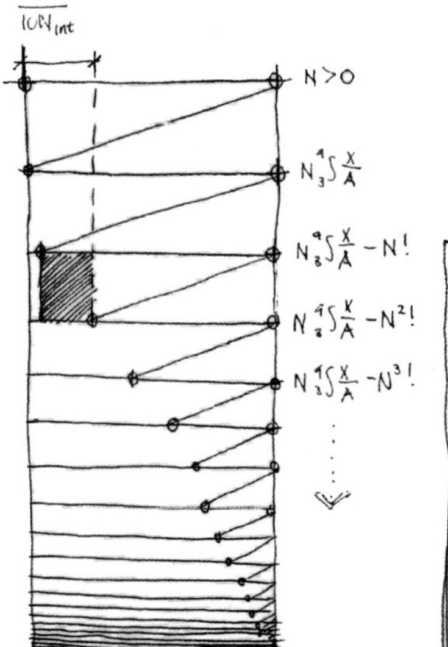

This is an especially strange feature of my journals ... my ongoing studies of temporal displacement ... the equivalent of doodling in class, but it seems to spark my interest in the fields of math and science at that same time ... makes me wonder ... makes me dream ... maybe someday ... someday some scientist will be able to apply these studies to real experiments in time travel ... I know ... I'm a dreamer

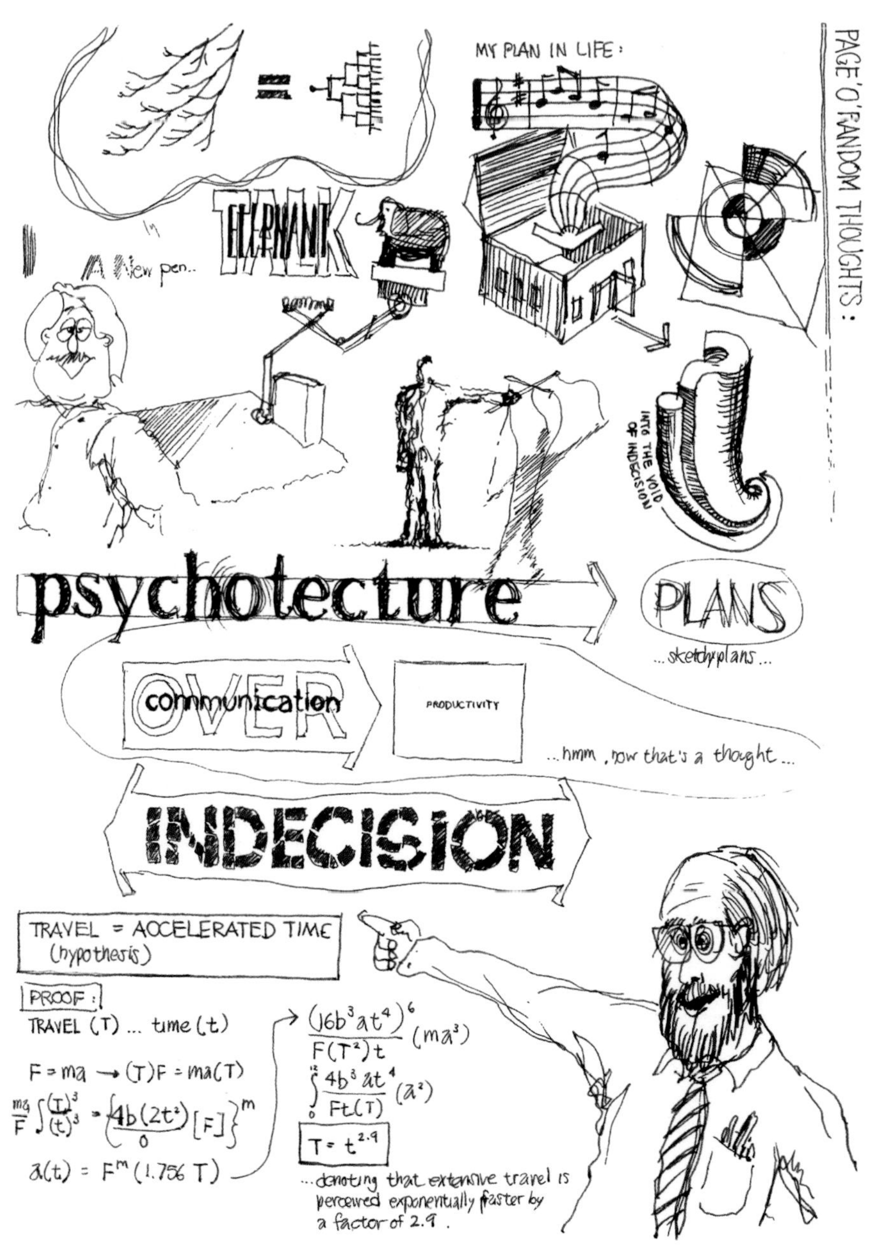

Time Travel: Sketching your daydreams of fantastical time travel equations and other theories may help explain that sense of déjà vu when visiting a destination for the first time -- and understanding that feeling as if you've been there before!

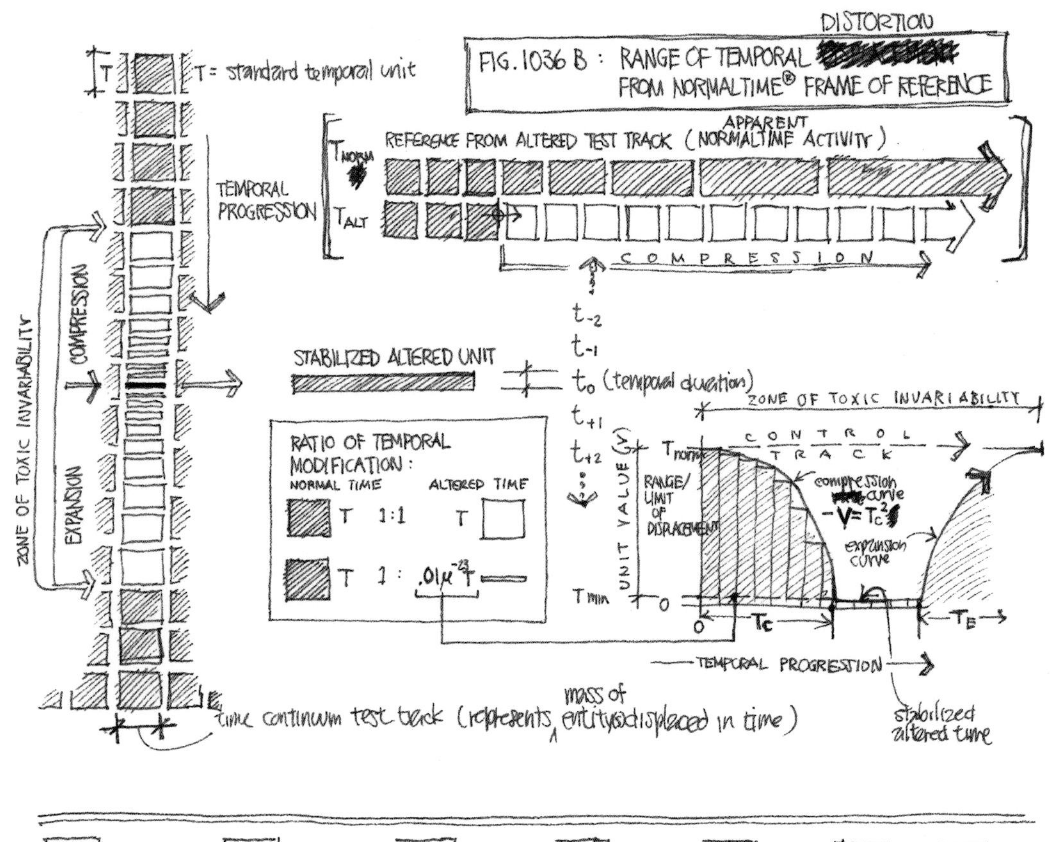

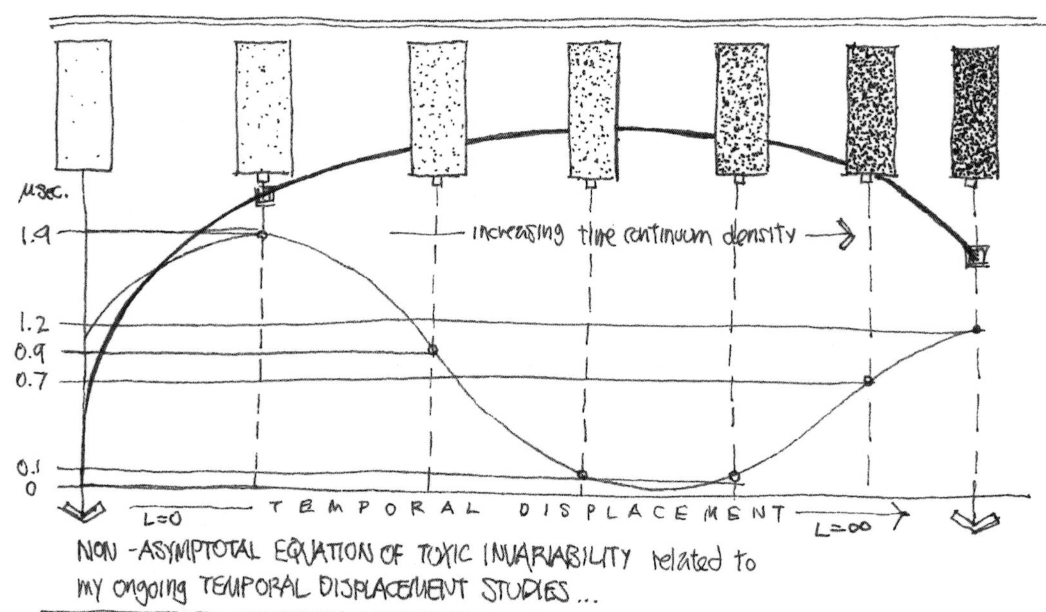

NON-ASYMPTOTAL EQUATION OF TOXIC INVARIABILITY related to my ongoing TEMPORAL DISPLACEMENT STUDIES...

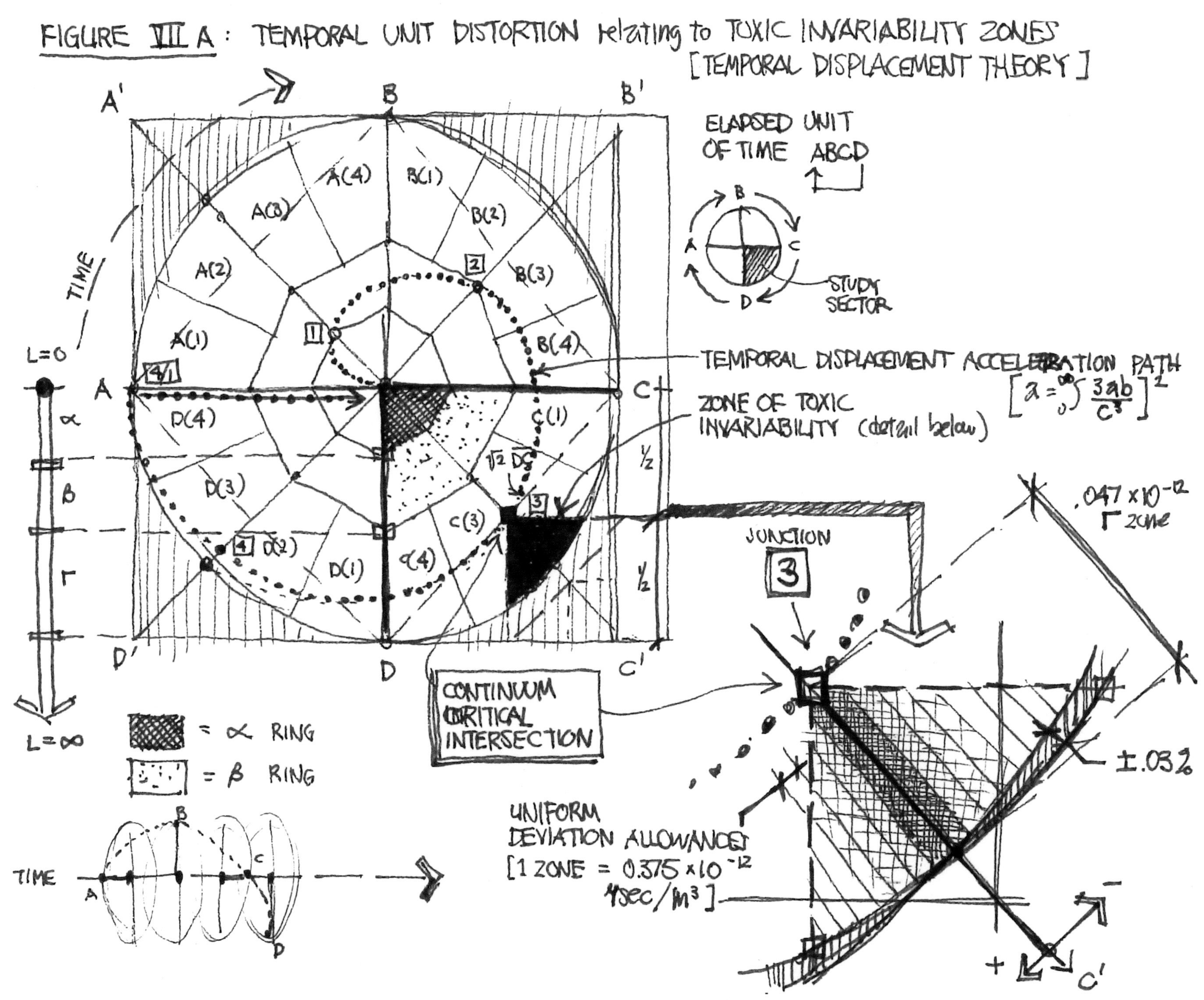

FIGURE III A: TEMPORAL UNIT DISTORTION relating to TOXIC INVARIABILITY ZONES
[TEMPORAL DISPLACEMENT THEORY]
A'
B
B'
TIME
L=0
A(4)
B(1)
A(3)
B(2)
A(2)
2
B(3)
A(1)
II
B(4)
4
A
D(4)
C(1)
√2 DC
B
D(3)
3
C(3)
4 D(2)
C(4)
D(1)
Γ
D'
D
C'
L=∞
= α RING
= β RING
TIME
A
B
C
D
ELAPSED UNIT OF TIME ABCD
B
A
C
STUDY SECTOR
D
TEMPORAL DISPLACEMENT ACCELERATION PATH
½
ZONE OF TOXIC INVARIABILITY (detail below)
½
CONTINUUM CRITICAL INTERSECTION
JUNCTION
3
.047 x10⁻¹²
Γ zone
±.032
UNIFORM DEVIATION ALLOWANCE
[1 ZONE = 0.375 x10⁻¹²
4sec/m³]
+
C'

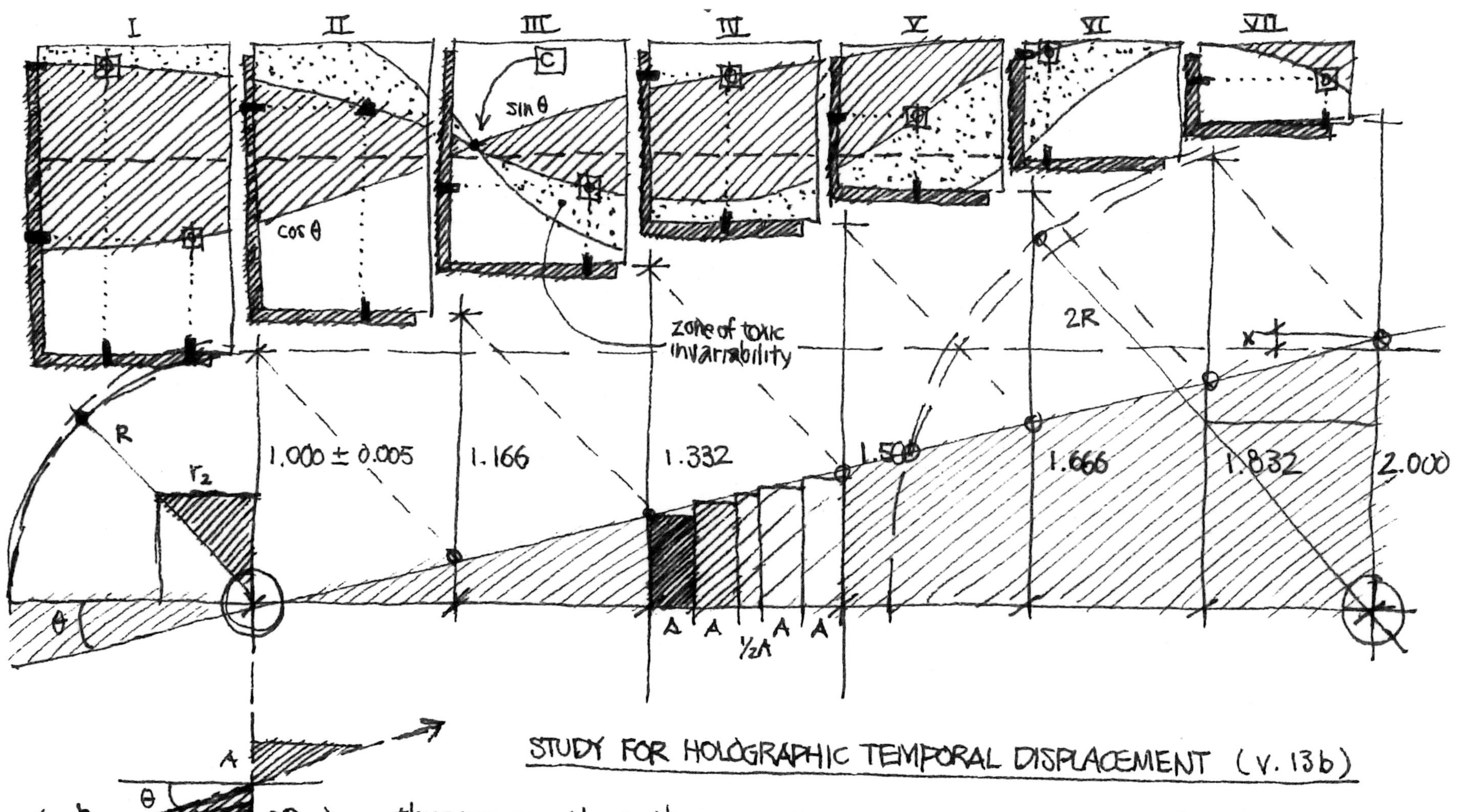

...thus proving that the critical continuum overlap node (c) is isolated by the intersection of the cos θ and sin θ in sector III (sector of minimal toxic invariability)...

SIGNIFICANCE: a shift in temporal displacement can only be detected within a sector of minimal toxic invariability,

hence,

$$\tan \theta \times \frac{c}{X\,\pi 2R} = \text{elasticity quotient for temporal displacement}$$

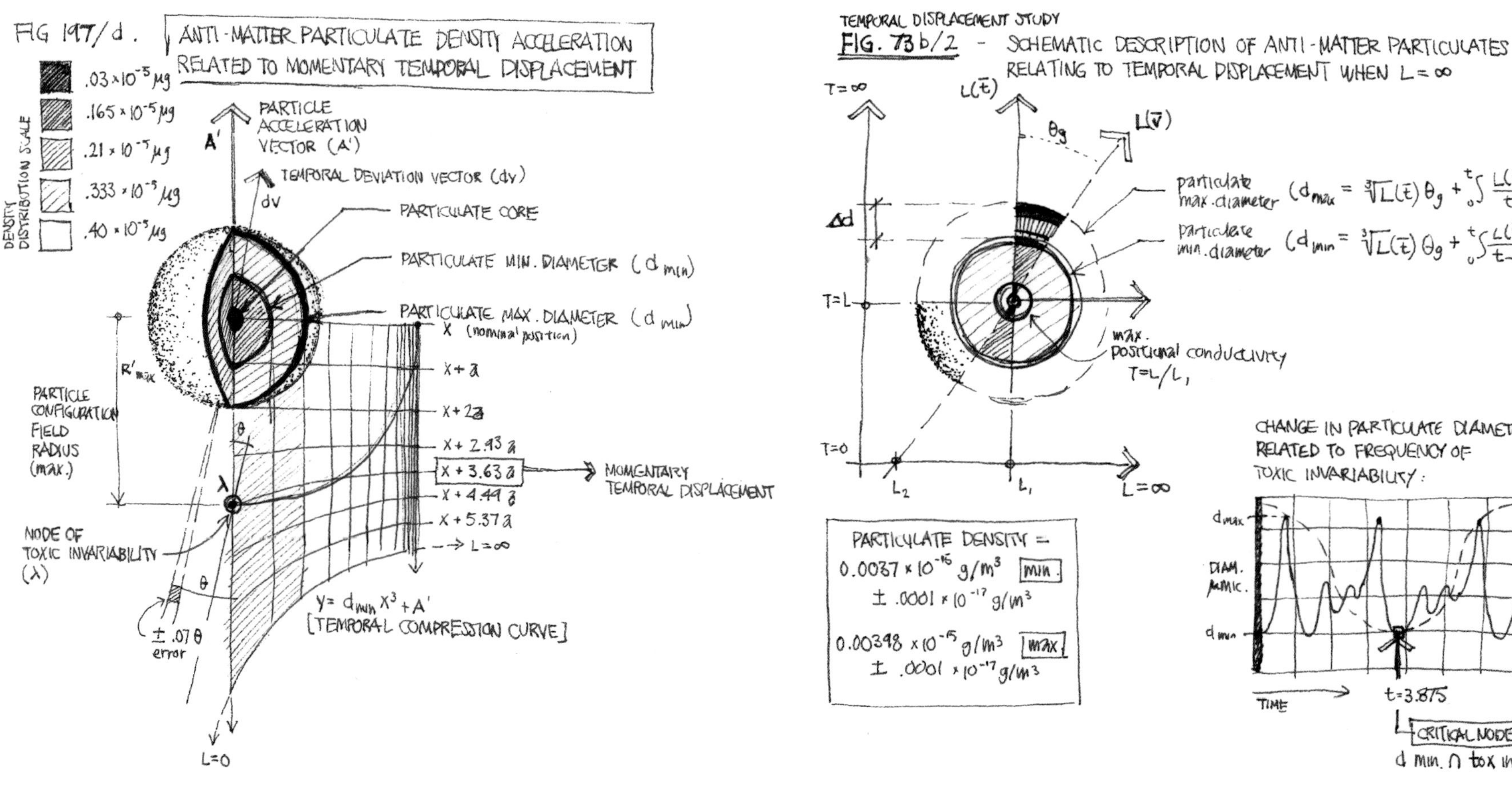

Back to the Future: Once you've found the secret to time travel and you realize that you've actually already been to all the places you've been yearning to visit -- and sketched them in a previous life -- it's time to rest and to note your observations -- and revelations -- in your sketchbook!

DRAWING RESOURCES:

TRAVEL SKETCHING:

Urban Sketchers

http://www.urbansketchers.org/
Urban Sketchers is a global community of artists that practice drawing on location in cities, towns and villages they live in or travel to.

Artists Network

https://www.artistsnetwork.com/
Membership-based resource to hone your drawing skills through videos, ebooks and magazines.

ARCHITECTURAL ILLUSTRATION:
There are professional societies for architectural illustrators and those who draw the built environment -- here are a few to inspire you:

American Society of Architectural Illustrators (ASAI)

https://www.asai.org

Society of Architectural Illustrators (SIA)

https://www.sai.org.uk

Japan Architectural Renderers Association (JARA)
http://www.jara-net.com

DRAWING SUPPLIES:
Some of the world's best art supplies are just a mouse click away:

Blick Art Supplies
https://www.dickblick.com

Michaels
https://www.michaels.com

Hobbycraft
https://www.hobbycraft.co.uk

TRAVEL RESOURCES:

TRAVEL & BACKPACKING:
There are a million resources related to travel, backpacking, and associated gear; here are just a few:

Lonely Planet
https://www.lonelyplanet.com

Rough Guides
https://www.roughguides.com

REI Co-op
https://www.rei.com

Eddie Bauer
https://www.eddiebauer.com

Victorinox
https://www.victorinox.com

Pack Hacker
https://packhacker.com

Eagle Creek
https://www.eaglecreek.com

Switchback Travel
https://www.switchbacktravel.com

Backpacker Magazine
https://www.backpacker.com

Travel + Leisure
https://www.travelandleisure.com

And if you still can't find what you're looking for, you can always try:
Amazon.com
https://www.amazon.com

DISCLAIMER: The above resources are provided for information only; the author and publisher accept no responsibility for the content of third-party websites.

ARE YOU READY FOR ANOTHER ADVENTURE?

If you liked this book, then you'll love the educational graphic novels that were inspired by my travel sketches!

The Bumbling Traveller - Sketching The World is part of the *Bumbling Traveller™ Adventure Series*, a book series that seeks to promote environmental and cultural awareness through entertaining mysteries and adventures -- and encourages people to be curious about the world around them.

CHECK OUT THE OTHER VOLUMES IN THE AWARD-WINNING BUMBLING TRAVELLER™ ADVENTURE SERIES!

VOLUME 1: BUMBLING THROUGH BORNEO
by Tom Schmidt | ISBN 978-988-18066-5-9

Share an arduous journey with Bumbling Bob up the fabled Rejang River to experience life in a traditional longhouse -- ending in a deadly race through virgin rainforest aboard runaway logging trucks to a world of subterranean splendor. Discover the Malaysian state of Sarawak, a land abundant in nature's treasures ruled by a melting pot of cultures on a collision course with environmental catastrophe!

- **Silver Medal Winner** - Independent Publishers Book Awards
- **Bronze Medal Winner** - Moonbeam Children's Book Awards
- One of **"Ten Best Books on Borneo"** - Summer 2012 Borneo Insider's Guide

VOLUME 2: BUMBLING THROUGH SUMATRA
by Tom Schmidt | ISBN 978-988-18066-6-6

Share a harrowing nautical sojourn through the pirate-infested waters of the Strait of Malacca, misadventures in ports along Malaysia's west coast, and an arduous overland journey across Sumatra ending with a mystical encounter with the shamans of the indigenous tribes of the Mentawai Islands. Discover Sumatra -- a land rich in ancient treasures whose fate teeters in the environmental balance!

- **Bronze Medal Winner** - Independent Publishers Book Awards

VOLUME 3: BUMBLING THROUGH HONG KONG
by Tom Schmidt | ISBN 978-988-18066-7-3

Share a fast-paced adventure through one of the most densely inhabited population centers on the planet, and a series of educational discoveries while the bumbling travelers search for an elusive doctor who holds the key to a lingering mystery. Discover Hong Kong -- a land rich in natural assets and cultural treasures whose fate teeters in the environmental balance!

- **Silver Medal Winner** - Moonbeam Children's Book Awards
- **Bronze Medal Winner** - Independent Publishers Book Awards

AVAILABLE AT BOOKSTORES, OR ORDER ONLINE AT **WWW.KAKIBUBU.COM**
PayPal / credit cards / other electronic payments accepted

About the Author:

Tom Schmidt is an award-winning
architect, writer, illustrator, musician, and
stand-up comedian.

Born in the United States, following his
studies of Architecture and Environmental
Design at the University of Colorado,
his wanderlust has carried him through
various bumbling adventures in more than
70 countries around the world and across
all seven continents.

Schmidt is a licensed architect in the
USA and New Zealand, an Accredited
Professional in the LEED® and WELL
building certification programs, a
founding member of the Hong Kong
Chapter of the American Institute of
Architects (AIA), and a member of the
American Society of Architectural
Illustrators (ASAI).

Schmidt is the Founder and Managing
Director of Sepia Design Consultants
Limited, a hospitality design consultancy.
www.sepiadesign.com

He has resided in Hong Kong since 1997.